The Art of Kula

The Art of Kula

Shirley F. Campbell

Oxford • New York

First published in 2002 by
Berg
Editorial offices:
150 Cowley Road, Oxford, OX4 1JJ, UK
838 Broadway, Third Floor, New York, NY 10003-4812, USA

Berg is the imprint of Oxford International Publishers Ltd.

Library of Congress Cataloguing-in-Publication Data
Campbell, Shirley F. (Shirley Faye)
    The art of Kula / Shirley F. Campbell.
        p. cm.
Includes bibliographical references and index.
    ISBN 1-85973-513-4 – ISBN 1-85973-518-5 (pbk.)
    1. Ethnology–Papua New Guinea–Trobriand Islands. 2. Kula exchange.
3. Wood-carving, Papuan–Papua New Guinea–Trobriand Islands. 4. Sex role–Papua
New Guinea–Trobriand Islands. 5. Trobriand Islands (Papua New Guinea)–Social
life and customs. I. Title.
    GN671.N5 C36 2002
    305.8′009954′1–dc21

                                                              2002008613

British Library Cataloguing-in-Publication Data
A catalogue record for this book is available from the British Library.

ISBN 1 85973 513 4 (Cloth)
    1 85973 518 5 (Paper)

Typeset by JS Typesetting Ltd, Wellingborough, Northants.
Printed in the United Kingdom by MPG Books, Cornwall

**To my mother, Pearl Campbell,
who gave me the vision**

Contents

List of Plates

List of Figures

List of Tables

Acknowledgements

A word of thanks to the people of Vakuta:

Milu Vakuta, komwaidona, agutoki besa uula, kuyamatagusi e kuvitolokigusi. Mapilana booki gala bagini kalayam yokwami gala pilasegu. Sena mwau nanogu gala abani ula keda, bama davaluasi. Lopogu sitana mwau migisi gala agisa kwaitala tcitu, kwaitala teitu. Taga, adoki babani ula keda e bama ovalu 2003, kaina 2004. Mapilana booki ula stori, kaina mokwita, kaina gala. Lapisewa peura labani biga mokwita. Taga aseki besa booki yokwami.

Magigu baluluwai Rurupa toya Kasanai, tamagu e inagu. E, bwadagu, Bukeravana mtoya Bagitaria. Aseki beso yokwami sena kwaiveka agutoki. Ruguna, Youwa, Kaitotu e Gigimwa mokwita tokabitam, mibiga kupilasegusi sopila Vakuta e sopila Kitava. Kunabu, Bomtarasi, Daiyaga, Ineiya, Boredoga, Magisibu, Naomi, Samisoni, Pilimoni e bidubadu numoya tomoya, aluluwai yokwami olopogu. Ula biga bogw itamwau, gala babigatona mokwita. Agutoki kwaiveka. (Seli)

There is an immeasurable debt I owe the people of Vakuta for the inevitable intrusions I made into their lives. I only hope that this book in some way conveys to them my gratitude and appreciation for the hospitality and good humour they graciously showed me. The fond memories and the warmth I feel for so many Vakutans are my fortune. It would be nice to think that some measure of this also exists in the hearts of my closest friends. It is my fervent desire that I have been able to portray their view of the world as accurately as is possible by someone raised in a totally different one.

The research for this book began in 1974 and has become a long-term project now, finally, coming to fruition. As a result, there have been many people who have contributed in various ways but who have now moved on in their lives, as well as those who have sadly passed beyond it. I am indebted to so many for their assistance when I was in need, for their emotional support when I was depressed and for their intellectual stimulation when I was truly lacking inspiration.

In particular, I am perhaps most indebted to the late Anthony Forge, who not only gave me the chance to pursue a long-standing interest but also assisted in the administration of my research and the intellectual supervision over the course of my analysis. Meeting in London prior to his departure for Australia to take up an appointment as the first Chair in Anthropology in the Faculties at the Australian National University, Anthony said, 'Well, dolly-bird, if you get there, I'll consider taking you into the graduate programme.' To his surprise, I landed in Canberra shortly after his own arrival, and thus our relationship was born. I hope that this book offers some justification for his willingness to take on a Yank from an American college where honours degrees do not exist.

Recently renamed the School of Archaeology and Anthropology, the old 'Department' has been my intellectual base throughout. Now, as a Visiting Fellow, I look back over the years and 'see' many faces – graduate students, administrative and academic staff – all belonging to people who have provided welcome assistance when called upon. In particular, I would like to thank Graziella Wurmli, Debbie McGrath and Sue Fraser for their superb handling of all matters administrative as well as their compassion and friendship. I am grateful for the financial and administrative assistance provided by the Australian National University, enabling me to carry out fieldwork in the Trobriand Islands between September 1976 and March 1978. More recently the University Publications Committee has awarded me a Publications Subsidy to cover the costly production of three colour plates. As colour is an integral part of the process of communicating information, and an important component of the following analysis, I am very grateful for this support.

A starting premise for this research was that art belonged to a communication system akin to, but separate from, other means of communication. As such, it was clear that for me to hope to grasp what was communicated by art I would need a fairly comprehensive understanding of the language. I devoted the first three months entirely to this end with the result that I was reasonably fluent in the Vakutan dialect. My success in this endeavour was due to the untiring tuition of the Vakutan people and to Ralph Lawton, who, while compiling a complete grammar of Kilivila, writing an MA thesis on the Kiriwinan classifier and working on a translation of the Old and New Testaments, kindly gave me some initial instruction in the language prior to my departure. With an understanding of the structure, and armed with a basic vocabulary, I was able to advance my language skills with less difficulty than would otherwise have been the case.

I wish to acknowledge the assistance of the staff from several museums in Australia who made it possible for me to access their Massim collections. In particular, I would like to thank David Moore of the National Museum of Victoria, Jim Specht of the Australian Museum in Sydney, Michael Quinnel of the Queensland Museum, Mrs Keith of the now defunct Institute of Anatomy in Canberra, and Mrs MacIntosh and Wally Caruana of the National Gallery of Australia also in Canberra.

While in Port Moresby I had occasion to seek the help of others who were always willing to listen to my problems and offer advice and assistance when appropriate. I would like to thank Ron and Judy Fergie who were my 'family' in Port Moresby, members of the Department of Anthropology and Sociology at the

University of Papua New Guinea and Ron May for cautionary words about the political situation on Kiriwina Island. My research was supported by the National Museum and Art Gallery of Papua New Guinea. My gratitude goes to the late Geoffrey Mosuwadoga, a Trobriander and the first Director of the National Museum, who not only sponsored my research visa but also provided me with good advice and letters of introduction. My thanks to Brian Egloff and Dirk Schmidt who, in their own ways, helped me to articulate, through their probing questions, some of the ideas swimming around in my head.

While on Kiriwina Island I received considerable support from a number of people. In particular, the Uniting Church at Oiyabia and members of the congregation gave me a place to stay and provided welcome hospitality. The late Lepani Watson showed great interest in my work, writing a letter of introduction to give to the people of Vakuta. Jill and Frank Holland of Trobriand Fisheries gave me their friendship and logistical support whenever possible. It was their good humour and Aussie generosity that saw me through the pangs of homesickness.

A supervisor, ongoing mentor and close friend, Michael Young, has given me more than any other. His generosity is greatly appreciated, as are the many conversations in which we shared the minutiae of specialists. Michael scrupulously read and commented upon each successive draft of this work through its various transformations. Although he is perhaps most responsible for instilling in me dark periods of self-doubt, he has done so as a close friend. If there is any eloquence to be found in my prose, it is due to Michael's untiring efforts to find clarity in my writing.

Howard Morphy, too, has been an unfailing friend and inspiration, having read various versions and engaged me in many memorable conversations that have helped to formulate my thinking. Chris Gregory also deserves special mention. He has been a constant source of encouragement, providing sound advice and direction. Many colleagues have read parts of this work in its various guises. I would like to thank Don Gardner, Allan Darrah, Jimmy Weiner, Mike O'Hanlon, Nic Thomas, Bob Tonkinson, Fred Damon and Harry Berran, as well as the examiners of my doctoral thesis, Nancy Munn, Alfred Gell and Marilyn Strathern, for the incisive and critical comments they offered as they pressed for its speedy publication. Alas, speed has been a stranger to this work.

Finally, the boundless encouragement from my mother and father, the faith of my three sisters and the patience of my two boys have seen me through many a doubtful moment. However, it is to my partner, Paul Ratcliffe, that my thoughts turn. He has not only endured the countless transformations this work has undertaken, read draft after draft and given all manner of technical help, he has never ceased to doubt that its completion would eventually come to pass. Thank you.

Introduction

On the island of Kiriwina one tropical Monday morning in October 1976, while I was recording a meeting with the people of Olivilevi who had agreed to let me settle with them to conduct fieldwork, there came a knock at my door. I had temporary lodging at the Uniting Church Mission at Oiyabia while I searched for a permanent field site on Kiriwina. The wonderful month that I spent at Oiyabia enabled me to concentrate on my acquisition of language, with a constant stream of curious Kiriwinans, mostly children, coming to inspect this white stranger, or 'dimdim'. My visitors were admirably patient as I collected words for everything that I could point to. From this base, located between Kavataria and the government station at Losuia, I was able to travel to different parts of Kiriwina in search of a suitable village. As my research interest centred on the carvings that made these people particularly well known to outsiders, my search was focused on those villages renowned for their carving output. I had already visited several and had been largely unsuccessful: either the villages lacked working master carvers or they were disinclined to accept the pesterings of some 'dimdim'. Olivilevi was an exception. Not only were master carvers still working for local consumption and the tourist trade, but they also seemed excited about the prospect of my settling with them for the next eighteen months. I was adopted into a family and told that they would start building a house for me immediately. We agreed on a site, and an appropriate remuneration for the work, and I was sent away to await news that my house had been built and I could move in. The knock on the door changed everything.

Four young men dressed in their finest, with bodies oiled and delicately sprinkled with the yellow pollen of hibiscus, faced me. They said they had come with a message from Olivilevi. I was told that if I wanted to live there I was required to pay the village headman on a daily basis what was then an exorbitant amount of money for a student on a research scholarship. Once over the initial surprise in this change of circumstances, I tried to make sense of it. Upon reflection, it seemed to me that these demands were no less than a refusal to host my work. I became quite depressed about any prospect of working in the Trobriand Islands, and seriously considered packing up and heading back to Australia. I wrote to Anthony Forge, my supervisor, with news of the situation, adding that I would try the island further south as a last effort to establish a research site in the Trobriands. Feeling defeated, I recalled the numerous friendly warnings against working in the Trobriands while I was in Port Moresby. Well-wishers cited recent troubles between two rival factions and the sophisticated tactics of the people in their dealings with 'dimdims'; no doubt a result of many years of dealings with foreigners, all trying to get something out of the islanders.

The fame of the Trobriand Islands is not a recent phenomenon. Indeed, the entire culture area known as the Massim[1] had a certain reputation, shaped in the tales carried home by the earliest Europeans to visit in the middle of the nineteenth century. Frequented by explorers, whalers, pearl and gold prospectors, followed by traders, government and missionary personnel, the sexual freedom enjoyed by unmarried youths, as well as the particularly fine wooden carvings produced by Massim craftsmen, gave the foreigners something to talk about and carry away. The islands of the Massim became a magnet for people seeking adventure and riches. The wax and wane in the market value of *bêche-de-mer*, pearls, copra and fish all contributed in attracting a wide range of people who set up residence for varying lengths of time. Although not seeking his fortune in exportable riches, the young Bronislaw Malinowski travelled to the area early in the twentieth century looking for insights into the human condition through the social and cultural lives of 'primitives'. He too became a resident, initially spending eight months from June 1915 to February 1916, followed by a slightly longer period from December 1917 to September 1918 on Boyowa, or Kiriwina Island. His research in the Trobriands led to a number of publications detailing the life and customs of the people, while simultaneously constructing ground-breaking theories in the social sciences. There would be few anthropologists who could avoid a diet of Trobriand ethnography in the first years of their training. Malinowski wrote prolifically on nearly every aspect of Trobriand life, but nowhere does the art come under his otherwise meticulous scrutiny. Malinowski's 1917–18 fieldwork diary, however, reveals his intention to write an extensive monograph on the people and their culture, to be named simply 'Kiriwina'. Drafts of the structure of his work are in the London School of Economics archives and indicate that the book would have been divided into seven major sections. The last section was to be devoted to art (Young 1998). This compendious tome was never completed, and during the course of his career Malinowski drafted the main sections into his various publications.

Over the latter part of the twentieth century the rich cultures of the Massim and the writings of Malinowski have continued to lure other anthropologists. I am one of those drawn to the islands. In particular, my research interests are explicitly focused on the tradition of carving, uniquely Massim and recreated over generations by carvers whose works are now housed in museums and personal collections around the world. I had already completed a formal analysis of Massim carvings found in Australian museum collections in 1976. A significant aspect of my research project had been to avoid any interpretive consideration of indigenous exegesis in the analysis of the formal properties that embellished the carved surfaces. Following completion of the analysis, I identified what I thought were the formal properties mediating the system of stylised representation. The next stage of my research was to test whether I had indeed been able to 'see' the significant forms that conveyed meaning in its indigenous context. This book is the result of that effort to link form and meaning.

The significant volume of carvings originating from the Massim and now found in collections around the world is testament to the high regard in which these were held by Europeans. The extent to which carvings were collected and taken back to European and Australian ports, however, is not easily determined, particularly in the initial phase of contact with whalers and explorers. The earliest evidence we have of European interest in Massim carvings derives from the collecting activity of the first missionaries. These were Italian Marists who arrived on Muyuw (Wood-lark) Island on 15 September 1847 (Afflect 1983). In 1863 a shipment of artefacts from the Seminary of Foreign Missions at St Calocero arrived in Milan and included objects from the Massim. These were displayed at the Civic Museum in the same year, for which a catalogue was produced detailing each artefact (Afflect n.d.). The collection was subsequently destroyed during the bombings of 1943.

In an unpublished index of specimens held in the British Museum, one artefact is listed as having been collected by Captain Owen Stanley while exploring the Louisiades on HMS *Rattlesnake* in 1849 (Halls n.d.). In his book, *Art and Life in New Guinea* (1936), Raymond Firth included one item collected by Admiral J. Erskine around 1850 and seven pieces collected prior to 1875 by Captain Moresby of HMS *Basilisk*. Sir William MacGregor, the first Lieutenant-Governor assigned to British New Guinea, was a keen admirer of Trobriand carvings (Quinnell 2000), as was the Reverend George Brown, who had a large selection of Trobriand artefacts in his collection (Gardner 2000). By 1895 a considerable number of specimens of Massim art, and in particular Trobriand carvings, had found their way to various museums in Britain, Holland and Australia. A. C. Haddon made use of these collections in the development of his theories towards an analysis of 'primitive art' (1893, 1894, 1895).

European response to Massim art in the early years of the twentieth century was generally favourable, though some voices raised the issue of degenerating quality. Further, there arose a concern for artistic 'purity' as colonial consumers began to impose preferences and influence the productive talents of the 'natives'. This issue filtered into several descriptions of the art (Finsch 1888; Haddon 1893, 1894, 1895). Fears for what was considered an inevitable decline in Massim peoples' material and cultural lives, as a result of European contact, incited a 'salvage' mentality amongst collectors. A. C. Haddon wrote:

> Degeneration in artistic excellence is the almost universal result of the influence of the white man . . . The natives have, by this time, sold a considerable portion of their old

and well-carved objects, and they find that the trader does not insist upon perfection in more modern objects. As far back as 1885, Dr. Finsch found that even shields were made to sell to the white-man. (1894: 203)

Much later, Austen lamented that 'most of the stuff I have seen being turned out was cruder and more hastily finished than in the past' (1945: 193). Even more recently (1978) the Kiriwina Lodge proprietor Ray Hargraves confided in me that there had been a 'marked decrease in quality within the last four years'. Like Haddon some seventy years earlier, he blamed artistic degeneration on the indiscriminate buyer – together with the frenzy amongst carvers to acquire cash.

While public and private collections were being filled with Massim carvings, little attention was invested in discovering the cultural context for which the art was intended. Haddon was the first and last in over eight decades to publish a serious analysis of art from the Massim.[2] He concentrated primarily on describing several of its formal characteristics, comparing them to other artistic traditions found in British New Guinea (1894, 1895). This focus, however, was not necessarily an indication of a lack of interest in the meanings that may be associated with islanders' art. Indeed, in 1916 Haddon wrote a letter to the young student of C. G. Seligman in the Trobriands, Bronislaw Malinowski, pressing him to ask for local exegeses pertaining to various designs carved and burnt into the artwork. Alas, Malinowski wrote back, lamenting 'there is no sense, no meaning in the whole of a design . . . No deeper magico-religious meaning, absolutely none – and this applies to their art throughout.'[3]

It wasn't until the early 1950s that the art of the Trobriand Islands came under close scrutiny again. A. J. Halls, formerly the Art Officer attached to the Department of Education in Papua and New Guinea, took a personal interest in the formal construction of Trobriand carving. He developed his work into an unpublished, four-volume manuscript deposited with Raymond Firth in 1952. One volume was devoted to an analysis of formal elements and the process of design development. The remaining three volumes contain detailed drawings of specimens held in various museums in Europe and Australia. It is unfortunate that this material remains unpublished as its value lies in the analysis of formal elements comprising Trobriand carving. The meaning encoded in these elements, however, escaped Halls's attention.[4]

Edmund Leach broached the subject of meaning associated with Trobriand art in an article offering an innovative interrogation of a Trobriand war shield (1954). Working from a published image by Fellows (1898b) of a shield which included Trobriand names for various designs, Leach argued that the designs were meaningful and communicated information to those who could understand them. Not only was the shield itself functional, but the designs, too, had a 'functional significance' (1954: 105). His analysis drew heated controversy (Berndt 1958;

Leach 1958; Reynolds 1958; Salisbury 1959; Tindale 1959) and, somewhat later, stimulated another analysis of the shield by Patrick Glass (1978). Glass attempted an interpretation of the designs as elements of a 'code' referring to the existence of a 'secret fertility cult' in the Trobriand Islands. His evidence is drawn from selective, and liberally interpreted, fragments of the Trobriand ethnographic corpus. Although highly creative, his conclusions bear only tangential resemblance to Trobriand social and cultural life.

G. G. Scoditti was drawn to a study of the kula canoe prow and splashboards carved on Kitava Island. His interpretations have led him to the view that the 'congeries of concepts and symbolic meanings' are a representation of a secret myth about a culture hero named Monikiniki (1980: 77; see also 1975, 1977, 1990). According to Scoditti, the designs represent the mythical adventures and attributes of this hero and form a 'historical interpretation' of them (1980: 78). Although my interest is likewise drawn to the carved boards used to beautify kula canoes on Vakuta Island, my approach leads me to very different interpretations. Whereas Scoditti was disposed to link Kitavan conceptualisations to those held initially within the Greek Hellenistic tradition, and later developed in other 'high' periods of European art as philosophical reflections on a universal human aesthetic, I am concerned with describing the relationship of the carvings to Vakutan values and the meaning evoked by the designs within a purely Vakutan context. In more recent discussions of Kitavan representation, however, Scoditti's emphasis has returned to the Kitavan context with an identification of local exegesis. In particular, he has drawn attention to the 'aesthetic' discourse that these carvings and their designs evoke for Kitavans (1990).

Nancy Munn, although analysing Gawan canoes as opposed to Gawan 'art' *per se*, comes closer than anyone working in the Massim to an interpretation and integration of meaning as this is conveyed through a material object (1977, 1986). She develops a sophisticated analysis of the means by which the kula canoe represents men's corporate and individual pursuit of identity, constructed by various 'time/space' transformations and propelled by means of the vessel.

Other than the earliest descriptions of Massim art, Harry Beran is the only scholar to have viewed it as a recognisable corpus of great beauty and aesthetic appeal readily appreciated by Western consumers. Beran has produced a number of publications describing the formal properties that identify a diverse genre of carved artefacts produced by Massim craftsmen. He has drawn together those common elements that clearly identify the art in terms of regional styles, and even attempted to distinguish the styles of particular artists from works now held in private and public collections (1980, 1988, 1996).

My own research has much more in common with the work of Munn. The analysis that follows is concerned with the carvings produced by artists for consumption within their own society and for which there is a practical use and associated value. Whereas Munn uses the canoe as the vehicle through which to analyse the projection of Gawan men through time and space, I enlist the carvings placed on the kula outrigger canoes as consummate visual 'texts' defining how men would like their renown to be perceived. However, as these are produced to enhance the success of men engaged in kula, the analysis extends to the broader institutions related to kula and the relentless pursuit of shell valuables – long after Malinowski predicted its demise. My analysis explores the feedback generated between an artist and the community for which he works, his training, the value of his work as a practical object and its power as a vehicle for symbolic repres-entation.

To this end, the analysis concentrates on the system of meaning encoded on the kula canoe prow and splashboards. The prowboard, carved and painted on both sides, sits along the length of the prow as an extension of the canoe, while the splashboard sits across the end of the canoe's hull. Because I consider the formal system of design construction an essential component in the process of commun-ication, significant attention is devoted towards an analysis of design orientation and placement. Further, the design elements chosen to express certain concepts receive attention, together with those aspects of the natural environment singled out to express these. Finally, as a medium of communication, the carvings become more than just the decorated surfaces embellishing outrigger canoes. By integrating the encoded meanings carved and painted onto the prow and splashboards with the rituals of kula and the broader context of Vakutan life, I hope to suggest the role these carvings play in their reflection of Vakutan concerns. In particular, the boards support a narrative defining the goals of Vakutan men in search of their mortality and the projection of a man's name through space and time.

Any analysis of non-Western art, with the aim of coming to some understanding of what it is 'about', is fraught with difficulties (Forge 1973; Gell 1998; Layton 1991). Significant questions loom in relation to the 'accuracy' of an 'outsider's' interpretation and the maintenance of a sufficiently neutral or overly self-conscious 'objectivity'. Issues of historical relevance and the influence of colonisation also 'muddy the waters' (Phillips and Steiner 1999; Thomas 1991). Concerns over authenticity and debates seeking to distinguish tourist art from 'traditional' art continue unabated (Caruana 1993; Graburn 1976; Morphy 1983). Because there seems no escape from these problems the validity of such analyses has been open to attack (Gell 1998; E. R. Leach 1973; Sperber 1976). Although it is often not hard to establish that art in one way or another evokes responses from a viewing public, it is far trickier to demonstrate convincingly what the nature of those responses is and on what basis people continue to seek expression through art. Discovering meaning is not only problematic, it is frustratingly elusive.

Many analysts of so-called 'primitive art' have avoided the dilemma inherent in the search for meaning by sticking to formal analyses and the delineation of style. Indeed, it was Haddon (1893, 1894, 1895), followed by Boas (1927), who first launched into the stylistic analysis of non-Western art. Both adopted a formal approach to form and the origin and development of style. Analyses often focused on whether the art was abstract or representational, decorative or narrative, sculptured or flat. Later, Reichard explored Melanesian wood and tortoiseshell carvings (1933), detailing the elements of design composition and style. In 1939 she published an analysis of Navajo sand paintings in relation to their associated legends. In this work Reichard moved further into the interpretive realm but fell short of exploring the relationships linking the two. Thus a broader discourse on meaning was not attempted. Apart from these, and with the notable exception of Firth (1936), non-Western art systems have, until the latter quarter of the twentieth century, remained the sole interest of museum research. In this milieu, however, attention given to the art as artefact has largely been focused on attributing style to regional and cultural locations, as well as developing typologies to define and categorise material culture.

With the increasing sophistication and analysis of linguistic models, in particular the transformational grammar proposed by Noam Chomsky (1957, 1966), a few anthropologists began to turn their attention to non-European art in efforts to construct 'grammars' of design composition and transformation. Examples of this approach can be seen in Watt's analysis of Nevada Cattle brands (1966–67, 1967), an analysis of Nuban body painting by Faris (1972), and Greenberg's formal analysis of form and the organisation of Hopi pottery designs (1975). These analyses adopted a systematic approach to art as non-verbal systems of communication. They argued that in identifying the separate design elements operating within these respective systems analysts could establish rules and patterns of design orientation, organisation, transformation and motivation. But they shied away from locating the formal characteristics of these systems within the cultural context for which they are presumed to operate. Analyses about *how* systems communicate certainly delivered some interesting findings, but if we accept that art is a kind of grammar, we could expect that what the grammar delivered by way of meaning would be a legitimate question worthy of investigation. Holm justifies his formal approach to the analysis of Northwest Coast Indian art by arguing that the meanings associated with design elements are of secondary significance to the formal properties of the art; 'the formal element of the designs very often takes on such importance as to overshadow the symbolic element to a point where the symbolism becomes very obscure' (1965: 11). Attempts to make sense of labels attached to designs are often unsatisfactory, in many cases suggesting little more than completely chaotic and/or arbitrary associations. No doubt this led Holm to find the symbols obscured by the 'meanings'. Finding meaning in art is more than mere translation, however. It requires many strategies to discover the way meaning operates within the formal 'grammars' of art (Campbell 2001).

Three major studies in the 1960s and 1970s, with the expressed aim of analysing the relationship of art as a system of communication within the context of the society it was produced, have greatly influenced my own approach: Munn's analysis of Walbiri ritual paintings and sand-drawings (1962, 1973a, 1973b); Forge's analysis of Abelam flat painting (1966, 1970); and Morphy's analysis of Yolngu bark painting (1977a, 1991).[5] For the most part, the theoretical basis for these analyses also derives from theories developed to illuminate language. More specifically, the value of the Saussurean concept of the sign and the way it encodes meaning was a model for these analyses of form in art.

There have been further analyses of non-Western art since these three exemplary studies, each in one way or another adopting similar ways of investigating art within different cultural contexts. Originally, my own approach was likewise greatly influenced by sociolinguistics, particularly that of Roland Barthes, who further developed the Saussurean concept of the sign (1967). However, as is the case for many now writing about the way in which meaning communicates through art, there has been a loosening of the ties to the original linguistic models as anthropologists have become more comfortable with writing about the ways in which individual systems operate. The importance of linguistic theory to the anthropology of art is that it provided the means by which analysts could negotiate alternative paths through the rich labyrinth of non-Western art systems to demonstrate that meaning had an inherent connection to the 'signs'.

In his final contribution to anthropology, Alfred Gell took a bold step to reassess what is and what should be included in an 'anthropology of art' (1998). Unhappy with the direction investigations of non-Western art had taken, particularly those intent on examining the aesthetic contexts of art and analyses investigating art as visual codes of communication, Gell proposed a 'programme' that returns to what he argued are the basic interests of anthropology. In other words, an anthropology of art should be about social action: 'I view art as a system of action, intended to change the world rather than encode symbolic propositions about it' (1998: 6). While I have some sympathy for Gell's desire to define the anthropology of art more clearly within the confines of the discipline, an act that implicitly returns to the grand narratives of our anthropological ancestors, cannot, I submit, be sustained. It is too restrictive. While I agree that an examination of art as a vehicle for social action, incorporating 'agency, intention, causation, result, and transformation' (ibid.), offers an intriguing investigative process, perhaps enabling a better understanding of how artistic systems articulate with human lives, I hesitate to cast aside those approaches that examine the way formal elements encode meanings and the processes of representing significant relationships and the context in which these communicate. In this present work I shall demonstrate that it takes many kinds of approaches to understand the value of art beyond its decorative appeal.

The 'ethnographic present' throughout the book is taken from the late 1970s while I had the opportunity to live on the island and become as much a part of daily life as one can. While I have no reason to believe that the art produced for kula has undergone significant changes since that time, the reader should be conscious that Vakutans do not live in a timeless 'present'. Changes have made, and will continue to make their mark on Vakutan life. I have divided the book into three sections. Part I outlines the social setting. The Trobriands are known from Kiriwinan ethnography. Therefore, I have devoted some space to providing a Vakutan version of island life. As will be seen, there are several divergences from what is known about Kiriwinan society. Further, as Vakutan life is a consequence of its past, a brief look backwards from both Vakutan and European perspectives will serve to set the context in which the art of kula is produced. It is to the art that Part II turns. A formal analysis examines how the system is internally structured and identifies the relationship between its formal elements. A representational analysis introduces the system of 'labels': the association of form to the natural elements that Vakutans single out from their environment for representation. An analysis of colour extends the emergent meanings into a wider Vakutan context. This section concludes with a review of all approaches to the art in an attempt to pull together the various strategies leading to an interpretation of meaning. The rituals of kula become the focus of Part III. Finally the kula boards take their place on the outrigger canoe, ready to dazzle the kula partners of Vakutan men so as to enable the latter to attain wealth and renown.

Part I
In the Beginning

–1–

'Before, There was Nothing'

At a time when the islands basked peacefully in sun and sea, Togamolu emerged from the ground:

Before, there was nothing on Vakuta. Just the woods. Then my ancestor, Togamolu of the Susupa *dala* [Malasi clan] rose from a hole in the ground. Here, between Oluwala [hamlet] and Kuweiwa [hamlet]. He jumped up from the hole in the ground and he saw only woods. He was the only one here, only one man, my ancestor.

Togamolu's sister, Ilumaimaiya, lived in a hole. During the day she rose from the hole and at night she returned to the 'stomach' (*olopola*) of the earth. One night Togamolu went fishing and he caught his sister and pulled her to the ground. There she remained.

Lepani's ancestress,[1] Ilubonotu [Lukwaisisiga clan] came to Vakuta from Kilivila [Kiriwina Island] and Togamolu married her. He gave her Kuweiwa hamlet because it was not far from his village, Orodoga, where he rose from the earth. Lepani and I have much land, more than others because my ancestor was the original man on Vakuta and Lepani's ancestress was his wife.

People came to Vakuta and Togamolu gave them land: Oluwala, Kuweiwa, Osaroru, all the hamlets and villages on the island. He did not demand payment because he was happy to have people to talk, work and play with. (Ruguna, Kuweiwa Hamlet, Vakuta village)

The Land

The Trobriand Islands encompass several raised coral shelves located some 160 kilometres north of the eastern tip of Papua New Guinea (Figure 1.1). With little regard for what local people called their islands, this group was named by the explorer D'Entrecasteaux in honour of his first lieutenant, Denis de Trobriand of the frigate *L'Esperance*. Sir William MacGregor continued to refer to this group in the same way, securing this as the official name (1890–91: 7). The people who have for generations made these coral islands their home, however, know them by their individual names. There are seven inhabited islands in the Trobriand group.[2] The largest of these is Kiriwina (Boyowa), with Kaileuna (Kadawaga), Kitava, Vakuta, Tuma, Kuyawa and Manuwata Islands in descending order of size.[3] There are several smaller, uninhabited islets also connected to the group

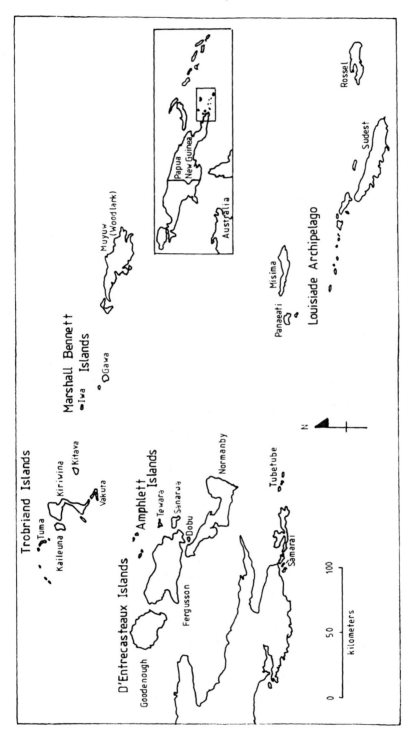

Figure 1.1 Location map of the Massim, Papua New Guinea

(Figure 1.2). The whole are thought to have formed the upper, eastern edge of an ancient atoll which in earlier geological time subsided into the Solomon Sea (Allied Geographical Section 1942: 33). Today they present the typical profile of low-lying coral islands.

Vakuta Island is located approximately 35 kilometres south of the government station at Losuia on Kiriwina. The island emerges as raised coral from the sea and presents a continuous low cliff along the eastern edge pocketed with caves. The land slopes gently towards low-lying swampland on the western shore. The southern portion of Vakuta is almost entirely swampland, while in the northern portion the soil is very rich, yielding good harvests. Vakuta is approximately 20 kilometres in length and no more than 4 kilometres at its widest point. Several tidal creeks cut into the island from the lagoon at its western shores (Plate 3).

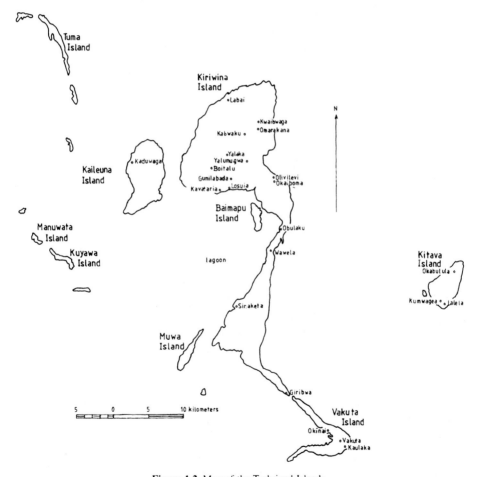

Figure 1.2 Map of the Trobriand Islands

A Vakutan View of History

Like the origin myths of Kiriwina (Malinowski 1922: 304, 1932: 418–420, 1948a: 111–126; Weiner 1977: 38–42, 1988: 99–101), Ruguna recalls how his founding ancestors emerged from the earth to claim Vakuta Island. However, the origin myth of Vakuta gives a different account of the way others came to the island. Whereas Kiriwina was populated by the emergence of autochthonous representatives for most of the clans and sub-clans who, emerging from holes throughout the island, lay claim to various parts of it, Vakuta was populated largely by immigrants. Only one *dala* (sub-clan)[4] emerged from the Vakutan soil, Ruguna's ancestor and his sister.[5]

From this point, the oral history of Vakuta contracts to focus upon events thought to have occurred just prior to contact with Europeans. It is said that for much of Vakuta's history people from the Lukuba clan were the most powerful group, although some people from the Malasi clan were also influential. Then the 'wars' began sometime before the arrival of missionaries (one man felt the need to supply me with exact dates, 1804–12!). Vakutans often referred to these as the Vakutan wars, which seem to have coincided with the arrival of the first Tabalu Malasi from Kiriwina Island:

> Towegai's [Tabalu Malasi, Kumvivi hamlet] family came from Kiriwina. He was the first Tabalu on Vakuta. Taibutu's [Tabalu Malasi, Omarakana hamlet] family were the second Tabalu to arrive. They arrived for the beginning of the wars. Rurupa's [Tabalu Malasi, Oluwala hamlet] family came from Dobu.[6] They came and started a war against Youwa's [Yagwabu Malasi, Wakwega hamlet] family.[7] Towegai's family helped Youwa's family fight Rurupa's family, but Rurupa's family won. (Artur, Kumvivi hamlet, Vakuta Village)

In this account, Artur describes the order in which different branches of the Tabalu Malasi arrived on Vakuta and the ensuing events that brought about shifts in an apparent struggle for dominance. It is therefore not surprising that the tensions that existed while I was there reflected the conflict between groups mentioned in Artur's account. Either contemporary political alliances form along similar lines recalled in the oral tradition or current conflicts are justified through a constructed account of the past.

Shortly after the Tabalu success in gaining a foothold on Vakutan soil, the British New Guinea colonial government established their presence in the area. It was perhaps this state of affairs that Lieutenant-Governor MacGregor found when he arrived on Vakuta Island and may explain the official recognition of the Tabalu Malasi as the 'chiefly' family on Vakuta, eventually leading to Rurupa becoming the 'chief' while I was on the island. The events taking place on Kiriwina following contact with European whalers, government officials, traders and missionaries, though distant, had their ramifications on Vakutan life. As many of these were recorded in official documents and personal diaries, we will turn our attention to a history of the islands from the perspective of foreigners.

Contact Experience of the Trobriand Islanders

It is difficult to establish a precise date for European contact with the Trobriand Islands prior to the middle of the nineteenth century. It is likely, however, that the islanders had seen European crews by the end of the eighteenth century when whalers began to frequent the islands of eastern New Guinea. Recall that in 1782 D'Entrecasteaux sighted and named many of the islands in the area. The trading of yams for iron hoops occurred during the early nineteenth century according to reports in *Nautical Magazine* (1839: 37–9), while illegal labour recruiters known as 'blackbirders' were scouring the islands in the latter quarter of the nineteenth century (Young 1983c).

The earliest settlement of Europeans in the area was probably established by the Italian Marists, who constructed a mission on Muyuw (Woodlark) Island from 1847 to 1852. It is uncertain whether they had any first-hand contact with the Trobriand Islands; however, their influence could only have been minimal. There is no recorded contact, nor recollections by Vakutans. If there had been contact, it probably was only of a fleeting nature.

In 1880 two traders, William Whitten and Oscar Soelberg, settled on the northwest of Kiriwina Island and set up a fishing station (Austen 1936: 10). This marked the beginning of the islanders' direct and extended contact with Europeans. From this point on many traders, pearlers and others seeking their fortune, followed by missionaries and government officials, settled in the Trobriand Islands. Other contacts prior to government control are reported to have been made by Germans from New Britain who sailed to the Trobriand Islands to buy yams (MacGregor 1890–91: 7; Austen 1936: 11).

The first contact Trobrianders had with the government of British New Guinea was MacGregor's inspection of Kiriwina, Kitava, Kaileuna and Vakuta Islands in August 1891 (MacGregor 1891–92: Appendix A). During his investigatory tour, MacGregor was determined to demonstrate to the 'natives' the power and supreme authority of the government. To this end he sought out and established a hierarchical relationship between himself and the various 'chiefs' he could locate. He paid particular attention to the chief of Omarakana village on Kiriwina Island, Enamakala, playing upon the old man's seemingly 'paramount' authority over the Trobriand people. His goal was to establish an official relationship between the people of the Trobriand Islands and the British Government via the Paramount

Chief. In this first encounter with Trobrianders, MacGregor found them 'kind, hospitable, and unsuspicious' (1891–92: 6), sentiments further reflected in his report:

> In all probability it will be found that the missionary will make more way and produce a deeper impression in Kiriwina than elsewhere in the possession; and it is not unlikely that these tribes may possess some trace of that religious sentiment which is so conspicuously absent in the Papuan generally. As a mission field it could hardly be surpassed. If some new industry could be introduced which would create something for export, there can be no doubt that Kiriwina would become an important trading centre. (1891–92: 7)

While the initial impressions held by government officials and missionaries have been well recorded, it is perhaps not surprising that little is known of the islanders' views. One can only infer that the Trobrianders themselves were content with the as yet limited intrusion of Europeans into their lives. Reports suggest no displays of hostility, nor any apparent fear of the intruders. This may be interpreted as merely complacent behaviour following several decades of contact with all sorts of visitors from overseas, or that any discontent harboured by the islanders was simply not reported to the newcomers.

Sometime before 1894 Whitten discovered pearls in the Trobriand lagoon, leading to a substantial increase in 'foreign' traders. Shortly after the discovery was announced there were some nine to ten traders living permanently on Kiriwina Island (Moreton 1894–95: 71). It was also in 1894, on the 27th of August, that Reverend S. B. Fellows of the Wesleyan Methodist Mission in British New Guinea dropped anchor in the Trobriand lagoon and ferried ashore timber, iron and personal belongings for himself and his wife in preparation for establishing a mission.[8] His arrival marked the commencement of a long-term effort to bring Christianity to the Trobriand people.

In his diaries Fellows recorded many frustrations in the advancement of his work, belying MacGregor's earlier predictions. From 1894 government reports made by the resident magistrate based on Samarai Island, 240 kilometres to the south, often recorded incidents illustrating an uncooperative 'native' with an 'addiction for thieving' (Moreton 1896–97: 21). There were also reports of petty fights, together with a serious challenge to the position of Enamakala. These finally resulted in a war between rival factions on Kiriwina and sparked threats to the lives of Reverend Fellows and the Mission teachers. When on 3 July 1897 MacGregor, together with the resident magistrate, M. H. Moreton, arrived on Kiriwina in response to concerned missionaries (MacGregor 1897: 37), initial skirmishes provoked the constabulary to open fire. As a result, Trobrianders called a halt to their own fighting, giving in to the superior weapons of the government.

Towards the end of the nineteenth century, while C. A. W. Monckton was resident magistrate for the Eastern Division, an assessment was made on the 'condition of the Trobriand people' following several years of 'contact with a higher civilisation' (Austen 1936: 11). By way of comment upon the work of Fellows, Monckton made a pessimistic observation, 'a fine type of man who, with his equally devoted wife, was endeavouring to stay, with as I could see, little hope of success, the rapid deterioration of the islanders' (Monckton 1921: 75). Monckton further noted that, 'Throughout New Guinea the group was famous for three things: the cowardice of the men, the immorality – or rather I should put it the total unmorality – of the women, and the quality of its yams' (1921: 74–75). While the 'rapid deterioration' of the islanders' moral and social integrity was blamed upon the 'low-class whites and Asiatics' who had taken up residence (Austen 1936: 11), the islanders' physical condition was also under threat from venereal disease. The infection became so widespread that the administrator at the time, Captain F. R. Barton, moved to open a hospital on Kiriwina Island in 1905 (Black 1957: 233). Dr R. L. Bellamy was appointed to the Trobriand Islands and given the powers of an assistant resident magistrate. Bellamy's appointment marked the first permanent government station at Losuia on Kiriwina Island. When Bellamy arrived on 6 October 1905 there were twelve Europeans living there, 'of whom three women and one man were at the mission station. The remaining eight males were engaged in trading and pearling' (Black 1957: 233). In October 1906, Bellamy reported to a Royal Commission on Papua that venereal disease afflicted approximately 10 per cent of the whole population. By the time he left in 1915, he had reduced this figure to only 1 per cent (Austen 1936: 11; Black 1957: 234).

With the permanent presence of a government station in the Trobriands, a more settled island life was achieved. The cause of recorded troubles in 1894 may unwittingly have been provoked by the government when they established the supremacy of Enamakala and his followers. With government operations located on Samarai, official dealings with Trobrianders were made through Enamakala in Omarakana, establishing a level of authority that may not have sat well with other Trobriand communities. Trobriand unrest may further have been a reaction to the unwelcome intrusion of an increasing number of outsiders, or it may have been part of a recurring instability initiated by various local political factions. Whatever the cause, Assistant Resident Magistrate (ARM) Leo Austen, residing at Losuia Station, wrote in 1936:

As regards the natives themselves, they can be considered as a most law-abiding lot. They have their squabbles and their jealousies like any other human beings, but for the most part their breaches of the law are of a petty nature, and the A.R.M. and his three native armed constables are quite able to control the 8500 natives in the Group. (1936: 11)

With the Japanese occupation of Rabaul on 23 January 1942, Trobriand Islanders were drawn into the Second World War. 'On the same day that they [the Japanese] landed at Rabaul they occupied Kavieng, and their aircraft raided the Trobriand Islands' (McCarthy 1959: 39). Following the unsuccessful invasion of the Milne Bay by 2,000 Japanese in August 1942, the area became a strategic base for Allied Forces. Officers were scattered amongst the islands primarily to watch for any evidence of Japanese movement. The Trobriand Islands were occupied by Allied Forces throughout this period (Saville 1974: 15). The troops organised Trobriand labour to help build an airstrip in the north of Kiriwina Island. Their occupation introduced the people to army rations of tinned meat, rice, sugar and other sundries. Today Trobrianders still recall the relative generosity of the Americans over that disposed by Australians, although this observation might have been made for my benefit.

MacGregor's desire to establish an export industry found some difficulties in its execution. The introduction of cash crops has largely been unsuccessful in the Trobriand Islands. At the turn of the century pearling brought considerable cash to lagoon villagers, but the soon-depleted beds left them with poorly maintained gardens and not enough cash to buy rice. Instead of bringing in a steady flow of cash to benefit the local population, a few white traders made a living from the lucrative pearl market. In 1910 a massive programme to plant coconut palms was initiated by Bellamy. Although this was primarily aimed at improving the islanders' diet, a secondary benefit was its potential value as an export industry in the form of copra (Black 1957: 237). Today copra is produced and sold on a small scale by individual Trobrianders. Fishing was also attempted on several occasions as a means of increasing the income of outsiders. All these enterprises have failed in the long term. Today some islanders are able to extract a small, irregular income. The production of carvings for sale to tourists has perhaps been the most lucrative industry for the islanders. We will return to this industry in the next chapter.

Some men and women leave the islands to settle in urban centres. Here they find employment and are able to sustain a modest living. Strong ties are maintained, however, and much of the available cash comes from the expatriate Trobriand population. In general, the islanders continue to rely primarily upon the produce of their gardens for subsistence.

Access to the Trobriand Islands today is principally by air, although transport can sometimes be arranged on various supply boats delivering trade goods throughout the region. After the Second World War, a second air strip was built on Kiriwina Island where aircraft now land to disgorge visitors and returning Trobrianders. Occasionally, 'wealthy' strangers sail into the lagoon aboard yachts, while cruise ships sometimes drop anchor off the deeper waters of northern Kiriwina to allow tourists an evening's entertainment of exotic and highly suggestive dances put on specially to delight the visitors.

As in the past, access to Vakuta Island from Kiriwina remains primarily by outrigger canoe. Occasionally a ride on a government launch can be organised, but visits by government agents are rare. A few people on Vakuta Island own outboard motors and attach these to either a canoe or an aluminium dinghy. The use of outboard motors, however, is rare owing to the uncertain availability of fuel and the difficulty of locating spare parts for broken engines. As today, poor access to the island in the past made visits by Europeans sporadic. Consequently, and in contrast to Kiriwina Island, relatively little is known of Vakutan reactions to European colonisation.

MacGregor first made contact with the people of Vakuta when travelling to the lagoon villages by whaleboat and thence inland. On 27 August 1891 he reached Giribwa village, located on the southernmost tip of Kiriwina Island, and from there he travelled down the lagoon coast of Vakuta Island to the two villages 'Bokinai' and 'Toula'. Upon this first encounter MacGregor records that the people had for some time been well aware of the government and its policies towards the islanders:

> When discussing administrative matters with them they declared they would not fight because they were afraid of the Government. They said they had heard all about the Government from Murua [Woodlark Island] . . . and had long been expecting me at Vakuta. (1891–92: 6)

On this inaugural visit to Vakuta, MacGregor's impressions compared favourably with those he formed of Kiriwina. He adds, however:

> They appeared to me to be of coarser features generally than the Kiriwina people, with round, wide nostrils and a thick nose; and there are not a few genuinely red-haired people, none of whom were noticed on Kiriwina. This admixture is probably to be traced to the more maritime habits of the Vakuta people. (1891–92: 6)

In the following year MacGregor made another survey of Vakuta, this time visiting the larger, inland village of Vakuta. Of this village he wrote: 'The principal village . . . is of unusually large size. The people appeared to be perfectly peaceful and very friendly, and to give more than ordinary obedience to their chief. Food was very abundant' (1892–93: xiii). This reference to 'their chief' and their 'more than ordinary obedience' is curious given comments by Vakutans today regarding rank and my observation that hierarchy is only weakly acknowledged.

In August 1893 MacGregor again anchored in Vakutan waters and in his report records Vakutans' apparent desire to conform to all that the government wanted:

> There I found the chief seated in state on a small platform in the square of his own quarter. We were surrounded by hundreds of resonant throats. The noise, of a friendly and jubilant character, was dreadful, so great that at last the chief took up a gun and,

presenting it at the crowd upside down, put hundreds of them in flight. The chief assured me there had been no fighting or quarrelling in the tribe. He said they wished to have a mission settled there and he promised a site for that purpose. (1893–94: 18)

According to the entry in Fellows's diary of 14 August 1895, John Andrews of the Wesleyan Methodist Mission sailed earlier that day for Vakuta Island to set up a station. Several days after his arrival he sent a report to Fellows saying that he had been well received and had little difficulty in organising labour to build a church and residence for himself and his wife. By 12 June 1896, however, Andrews and his wife left Vakuta due to poor health following several bouts of 'fever', presumably the effects of malaria. Fellows subsequently sent various Fijian and Samoan teachers to Vakuta. All had little success, however, due to chronic sickness followed by requests for transfers. By the end of 1899 Fellows attempted to buy more land further inland from the swamp, apparently convinced that proximity to the water was the cause of the recurrent illness of his teachers. In his diary entry for 10 December of that year, Fellows vowed not to send any more layman if he could not obtain the parcel of land further inland. It appears that nothing had happened by the time of Fellows's last entry in his diary of 7 October 1900, when he left Kiriwina Island. Although there is no known date for the recommencement of the mission station on Vakuta, this probably occurred shortly after the Reverend M. K. Gilmour took over the Mission on Kiriwina Island following Fellows's departure.

Malinowski visited the island briefly, arriving on 15 April 1918 and departing shortly after somewhere between 23 April and 2 May (Wayne 1995: 128–136).[9] By and large, Malinowski's account of his visit reflects considerable enthusiasm for the place and people, 'I am quite in love with Vakuta . . . the main thing is . . . the opportunities for work, and these are excellent here. The information is not pouring in but simply gushing . . . The reason is that . . . they are considerably more civilized by the Mission and work with white men' (Wayne 1995: 130). In the short time he was there, he was able to 'discover' new information, engaging in some lengthy discussions with carvers. However, his attempts to discover anything but a few rudimentary labels for some of the designs confirmed his sense that there was,

neither mythical nor individual explanations as to the meaning of their compositions. The reasons why such and such ornamental motives [*sic*] are combined in a definite manner on a LAGIM [splashboard] or TABUYO [prowboard] of their canoes cannot be squeezed out of [them] and only a very few motives [*sic*] have names and still fewer are referred to natural objects as sources. (Wayne 1995: 133)

With Malinowski's departure no further documentation of events on Vakuta is available, leaving only records kept for Kiriwina to shed some light on local developments on the outlying islands.

The effect of the Second World War on Vakutans can only be estimated. While Kiriwina Island hosted American and Australian Allied Forces, Vakuta was no doubt visited for purposes of reconnaissance. However, Vakutan village life was probably little affected by the events of the war. Several people told stories about their fathers who had worked periodically for the troops on Kiriwina. One man, who had lived as a boy in Giribwa village, told me that his father had harboured a Japanese soldier for a time. The tendency for people of southern Kiriwina and Vakuta to express little allegiance to either side of the conflict may further indicate their minimal involvement.

Tourism, likewise, has had only marginal impact on Vakuta. This is due mostly to the poor accessibility of the island. Although Vakutans are well aware of events occurring on Kiriwina, and to a certain degree receive indirectly the repercussions experienced by Kiriwinan people in their contacts with the outside world, they are by and large unaffected by Kiriwina and remain self-consciously distinct from their northern neighbours.

In the mid-1970s Vakutans were encouraged by Frank Holland, the proprietor of Trobriand Fisheries, to extend their fishing activities and sell the larger part of their catch to him. Freezers were installed and powered by generators. Holland made regular trips from Losuia to empty the freezers and pay the fishermen. By January 1978, however, the freezers were no longer operating, and not long after that Trobriand Fisheries closed and the proprietor took his family off Kiriwina Island.

It was also in the mid-1970s that a self-help development movement named Kabisawali, under the leadership of John Kasaipwalova, was gaining momentum on Kiriwina Island (Kasaipwalova 1975a; Leach 1978, 1982). This provoked a conservative reaction (Tonenei Kamokwita – TK) by those who sought government development and aid. A polarisation occurred within the islands, and alliances were secured according to a complex rationale based upon traditional and contemporary political interests. Vakutans were strongly opposed to the Kabisawali 'upstarts' and pronounced themselves TK supporters. Vakutan alliance with the TK opposition, however, was largely influenced by Lepani Watson (the living descendant of the wife of Togamolu, the first Vakutan), the elected chairman of the TK executive in 1974.

Settlement and Local Groupings on Vakuta

In 1891 MacGregor recorded that there were six villages on Vakuta: 'two large villages on the coast – Bokinai and Toula.[10] They say there are four other villages on the island . . . There are seventy-six houses in Bokina [*sic*] and about the same number in Toula' (1891–92: 6). On the sketch map accompanying his report, however, there are only three villages indicated: Sikwea, Wokinai and Vakuta. On the map of the Trobriand Islands published by Seligman (1910: Figure 46) there are five villages identified on Vakuta: Sikei (presumably Sikwea), Vakuta, Wapaia, Kaulaka and Kwaidagila. Malinowski shows four villages (1922: Map IV): Osikweya, Okinai, Vakuta and Kaulaka. Leo Austen, however, recorded only three villages during his term as ARM: Okinai, Kaulaka and Vakuta (1936). On a map made by the Allied Forces in 1942 and based upon government records, Vakuta Island is again credited with five villages. Four of these are the familiar Osikwea, Okinai, Vakuta and Kaulaka, but there is the addition of Loriu village (Allied Geographical Section 1942). These inconsistencies raise the question of population dynamics in the first half of the century. There may have been a decrease in the Vakutan population, resulting in a contraction of villages and hamlets. Vakutans' own recollections suggest a considerable decline in their population. They pointed to areas around the main village, once the location of old hamlets long since abandoned.

Today there are three villages on the island: Okinai, Vakuta and Kaulaka. However, another village, Giribwa, situated on the southern tip of Kiriwina Island, claims political, economic and social affiliation with Vakuta. The populations of these villages are relatively fluid. There is considerable movement between them for the purposes of marriage, changing alliances and relocations following deaths.

The layout of Vakutan villages is very different from that described for the villages of northern Kiriwina, resembling more the coastal pattern described by Malinowski as presenting 'quite a chaotic appearance' (1922: 55; see also Powell 1969a: 188; Seligman 1910: 662; Weiner 1977: 33). Of Vakuta village, MacGregor wrote: 'The village is a very large one, the houses built in irregular batches to suit the rocky nature of the ground, so that it is not easy to form an idea of the exact number [of houses]; but there are probably 200 to 300'[11] (1892–93: 9). Although Vakutan villages may *look* irregularly arranged, they are in fact very precisely organised into distinct hamlets (Figure 1.3).

Vakuta village, by far the largest on the island, has fifteen distinct hamlets, each linked to the others by a network of well-worn footpaths.[12] Individual hamlets are more or less spatially organised around a central area, some more clearly so than others, with houses delineating hamlet boundaries. Although clustered around a central space, dwellings do not necessarily face towards the centre of the hamlet, as shown by the orientation arrows in Figure 1.3. Malinowski referred to the central spaces of Kiriwinan villages as *baku* (1922: 56). Vakutans do not regularly use this term, preferring instead to denote these spaces by hamlet name. Spaces between hamlets are incorporated into the social domain of each hamlet. Coral outcrops mark significant historical locations or the remains of a house belonging to a particularly important person. These inter-hamlet spaces are where recently deceased members of the hamlet are buried. Certain trees are planted in these

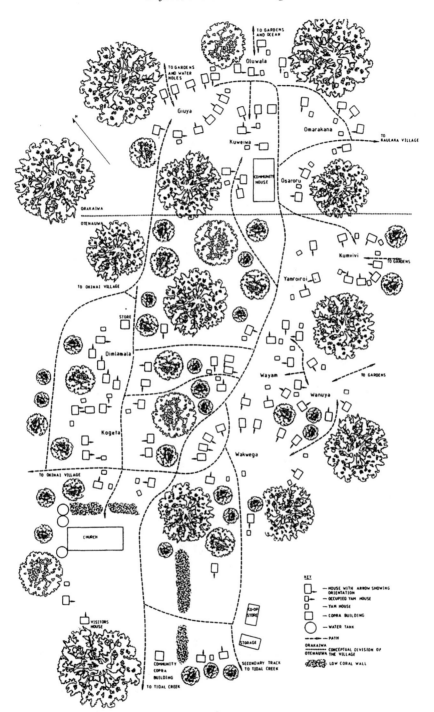

Figure 1.3 Plan of Vakuta Village

spaces, providing the residents with cherished *seida*, or 'native almond' (*terminalia catappa*)[13] when in season, as well as the produce from coconut and betelnut palms, mango and banana trees.

Vakuta village is conceptually divided in half. This division is associated with the spatial oppositions upper/lower and above/below (*orakaiwa/otenauwa*; see Figure 1.3). While there is no hierarchical relationship implied by this opposition today, people said that the division demarcated political alliances between past leaders. The distinction between upper/lower, above/below has further symbolic associations that will be discussed in greater detail later. At this point it is enough to note that this division is incorporated into the social mapping of the village.

In addition, each hamlet is further associated with one of the four matrilineal clans, or, more specifically, to a *dala*. Ownership of hamlet land is based upon mythological charters.[14] Although the Vakutan origin myth describes how the original Vakutan emerged from a hole in Kuweiwa hamlet, and his subsequent largesse in the endowment of land to latecomers, each owning *dala* of the existing hamlets maintains a specific 'origin' myth detailing how their ancestors came to be on that parcel of hamlet land, or specific events demonstrating their rights to the land. Senior male members of each *dala* are responsible for the 'foundations' (*tumila*) of *dala* land, and reside in their respective hamlets. This person has the right to determine who may or may not be buried on hamlet land.[15] While all members of the owning *dala* have a right to be buried within the hamlet, others must apply for plots and give valuables in payment for them. The valuables are distributed amongst other senior members of the *dala* who may or may not be resident within their *dala* hamlet. The senior male resident of the owning *dala* also has the ultimate say in who may reside in the hamlet and where houses should be built. Again, owning *dala* members claim a right to reside in their *dala* hamlet, while others must apply to the senior male resident. The ideal composition of the hamlet would include all male members of the *dala* from late adolescence to their death, together with their wives and children. However, this is far from the reality.

Residence patterns on Vakuta today do not follow those prescribed by avuncu-local residence rules described by Malinowski (1932) as typical. Instead, people choose where to live according to personal preferences, political expediency and mortuary obligations. Both Powell (1960, 1969a) and Weiner (1977) noted the low frequency of avunculocal residence in contrast to the popularity of other residence preferences. Powell argued that only in cases where a man was likely to inherit the 'ownership' of the village from his mother's brother did he make a definite move to his own village (1960). Otherwise most men were just as likely to choose alternative places of residence according to changing political and economic opportunities (see also Weiner 1977: 42).

In brief, residence on Vakuta is fluid. Apart from the effects of death, marriage or divorce on initiating movement between hamlets, men tend to change their place of residence in pursuit of better political and economic possibilities, acting as individuals in pursuit of their own opportunities to enjoy successful social lives. Women move with their husbands, or, following divorce, return to the hamlet of their birth where their mothers or other maternal kin may continue to reside. Thus, although there is a vague ideology favouring avunculocal residence for men, they choose alternative residence locations, indicating a complex range of considerations reflected in the high degree of mobility between hamlets. This tendency towards individual men being mobile and somewhat free of matrilineal obligations is echoed in the symbolism of kula, as we shall see later.

Generally, the sphere of influence enjoyed by the resident senior man extends only to those matters concerning hamlet land. The management of a *dala*'s garden land is not necessarily vested in this person, although if he is a man of general influence within the community he will have a great deal to say about the distribution of garden land. Contrary to the obligations of hamlet residents to the hamlet 'manager' described by Weiner for northern Kiriwinan villages (1977: 146), Vakutan hamlet residents do not specifically make gardens for senior men in the hamlet. They may, however, make gardens for these men in accordance with other exchange obligations.

Subsistence

Typically, the Vakutan economy centres on the yam garden. Yams not only provide the primary means of sustenance, they also act as essential objects of exchange in the complex network of community relations (Campbell 1989, n.d.[b]; Hutchins 1980; Malinowski 1932, 1935; Weiner 1977, 1988). A wide range of exchange obligations requires people to give yams at harvest time. Yams are distributed as payment for canoes, rights to the use of canoes, payment for domestic and yam house construction and the carving of boards for any of these. Further, payment in the form of yams for the use of land, for either a live pig or pork and for magic are only some of the exchanges using yams as the main item in reciprocal relations. Mortuary obligations can drain a large proportion of a man's harvest (Campbell 1989; Weiner 1977). Marriage payments are made in the form of yams as initial 'gifts', interest on 'gifts' and continuing exchanges related to marriage. The giving of yams forms complex relationships that can take several years, if ever, to finalise. Yams are also given as *pokala*,[16] a specific type of exchange to be described later. Finally, prior to colonial and missionary interference, yams were the focus of a system of magic, meticulously described by Malinowski (1935). Seed yams, tubers still developing in the soil, yam vines, freshly harvested yams and those stored in yam houses received considerable attention from men possessing special knowledge of spells designed to have some impact on the health of the tuber.

Ideally, Vakutans maintain three gardens at any one time.[17] Firstly, there is the 'old garden' (*origabu*) from which all yams have been harvested during the harvest 'month' (mid-July to mid-August). Villagers rely upon the *origabu* to provide them with a variety of foods throughout the year. Several varieties of taro, sweet potato, tapioca and pumpkin are also planted in these gardens. A second garden (*kamgwa*) is planted as an alternative garden and used to sustain a family when the old garden has been depleted and before new yams are ready for harvesting. As Bomtarasi of Kuweiwa hamlet put it, 'All wise gardeners make *kamgwa* to see them through the months of hunger.' The third garden (*kaimata*) is the main garden and is often referred to as the 'new' garden. In this garden, exchange yams, seed yams and yams for domestic use are grown. As a consequence, the status of the 'new' garden assures it the greatest attention during the year.

The Vakutan calendar revolves around the events taking place in this garden, with each lunation marking a new stage in the gardening cycle. The preparation of this garden for the planting of yams marks the beginning of the Vakutan new year. Once the garden is prepared only men's yams are planted. Vakutans make a distinction between men's yams and women's yams. Men's yams are grown for competitive display as well as for distribution and exchange. These can only be planted and harvested by men. Women's yams, on the other hand, are grown for family consumption and receive no collective attention. The annual cycle and all associated public activities in the garden are directed towards the production of men's yams. Women's yams are planted at any time along the tracks and in the borders of the *kaimata* gardens. They are harvested as needed.

Apart from the distinction between exchange yams grown by men and consumption yams grown by women other indicators also exist. When women's yams are used for exchange they are cooked and presented on a plate with other cooked vegetables to a particular person for a specific exchange purpose. Men's yams are usually exchanged in a raw state and carry quite different meanings.[18] Following the harvest of men's yams from mid-July to August, the *kaimata* becomes the 'old' garden and a new *kaimata* garden is cleared after the harvest celebrations. On Vakuta a man's exchange garden is the same as his main subsistence garden (cf. Weiner 1977, 1988).

It is difficult to compare the types of gardens on Vakuta with those of northern Kiriwina. Malinowski's distinctions are somewhat difficult to differentiate, particularly those which define 'fields', 'gardens' and 'plots' (see 1935 Vol. 1: 58, 87–91). Generally, however, it seems that Vakutans cultivate in any one season more than one 'field', to use Malinowski's term. Although Malinowski notes that more than one 'field' per village may be cultivated, these are for separate uses, none of which overlap: for example, one *kaimata* 'field' may be cultivated, while one *kaymugwa* 'field' (Vakutan *kamgwa*?) may be cultivated, and so on. On Vakuta, however, a man may have a *kaimata* 'plot' in the same 'field' as his *kamgwa* 'plot', or he may have a *kaimata* 'plot' in a 'field' where others have *kamgwa* 'plots'. In comparison with some areas on Kiriwina, land is not as scarce on Vakuta relative to the population it supports. Hence there seems to be greater flexibility in the allocation of land to the types of gardens that can be cultivated. Powell (1969b) and Brunton (1975) argued that the higher population density of northern Kiriwina 'caused' relations of hierarchy to emerge, resulting in the development of ascribed positions of rank. If this account is valid, the much weaker presence of rank within Vakutan social relations may be a consequence of lower population density and decreased pressure on land, a situation not dissimilar to other Massim communities.[19]

Further differences in garden utilisation between Vakuta and northern Kiriwina are evident from Weiner's data and the distinctions she makes between subsistence gardens (*gubakayeki*) and exchange gardens (*kaymata* and *kaymwila*). Weiner describes how in northern Kiriwina a family's subsistence garden is quite separate to the garden from which exchange yams are cultivated (1977: 137–138). As indicated above, this is not the case on Vakuta. The main exchange garden may also contain subsistence yams as well as other cultigens grown for consumption.

The natural environment is good to Vakutans, providing them with more than adequate food supplies. In fact, Vakutan harvests are known throughout the Trobriand Islands, and further afield, as being plentiful. When other areas suffer from poor harvests, Vakutans seem to fare better, their high yields sought by less fortunate Kiriwinans and people from the Amphlett Islands.

Apart from yams, several varieties of taro, sweet potato, tapioca, breadfruit, sugar cane, together with numerous kinds of plantain and banana, nourish the population. Pineapple and pumpkin are popular, while oranges, grapefruit, corn and beans are the least favoured of the introduced fruits and vegetables. Foodstuffs from the bush include various kinds of greens, herbs, nuts, mangos and edible flowers. These are available seasonally and offer some relief from the monotony of the yam diet.

As well as being prolific gardeners, Vakutans are very successful fishermen, the produce of the sea representing another important item for consumption and exchange. On average, a family eats fish five days a week. Men do all the fishing, although young unmarried girls may sometimes help their fathers, particularly if they have no brothers. The techniques used are numerous, with various kinds of net fishing, spear fishing, line fishing and poison utilised (see also Malinowski 1918). Pig, chicken and other birds are also a source of animal protein. Pork is particularly valued as a source of food and as a mark of prestige when given in distributions. It is eaten only on special occasions usually involving elaborate exchanges.

In the 1970s a couple of people maintained small trade stores on the island from which Vakutans purchased 'exotic' food, including sugar, rice, tea, tinned beef and fish, biscuits, tins of jam and marmalade, rice, oil, kerosene, tobacco and other goods commonly found in trade stores throughout Papua New Guinea.

Exchange

The use of exchange to create, define, validate, or challenge interpersonal and inter-group relations is one of the more characteristic features of Vakutan life. Everywhere, and on nearly all levels of interaction, activities associated with various classes of exchange take place. Vakuta, of course, is not unique with respect to the pervasive impact of exchange on social life. Malinowski recognised the intrinsic significance of exchange on 'primitive economics' when he argued that for Trobrianders:

> *the whole tribal life is permeated by a constant give and take*; that every ceremony, every legal and customary act is done to the accompaniment of material gift and counter-gift; that wealth, given and taken, is one of the main instruments of social organisation . . . (1922: 167)

Many writers have since emphasised the importance of exchange in Trobriand relationships (Leach 1983; Montague 1989; Powell 1960; Uberoi 1962; Weiner 1977, 1978, 1980, 1983, 1988). Although all of the Trobriand Island communities, and indeed other Massim societies, share a similar, almost fanatical preoccupation with exchange, it is clear that within each community exchange is used to define relationships differently. For the purpose of facilitating a comparative analysis at this point, it is helpful to distinguish between 'spheres' of internal exchange and 'spheres' of external exchange. In so doing, however, there is a risk that an over-simplification of the data may lead to a misrepresentation of exchange on Vakuta. Bearing in mind, however, that the distinction is an analytic one developed to help in the initial description of exchange, the complexities that actually exist will, it is hoped, emerge more clearly in the discussion. To a certain extent Vakutans, too, make a distinction between exchange between themselves and exchange with outsiders, although there is no word that succinctly marks this distinction. Nevertheless, Vakutans note that the overt behaviours, inherent in exchanges that take place between Vakutans, are different from the behaviours generated by exchanges between Vakutans and outsiders. Similarly, Vakutans distinguish between items they receive through exchanges entered into with other Vakutans (raw yams, pigs, fish, coconuts and cooked food) and exchange items obtained from outsiders (kula shell valuables, long yams or *kuvi*, ochre, pots and other exotics). Nevertheless, these exchanges inter-penetrate, crossing the boundaries between 'internal' and 'external', as will be shown later.[20]

Internal exchange takes many forms. Individual services are rendered in exchange for food or small items of sundry value. Examples include gifts given by a man when soliciting a woman's sexual favours or between husbands and wives. Vakutans warn that a man, once married, must continue to provide his wife with special food and small valuables lest she withdraw her sexual services (see also Malinowski 1922: 177–179). Services of a communal nature are also part of the exchange network. Whenever communal labour is required for garden work, canoe or house building, the labourers are rewarded immediately by food and refreshment and later by the reciprocal supply of labour for other projects. Some of the activities requiring communal labour also incorporate the exchange of men's raw yams as well as cooked food and refreshment.

Other forms of internal exchange occur exclusively between kin. Examples of these include informal reciprocal relations between 'sisters' and 'brothers', together with the more formal exchanges between this category of kin. An example of an internal exchange occurring between kin is demonstrated through *urigubu*.[21] On Vakuta *urigubu* is a gift of the fruits of a betelnut palm, a betel-pepper vine, pig, sugar cane, taro, yams or sweet potato to a man's sisters, daughters, sister's daughters or mother. For example, a man may grow and nurture a particular betelnut palm so that when it reaches maturity and begins to bear fruit he can give it to a woman close to him, saying, '*kam urigubu*' ('your *urigubu*'). The recipient becomes the 'owner' of the fruit, but not of the tree or land from which it grows. The giver retains the right of ownership over the tree and land but he can never take the fruit or harvest from the land which he has given as *urigubu*. The reciprocal exchange for *urigubu* is either in the form of a shell valuable or money. Concurrent with *urigubu* is another exchange called *vaula kaukweda*. Whereas *urigubu* is given to female relatives, men give *vaula kaukweda* to their sons. The exchange involves giving part of a butchered pig to a son, who then cooks and eats it. At the following harvest, the recipient gives baskets of yams to his father in recognition of the eaten pork.

Another form of exchange occurring between kin is that which establishes a formal relationship between a boy and his father's brother. This exchange relationship exists until the death of either partner. In its simplest form, the exchange involves a boy giving seasonal produce in its raw state to his father's brother and the latter making reciprocal exchanges of valuables and cooked food. It is noteworthy that this exchange complex occurs between people of different generations who have no formal economic responsibility to each other, unlike that between matrilineal kin and the social father. Instead, an economic relationship is artificially stimulated through this exchange. This relationship may also be seen as a mock kula partnership; a training period in which a boy learns the ways of exchange relationships and the advantages that they provide. The exchanges are between specific partners and involve delayed reciprocity. These exchanges are also a means by which young men acquire kula shell valuables, thus opening an avenue to initiate their kula career. Although occurring between people on Vakuta, this represents an example of the collapsing of boundaries between 'internal' and 'external' exchange. One of the principal items featured in these exchanges are kula shell valuables obtained from outsiders in external exchange.

The majority of formal internal exchange relationships occur between affines. Exchanges that occur at harvest time (Malinowski's *urigubu* payments, 1922, 1932, 1935), those resulting from mutual assistance between affines, the acquisition of essential exchange objects for major distributions, exchanges involved in boat-building, house and yam house construction, as well as marriage exchanges and the cycle of exchanges set off by a death – all involve relationships between people linked through marriage. There is an extensive depth and breadth of exchange networks activated between affines that require a more fully articulated explanation. However, my purpose here is simply to indicate the complexities of interpersonal relationships so as to provide the context for which the art of kula can be illuminated.[22]

Trade for Amphlett pots, long yams, ochres and other exotics occurs beyond the boundaries of Vakuta Island. Generally, these items do not feature in formal exchanges between Vakutans. Individuals obtain them by travelling to the areas of manufacture and cultivation. This is often accomplished during kula expeditions. Amphlett pots are sometimes given in marriage exchanges by the bridegroom's kin to the bride's kin (*takola*), but more usually these payments include kula shell valuables, axe blades, pigs and, today, money.

Unlike the social circumstances reported for Kiriwina (Leach 1983; Malinowski 1922; Powell 1960, 1969b; Weiner 1983) there is no internal kula within Vakuta. Vakutans consider kula relations to be highly volatile, and thus unsuited to the maintenance of social harmony amongst themselves. To engage in kula relationships with other Vakutans would, they believe, endanger the cohesiveness and perceived tranquillity of community life. Hence, kula activity on Vakuta is exclusively undertaken with outsiders. All Vakutan men are expected to participate in kula. Indeed, kula shell valuables are an essential item of exchange used in several of the internal exchange cycles. This makes it necessary for men to engage in kula activities to obtain these items and thereby enable their participation in domestic exchange.

Vakutans maintain kula partnerships with men on Kitava Island to the east, with men along the east coast of Fergusson Island, and with men of Tewara, Sanaroa, and Dobu Islands to the south-west. They have no kula partnerships with anyone on Kiriwina Island. As the following texts indicate, Vakutans consider Kiriwinans inexperienced kula operators with whom kula partnerships are undesirable:

A long time ago, before missionaries came, there was a big war in the Trobriand Islands: Kiriwina [n.b. Kiriwina here refers to north-east Boyowa and not the whole island],

Kaileuna, Kitava, Sinaketa, Vakuta, all were fighting each other. Before this war Kiriwina did not kula, only Sinaketa, Kitava and Vakuta. After the war, Kiriwinans saw the valuables and wanted to kula, but only with Sinaketa and some with Kitava. They were afraid to come to Vakuta because they would be killed here. (Kunabu, Kuweiwa hamlet, Vakuta village)

Mr Perosi (Reverend Fellows), Babari (MacGregor?) and Saragigi (Dr Bromilow) came from Australia to the Milne Bay [District]. They visited each island and stopped the fighting. They came to Vakuta, then to Kiriwina. Kiriwina stopped fighting and after that the Kiriwinans began to kula. (Youwa, Wakwega hamlet, Vakuta village)

Many years ago the people of Kiriwina did not kula, only Sinaketa and Vakuta. When the village was clean [no fighting] they began to kula. Saragigi was at Dobu, a missionary. He was the first to stop war. After the wars finished Kiriwina started to kula. (Sulubogi, Okinai village; originally from Tewara Island)

These three accounts question the involvement of men from northern Kiriwina Island in kula prior to the middle to late nineteenth century. All three independently describe a period of considerable unrest between the different communities of the Trobriand Islands.[23] Once hostilities were successfully curtailed by the colonial government it may be that Kiriwinans obtained safer routes through which to commence kula operations.

Vakutans worry explicitly over the explosive nature of kula partnerships. These are usually fraught with deceit and suspicion, particularly as the acquisition of kula shell valuables is one of the requisites for the achievement of status within the majority of kula communities throughout the district (Leach and Leach 1983). Vakutan kula partnerships are generally of short duration, as opportunistic individuals throughout the network increase their status and renown by manipulating lucrative pathways at the expense of their partners (Campbell 1983a). Vakutan men are constantly on the lookout for opportunities to enhance their influence within their own community and build up their renown throughout the kula network. For this reason they break up partnerships, set up new kula routes or reinstate old relationships. An example of the seriousness with which Kitavan and Vakutan men regard kula also illustrates the potential hostility and instability of kula partnerships.

In October 1977 Kitavan men, on the pretext of attending the Vakutan yam harvest festival, tried to reclaim an armshell given by one of them to a Vakutan who had gone to Kitava on a kula expedition earlier that year. They claimed that the armshell had been wrongfully enticed away from its proper path. The situation had developed because this Vakutan had successfully persuaded the Kitavan to relinquish it with promises of a superior shell necklace on its way to Vakuta from the south. The Kitavan, subsequently receiving threats of sorcery from his Dobuan and Gawan kula partners, thought better of his actions and wanted to redress the situation, hence his visit to Vakuta along with fellow Kitavans who supported his intention to reclaim the armshell. The Vakutan refused to surrender his armshell. The Kitavans, desperate at the refusal and the looming likelihood of sorcery attacks, tried to steal it during the night. The following day I was relaxing with friends awaiting the evening's festivities when heart-stopping screams shattered the tranquil sounds of village life. This was followed by much shouting and commotion as villagers ran to investigate the trouble. By the time I arrived at the scene dogs were barking, while women and children were screaming and crying hysterically. Men stood, frozen with fear not knowing what to do, their eyes fixed on the greater commotion at the centre of the crowd. The nucleus of the disquiet was a few men surrounded by others, poised with spears held high and ready for release. Finally, spears whistled through the tense air and the centre exploded with some men running in pursuit of escaping Kitavans, others spinning in confusion while calmer men tried to restrain them. The scene was one of complete pandemonium. Two Vakutan men became casualties in the commotion: one man was hit in the arm, the other in the leg, The Kitavans escaped the village and were later smuggled off the island without the armshell. In the days and nights that followed there was much talk of going to Kitava to fight those responsible for upsetting the community during harvest festivities, considered a time for rejoicing and relaxation. The raids were never made and the rage gradually subsided, although a serious rift remained between those directly involved.

Vakutans are less explicit about the role kula plays in the competitiveness of internal relationships. Men direct their aggression outwards in kula activities so as to veil the internal competition for status within their own community. This was deduced by Uberoi from Malinowski's (1922) and Fortune's (1932) descriptions of kula in Kiriwina and Dobu:

> the rites which punctuate the progress of an overseas expedition serve to mark out the social categories at home, within one district, and progressively loosen up their internal solidarity, so that canoe competes with canoe within the same fleet, and one man against another within the same canoe. (Uberoi 1962: 147)

The Vakutan Political Environment

> There really are no chiefs on Vakuta. In the past we did not have such a thing. A man was *guyau* [chief] if he was good at kula or in his gardens, but he was not always *guyau*, others were *guyau* too. We did not have *guyau* who were *guyau* because their ancestors were. (Vanisi Guyau, Dimlamala hamlet, Vakuta village)

> Within recent times, perhaps four to six generations ago, there came down and settled in [Vakuta] a branch of the real Tabalu, the chiefly family of highest rank. But their

power here never assumed the proportions even of the small chiefs of Sinaketa. In Vakuta, the typical Papuo-Melanesian system of government by tribal elders – with one more prominent than the others, but not paramount – is in full vigour. (Malinowski 1922: 69)

On Vakuta Island social relations are essentially egalitarian. Exchange between Vakutans operates to distribute wealth and is unaffected by the formal hierarchical constraints that impose economic inequalities in northern Kiriwina. Thus in the basic structuring of relationships within the community, Vakuta is much more akin to other Massim societies.

Although Vakutans share with other Trobrianders the labels identifying the different clans and sub-clans, there is no effective ranking system of these groups. It is not by virtue of birth that individuals on Vakuta claim special privileges. Rather, it is by industriousness, the ability to manipulate exchange networks and the demonstration of merit that individuals achieve status. While Powell (1960) and Weiner (1977, 1988) have modified Malinowski's characterisation of ascribed status and rank in northern Kiriwina by demonstrating that men of high rank compete for 'paramount' positions, it is still only from among the high ranks of Kiriwinan society that leaders are drawn. On Vakuta any man has the opportunity for achieving status. Individuals who desire prestige, however, must demonstrate their worth.

There is a man on Vakuta with the title of chief. He is referred to by the government administration at Losuia as the 'chief of Vakuta' and sometimes sits as figurehead at community meetings, although he does not officiate.[24] Other men, particularly those who have achieved status and influence at a given time, orate at length on the matters at hand, while a church councillor officiates. The man distinguished by the term 'chief' participates in these too, but to no greater or lesser degree than anyone else wishing to have a say.

A measure of this man's standing within the community may be deduced from the context of kula, itself a significant generator of influential men. In May 1977 the men of Vakuta were preparing for a kula expedition to Kitava Island. Although the 'chief' had kula business awaiting him on Kitava, he chose not to participate. It is not clear whether he was overlooked and not offered a place on any of the outrigger canoes making the voyage or whether he did not go for other reasons. As it turned out, he did have 'bad' kula business on Kitava.[25] Whatever the reason, a man with high ambition and a status to uphold is unlikely to forgo the opportunity to strengthen his position by avoiding a kula expedition. It was in this context that I was told that Vakutans did not consider the title of chief to have any relevance to their internal social relations.

The network of exchanges occurring between Vakutan men operates to equalise their economic position, unlike the prevailing conditions on northern Kiriwina where privilege accompanies rank to ensure that certain men are able to accumulate more wealth and thereby establish inequalities between themselves and others. For Kiriwinans this effectively separates those who are able to maintain their influence and authority from those who cannot. On Vakuta this cannot occur. In the absence of an institutional fixing of inequality, the accumulation of wealth on Vakuta is theoretically unobstructed; everyone has equal opportunity to acquire and use wealth to his or her own advantage. The ways in which one can obtain wealth are related to one's labour output. For example, if a man is a good gardener who works hard and has access to good garden magic which he has solicited (*pokala'd*) from a senior man, he will be able to harvest wealth in the form of yams. If he works hard at manipulating his kula routes, he will have wealth in the form of valuables that can then be transformed into other wealth (Campbell 1983a). Another way in which a man can accumulate wealth is through the fine management of all exchange relationships, ensuring that other people's labour is geared to the production of his wealth. Significant exchange relationships are those maintained primarily with affines. An illustration follows of how a man might set in motion processes by which he is able to maximise his ability to acquire wealth.

In one year a man might build a kula canoe for his sister's husband (*kaiyaula*). His payment is a very large proportion of his sister's husband's yam harvest (*karibudaboda*). He might have also transferred a kula shell valuable to internal exchange by giving it to a recently married man of his *dala* needing valuables (*takola*; referred to as *takwalela pepe'i* by Malinowski 1932: 76–80). *Takola* is a repayment for the wedding gift of raw yams (*pepeni*; Malinowski's *pepe'i*). He would then, at harvest, receive a very large proportion of yams given to the new groom by his wife's family (*vilakuri*). Thus in one year he would receive yams from his sister's husband in payment for a canoe, yams from a male kinsman in payment for a valuable given in a marriage transaction, and yams from various other exchange obligations. He would also harvest yams from his own garden. This large accumulation of yams he could reinvest by giving some as seed tubers to his sister(s) (*kabisivisi*), whose husbands are then obliged to repay them in the form of kula shell valuables (and nowadays money; *takola*). One of these valuables would have to be put into kula to replace the one removed to help his married clansman pay for the *pepeni*. The other valuables he could call his *kitoum* and invest as he wishes.[26] Other yams he might earmark for a female relative rumoured to be nearing marriage (a new *pepeni* gift). The payment for these would be shell valuables or other 'male' valuables such as pigs, pots and axe blades (*takola*). He could give more of his yams to a senior man who possessed land, trees (betelnut or coconut) or a specific form of magic in the hope of eventually acquiring one of these (*pokala*). This is, of course, a considerably simplified account of the possibilities available to a man in the management of his wealth. The example, however, demonstrates the interpenetrating nature of various exchanges and how directing valuables acquired from external exchange into internal exchange leaves a deficit that needs to be recovered.

While wealth is a measure of one's industriousness and the ability to mobilise exchange relationships, it is essential to keep it moving. The distribution of wealth forges alliances, which in turn generate more wealth in returned gifts. Failing to distribute one's wealth is considered anti-social. Hoarding is not only disdained, but also dangerous. Conspicuous accumulation of wealth is believed to attract the jealousy of sorcerers and witches.

Apart from the strong social pressure to distribute one's wealth as soon as possible, there are other 'equalising' mechanisms to encourage its dispersal. If, for example, a man 'comes first' in kula by acquiring the majority of valuables or receives an excessive amount of skirts or yams in a distribution (*sagali*), there is an institution that sanctions the wholesale appropriation and redistribution of it. This is called *kwaikwaiya*. The sanction is far from pleasant, and its threat deters anyone from a disproportionate accumulation of wealth. *Kwaikwaiya* is invoked if someone's excessive gain is not followed by its timely distribution. On a pre-determined night villagers meet at the 'lucky' person's hamlet and seize most of the material wealth from his and his neighbours' houses by distraint. If the victims want to retrieve their belongings they must redeem them by using other wealth items such as yams, betelnut and coconut from their gardens. I was assured that everything is removed: pots, pans, pigs, clothes, any valuables, even the bed the hapless householders may have been sleeping on!

A man who is able to accumulate wealth for distribution, as well as open and manage new exchange relationships, demonstrates confidence in his ability to plan and manipulate situations as they arise. This is a significant means of gaining esteem from fellow Vakutans. In contrast to the ascribed position of some men on Kiriwina who are expected to accumulate and display their wealth as a symbol of their position and the inherent powers of that position, Vakutan men compete with one another to achieve status through the distribution of wealth. By giving their wealth away, Vakutans establish support networks that can be used to steady tenuous positions of influence and leadership in day-to-day relations. Vakutans value the relationships created through the perpetual distribution of wealth. Weiner's analysis of Trobriand exchange (1977, 1978, 1983) demonstrates that exchange relationships created through the distribution of wealth are also valued among the non-ranked population of northern Kiriwina, but these relationships are not concerned with achieving positions of status and influence as is the case on Vakuta. Rather, exchange relationships in northern Kiriwina serve to recognise the relative status between people already established through birth. On Vakuta, birth merely identifies the group to which an individual belongs and from which he or she receives land. It does not establish an individual's relative status. This must be achieved through the channels opened via exchange.

As it does in other Massim societies, exchange binds the entire fabric of Vakutan life. In summary, wealth and its distribution is not only the means by which individuals achieve status, it is also a mechanism for the equalising of men's economic status *vis-à-vis* other men. In this regard, the distribution of wealth maintains an overt equality between them. Participation in kula is one of the principal means by which men achieve status within the Vakutan community. It not only provides men with the opportunity to demonstrate their skills in wooing external partners and risking the higher stakes of kula with renowned shells, it also provides men with an essential wealth item used to meet their community obligations. Shell valuables, acting as the currency of kula, are also necessary in many exchanges between Vakutans. However, the feeding of shell valuables into Vakutan exchange networks can be disruptive to the operation of kula as a separate, external system. This is manifest in the inability of men to put back into the external exchange system what was taken out for local use at any given time (Campbell 1983a). It is this inherent conflict that a successful man must negotiate, giving kula, in the one instance its allure, while at the same time holding within it the seeds of a man's destruction.

Reflections on the Domestic

There are seven main paths leading away from the village (Figure 1.3). One path leads north-east to the ocean and a favourite coral grotto where women go to wash their clothes on weekdays. On Sunday afternoons it is reserved for adolescent boys and girls who use it as a favourite meeting place after church. This path also by-passes an area of garden land, which was in a fallow state during my stay, the vines and creepers invading the once well-defined borders separating garden from unworked forest. Another path leads eastwards, linking the village to Kaulaka and the government school. A third path leads south to the tidal creek where the village's fishing and kula outrigger canoes are moored, while another path links Vakuta village to Okinai and the lagoon to the west. The remaining three paths lead out of the village towards separate garden areas.

As Vakutans are primarily horticulturalists, and fishermen only secondarily, the garden areas represent a very important focus of activity on nearly every day of the Vakutan year, finishing with a yam harvest celebration (*kovesa*) in mid-September/mid-October. On Vakuta, as elsewhere on the islands of the Milne Bay, people calculate time by the phases of the moon and the associated activities in their gardens.[27] At the end of the annual garden cycle, yams are harvested and celebration is in the air with the rise of the Milamalia moon.[28]

When the next moon rises it is time to commence another year with the clearing of new garden land. When the day's work has finished in the gardens and the time has come to return home, individuals meet on the various tracks leading to the village. On the way home many stop to wash: women congregate in one bend of the tidal creek while men wade into the deeper pools of another bend.

Quiet by day, the village is invigorated as people return. Stopping momentarily to greet friends and relatives, sharing some bit of gossip about the day's events, individuals continue along the path to their homes. People rarely return home empty-handed. Firewood is generally carried in by women. Groups of girls bring sacks of land crab, mud crab or crab taken from the coral reefs. This delicacy is distributed amongst family and friends to enjoy for their evening meal. Young men bring in fish for the family and other relations. These may be cooked immediately or smoked by the recipients. Married women usually enter the village laden with baskets of freshly harvested vegetables or foods gathered from the bush while married men return at dusk with bush knife and axe slung casually over their shoulders. On occasion a bunch of betelnut, delicately balanced on the tip of a bush knife, accompanies the men. It is often distributed and enjoyed during the evening's socialising.

Soon smoke rises from various houses as women prepare the evening meal. Young girls fetch water from the tidal creek for cooking. Coconut is scraped and the liquid squeezed from the flesh and added to the pot. Men sit and chew betelnut while talking of the day's activities, planning tomorrow's work and playing with their infants. Young children continue their day's amusements. They play with their age-mates in neighbouring hamlets, running off that last burst of energy before the evening meal makes them lethargic and a full stomach gradually entices them to sleep. Their chores over, young men and women plan their evening rendezvous and prepare for the night's pleasures.

As families sit down together to share in the day's harvest, much discussion continues as the members relay the continuing saga of recent intrigues, elaborating on the day's latest gossip. Once the meal has finished, betelnut is handed out and black twist tobacco rolled in strips of newspaper. Soon darkness settles. The wicks are lit so that the feeble flames of kerosene lamps dimly light the verandas of the village houses.

Visits are rarely made on rainy evenings. Adults and young children are content to stay by their warm hearths and chat amongst themselves before retiring early to bed. Young men and women are the only ones undaunted by a wet night. Equipped with rain mats, they make their rendezvous. Rainless nights, however, have a different character about them altogether.

On a moonless night the village tracks are filled with gently swaying kerosene lanterns casting an awkward light on the face of their carriers. The village paths are busy with people moving from one veranda to another; they crowd onto the well-lit verandas in preference to the darkness of the village. An occasional squeal, followed by a tirade of accusatory shouts and then laughter, interrupts the evening's discourse as two lampless people collide along one of the village paths. People rarely leave the village to follow paths leading outside it for fear of encounters with various supernatural pranksters or witches. Exceptions to this are men going fishing, women collectively heading for the mangroves to hunt crabs, or youths who organise an ambush on one of the inter-village tracks. Their purpose is to catch and punish a youth from another village who is suspected of organising an assignation with a girl from their own village. Although good relations between the youth of the three villages generally prevails, there is, on occasion, a show of possessive jealousy over the girls in one's own village.

If the night is lit by a full moon, a wider range of activities become possible. Villagers move away from the houses to the central areas of the hamlets. They gather to sing either 'traditional' Vakutan songs (*wosimoiya*) or multi-phonal religious songs introduced by Fijian missionaries. Alternatively they may enjoy the local string-band music. Other villagers may dance 'traditional' dances, or they may prefer the modern dancing accompanying island music. Still others may sit around a storyteller and listen for hours to his or her repertoire.

After the evening's activities reach a high-point, the participants gradually dwindle in number as tired men, women and children return to their houses and stretch out on sleeping mats. Young men and women, however, seeming not to tire, organise further gatherings or more private encounters. Eventually they too begin to wander off alone or as couples. A few men may remain on one of the verandas in the village discussing plans for a coming event or a particular ceremony. Soon they too retire to their sleeping mats and the village lies peacefully asleep until the early crow of the cock warns of the coming dawn and the beginning of another gardening day in the cycle of growth governing Vakutan life.

–2–

Craftsmen and Artists

For as long as Europeans have had knowledge of the Trobriand Islands they have remarked upon the proficiency of their carvers (Austen 1945; Edge-Partington 1969; Guiart 1963; Haddon 1893, 1894; Seligman 1910; Silas 1924, 1926). This is not simply a statement relevant to the past, for their prolific output has continued unabated since the beginning of the colonial period in the late nineteenth century (Beran 1980, 1988, 1996; Newton 1975; Scoditti 1975, 1980). The content of their artistic production, however, has undergone many changes. So, too, has the position of the artist been transformed within Trobriand society. In this chapter the contextual discourse continues to weave together historical perspectives recorded by visitors and short-term residents on the islands with Trobriand views about their traditions and how these have undergone transformation in response to changing opportunities. By examining the context of Trobriand carving over the last one hundred years, the unique position of Vakutans in relation to their artistic production and the status of the artist emerges in distinct contrast to that of their northern neighbours.

Artistic Production in the Past

In the latter part of the nineteenth century there were two classes of carver in the Trobriand Islands; those who carved with magic (*tokabitam*) and those who carved without magic. The latter hailed from the Kuboma district on Kiriwina Island and *tokataraki* scattered throughout other districts.[1] Those who carved with magic specialised in items of ritual and symbolic value, including yam house boards, canoe prow and splashboards, together with particular types of lime spatulae. The *tokataraki* and Kuboma carvers, on the other hand, produced items of utilitarian value: bowls, plates, lime spatulae, lime gourds, combs, walking sticks and clubs. The imposition of this distinction between symbolic and utilitarian production, together with the appropriate application of this made by Trobrianders, is consistent with what foreigners noticed when they first began to make the islands their home (Austen 1936, 1945; Fellows 1898a; Malinowski 1922; Silas 1924).

In the past, certain districts within the Trobriand Islands specialised in producing the bulk of artefacts. This specialisation, as Malinowski was at pains to point out

(1935 Vol. 1: 20–23), cannot be compared to specialisations found in societies where craftsmen rely on their work to provide an income. Although many of the specialists in the Trobriand Islands were less than self-sufficient, owing to the poorer quality of garden land in some districts, they did engage in subsistence activities. Nevertheless, these craftsmen used the trade of their handicraft to supplement the produce of their gardens.

> They [the people of Kuboma district] are . . . industrialists and craftsmen; and, as in any strict caste system, their high manual ability does not give them rank but rather places them among the despised. This refers especially to the most admirable of all Trobriand craftsmen, the inhabitants of Bwoytalu.[2] This village, which shares with its neighbours of Ba'u the reputation for the highest efficiency in sorcery, can certainly show the best results in carving; it is traditionally cultivated there and both for perfection and quantity of output is unparalleled in the region. From time immemorial its people have been the woodworkers and carvers of eastern New Guinea. And they still turn out wooden platters, hunting- and fishing-spears, staffs, polishing-boards, combs, wooden hammers and bailers in large quantities, and with a degree of geometrical and artistic perfection which any visitor to an ethnographic museum will appreciate. They also excel in plaited fibre work and in certain forms of basketry. During the wet season, when some other communities are busy preparing overseas expeditions, or engaging in festivities and ceremonial distributions, or . . . indulging in war, the men of Bwoytalu will day after day sit on one of their large covered platforms rounding, bending, carving and polishing their master-pieces in wood. It is a wholesale manufacture for trade and export. There is no magic whatever connected with their work, but from childhood skill is drilled into every individual, the knowledge of material, ambition and a sense of value. No other community can or tries to compete with them. (Malinowski 1935 Vol. 1: 15–16)

According to Malinowski's observations, there is a clear separation between the villagers of the Kuboma district and the rest of Kiriwina. This relationship found further ideological expression in a dietary schema distinguishing 'pure' and 'impure' food habits, with Boitalu villagers representing the epitome of all that was loathsome and despicable to other Kiriwinans. Boitalu people were known to eat the unspeakable bush pig and stingray, foods strictly taboo to other Kiriwinans (Malinowski 1922: 67, 1932: 420–421). Another isolating mechanism described by Malinowski was the virtual enforcement of endogamy within the Kuboma district. Other Kiriwinans maintained that no one from other districts would venture to marry the 'stingaree eaters' (1932: 385, 420–421).

In the Kuboma district most men were schooled in the craft of woodwork from childhood. Consequently, nearly all Kuboma men became practised craftsmen, their objective being to sell or trade their carvings rather than to work from commission. There was no special distinction between carvers and non-carvers in this area. Indeed, those who did not carve were an anomaly in the district and as such had an inferior social status in the same way that poor gardeners in other, essentially gardening, districts attracted ridicule. As Malinowski noted, the carvers of Kuboma worked without magic. Individuals were neither magically prepared for their craft, nor were the tools of their trade given magical attention. It was enough to be born into the Kuboma district.

The inhabitants were famed throughout the area for their work (Gilmour 1904–5: 72; Malinowski 1922: 67, 100; Seligman 1910: 529). Prior to embarking on trading and kula expeditions other villagers from northern Kiriwina, Vakutans, Sinaketans and Kaduwagans gave food and other valuables to villagers from the Kuboma district in return for their handiwork. These were taken overseas as solicitory gifts to 'soften' the minds of exchange partners (Austen 1945: 193; Fortune 1932: 207; Gilmour 1904–5: 72; Malinowski 1922: 99). Articles such as lime spatulae, lime gourds, combs, wooden bowls and plates, clubs, drums, grass skirts and baskets were traded for raw materials found only on adjacent, volcanic islands. In this way carvings predominantly from the Kuboma district were distributed throughout the region via trade networks linking the island communities of the Massim. It is possible that many of the artefacts held in museums with labels designating their origins as the Massim actually came from the Kuboma district.

Unlike their Kuboma counterparts, *tokabitam*, or master carvers, were men who received artistic status by imbibing carving magic. Young men who sought artistic renown solicited acclaimed master carvers to apprentice them so that they could be imbued with carving magic and trained as carvers. Only a few *tokabitam* lived at any one time. Great lengths were taken to maintain the relatively low ratio of artists to non-artists; principal among them was the rule that a master carver could give his magic and training to only one apprentice. This was meant to ensure the elite nature of their profession.

Men with *tokabitam* status could be found in villages outside the Kuboma district.[3] These men worked only on commission. They did not have to rely on the sale of their work to supplement their gardens. Like all other Trobrianders, they were principally gardeners. Their status as carvers of significant objects was separate to their gardening activities. Although their professional status as master carver enhanced their general standing within the community, a proficient master carver who could only manage small harvests could never be as prestigious as one who could fill several yam houses. While never spontaneously suggested, people admitted a potential flow-on effect from being magically prepared for carving knowledge and being specially endowed in other aspects of social life. Unlike the Kuboma craftsmen who supplied a local and overseas market, men with *tokabitam* status drew their clientele from within their immediate community. *Tokabitam* artists were exclusively commissioned to carve special boards for the yam house and kula canoe. Being largely inappropriate to people in other Massim communities, the carvings made by *tokabitam* attracted no demand from beyond the Trobriand Islands.

In contrast to *tokabitam*, there were men who carved without magic (*tokataraki*) apart from the Kuboma artisans. From an outsider's perspective these men displayed talent, but they lacked the necessary qualifications to make them 'artists' according to Trobriand criteria. Nor could they belong to the same class of carvers as the Kuboma craftsmen because they did not live there. They did not have the same 'inherent' attributes as their Kuboma counterparts. Generally, *tokataraki* were men who had wished to become master carvers and perhaps gone as far as to solicit patronage from a *tokabitam*. But in this endeavour they had been unsuccessful and therefore had to be satisfied with *tokataraki* status, if they continued to carve at all.

Tokataraki were sometimes commissioned to carve yam house boards or the prow and splashboards of the kula canoe by clients who did not feel inclined to pay for the work of a master carver. *Tokataraki* were cheaper, but their work was considered less efficacious. They lacked the magic that would provide them with the 'knowledge' held by master carvers. Difficulties also emerged when *tokataraki* tried to carve traditional designs. These were 'owned' by the *tokabitam* artists who had to be properly compensated for the use of their designs. The options open to a *tokataraki* carver were to produce entirely innovative works, for the most part unacceptable to clients seeking efficacious carvings, or to 'copy' and thus 'steal' the designs of a master carver. These options were not entirely conducive to the production of works by skilled craftsmen.

The Kuboma district carvers who worked to produce objects of general utilitarian value are contrasted with the *tokabitam* artists who were commissioned to execute items valued only by a local clientele for specific reasons. These two largely worked in separate domains. Overlapping both domains, however, were *tokataraki* carvers who had no real social mandate to carve at all. The association of Kuboma district carvers with craftsmen, on the one hand, and *tokabitam* with artists on the other is confirmed by the relative value placed on their work and their concurrent status within Trobriand society.

While Kuboma boys expected to be trained in the craft of carving as a part of their general socialisation, young men in other parts of the Trobriand Islands desiring master carver status had to engage in protracted offerings of gifts to a master carver. If successful they received magical preparation followed by intensive periods of technical and esoteric instruction. The value associated with the goods produced by Kuboma craftsmen was consonant with their utilitarian and trading value. Carvings produced by *tokabitam*, on the other hand, were valued because their productions were considered to be intrinsically powerful, having derived from magical substances and esoteric instruction. The fact that their enhanced ability was also spurred by considerable economic output could not have detracted from the public's assessment of their work. Finally, the relationship between the Kuboma craftsman and his clients involved a singular transaction whereby the item was simply exchanged for foodstuffs. The relationship between a master carver and his client, however, involved a long-term economic contract in which the client gave valuables before the commencement of carving, foodstuffs during the process of carving, followed by yams and valuables at the harvest after the completion of work.

The Artefact Trade

Late in the nineteenth century Trobriand craftsmen and artists alike found that their work appealed to the European newcomers. The interest Europeans exhibited had a marked stimulus on the production of carvings. As the demand increased, particularly in the late 1950s through to the early 1970s, the carving community multiplied and with it the level of production was augmented to satisfy this new and lucrative market. While surveying British New Guinea, making contact with the 'natives' and spreading the government's influence, MacGregor engaged in the significant collection of artefacts at every point of contact. In particular, he made a number of visits to the Trobriand Islands, making purchases for the 'official collection' and undoubtedly his own private collection (Quinnell 2000: 88). However, the missions were initially the biggest promoters of Trobriand artefacts and continued to have a prominent influence on artefact production until the early 1970s (Plate 4).[4]

At the end of the nineteenth century and beginning of the twentieth, the Reverend S. B. Fellows recorded in his diaries and letters to his wife the kinds of carvings produced, mentioning areas renowned for the quality of their work and specifying individual carvers. He encouraged European interest in Trobriand art by giving artefacts to government and church officials on their visits. For example, in his diary entry of 2 November 1895 he recorded, '[Reverend] Field left . . . I got him a large stock of curios'. The Fellows collection, held by the National Gallery of Australia, consists of some 240 items. Among the pieces are a number of model canoes with inscriptions to Fellows and his wife. One such model canoe/bowl reads, '*Naboailiga Sallie, Sena Kaiveka Boboailla. A saiki. Sam*' (Very beautiful/good hearted Sally, A very big thank you. I give you [this carving], Sam). Another model canoe is inscribed on the bottom, 'Rev. S. B. Fellows and Mrs. Fellows – landed Kiriwina Aug 28 1894 – left'.

Before becoming a resident magistrate, C. A. W. Monckton found little success in prospecting and diving for pearls. Instead, in 1895 he loaded up his boat with Trobriand artefacts intending to sell them at Samarai (Monckton 1921: 84). The large-scale promotion of Trobriand art for European consumption had begun.

However, this was initially accomplished by the collection of carvings predominantly made for local consumption but traded to Europeans in exchange for European goods. The carving of artefacts specifically for trade to Europeans had not yet taken hold.

It was in the early years of the twentieth century that carving production on Kiriwina Island increased significantly, together with the Trobrianders' growing awareness of the lucrative returns to be had by selling their carvings to Europeans. As Austen remarked:

> the people of Boitalu realised that there was a ready sale for their manufactures. They therefore produced larger *tokwalu*[5] pigs, birds and human beings than they had done in the past, when these carvings had been done more as an outlet for their artistic tendencies, and there was no sale for them in the villages. But once they found that the European would buy such articles, they began to create more. They saw that a table was necessary to the European, and that on it curios he had bought were placed. The Boitalu went one step further and made small tables of Melila wood, with a base and a top and two or three *tokwalu* as table legs. (1945: 196)

Mrs A. C. Lumley, the wife of a trader living on Kiriwina Island at the time, began to encourage carvers to create items solely for the European market. She instructed the carvers in the making of tables supported by human figures, pot stands and tables carved from a single piece of wood. Many new kinds of artefacts with particular appeal to the European buyer were also encouraged, such as stand-alone figures of humans, pigs and birds. She persuaded carvers to modify items traditionally made for the indigenous market, reconfiguring these so as to appeal to European tastes. As well as these changes to the nature of Trobriand carvings, Mrs Lumley encouraged men outside the Kuboma district to carve. In so doing, she instigated the blurring of indigenous boundaries separating carver from non-carver and craftsman from artist. Master carvers and *tokataraki* were carving similar objects and receiving comparative economic recognition for their work.

During the five years (1931–1936) that Assistant Resident Magistrate Leo Austen was stationed on Kiriwina Island, carving for commercial purposes continued to develop – or decline as Austen observed:

> Nowadays there is a small trade in these curios [wooden tables] which finds a limited local market in Samarai, but as the average 'table' is crudely carved there is little chance of the trade developing. As a matter of fact, it looks as though this side of woodcarving might eventually die out for lack of constant market. (1936: 20)

Later, however, he described how this development had progressed and indicated how he assessed the transformation of carving in villages not previously involved in this activity, especially the improvement in style and proportions of items such as tables and bowls. He noted for example: 'One table has a *tokwalu* representing a European on his verandah, with one foot resting on the rail, knee bent, chin cupped in hand with elbow supported by knee, and in his eyes the far-away look of the original *tokwalu*' (1945: 196).

For a period during the Second World War the Allied Forces occupied the Trobriand Islands. It is probable that Trobriand carvers continued to carve and sell their carvings to soldiers, although to my knowledge we have no evidence for this in published accounts.

In the 1950s the Kuboma Progress Society was formed for the purpose of marketing artwork from this district. The money earned from carvings was to be allocated to local projects. In 1964 the Society was reorganised to act as an unregistered cooperative selling artefacts and copra. Each member bought a share worth A$10 in the cooperative and in this way enabled the organisation to buy artefacts to provide a regular supply to retailers in Port Moresby. A marketing analysis of the Kuboma Progress Society's dealings showed that they made a profit of A$1494.30 in a three-year period (Wilson and Menzies 1967: 67).

By the mid-1960s the tourist trade had reached a peak and with it the production of carvings to feed artefact-hungry tourists. It was in 1962 that regular weekend charter flights began bringing tourists from Port Moresby. Tourists from Lae and Rabaul also arrived on monthly charters to Kiriwina Island. Each flight carried some thirty-two passengers. By 1967 visitors were arriving regularly throughout the week. As the tourists arrived they were accosted by a host of Kiriwinans trying to sell their carvings: 'There are usually 100–150 people at the airport, about 200 around the hotel and about 50–80 at each of the villages at which the tourists stop when taken on a truck tour of the island' (Wilson and Menzies 1967: 63).

In their report on the marketing and production of artefacts in the Sepik and the Trobriand Islands, Wilson and Menzies estimated that in a population of 12,000 on Kiriwina Island alone, some 300–400 (or 10 per cent) of the men were carvers producing artefacts for tourists. They estimated that in 1966 some A$20,000 worth of carvings were purchased directly from the carvers, while the traders on the island spent A$4,500, the mission A$2,000 and the Kuboma Progress Society some A$700 on carvings. This gave a net annual income of A$27,200, or an average of A$70 per carver.[6] They also calculated that the return for eight hours of carving was slightly more than A$1.00. The Society was forced to reassess its position as members compared the gains of the cooperative with those of individual carvers. They found that there were long delays between the shipment of carvings and the payment carvers received for their work. In contrast, carvers selling directly to tourists had an immediate return and usually higher dollar rewards for their work (Wilson and Menzies 1967: 67). With flagging interest in the cooperative, the Kuboma Progress Society was finally terminated. Carvers preferred to sell individually. When the tourists began to arrive regularly, the hotelier complained that the prices rose by 100 per cent while the quality diminished. Disregarding the implied inflation for a declining quality, these figures illustrate the extent to which a relatively large proportion of Kiriwinan men became engaged in carving activity. Both the traditional artists and craftsmen were thus engaged, competing for the tourist dollar.

In 1972 a recently completed 'international' hotel on Kiriwina Island burned down. With the cooling ashes, tourism to the islands went into sharp decline. Accommodation was reduced to one small expatriate-run guest house. Simultaneously, a local 'independence' movement (Kabisawali) was sweeping through the islands causing deep-rooted divisions within the communities, reflecting many traditional and historical resentments (J. W. Leach 1973, 1978, 1982). The local divisions stirred up by the Kabisawali movement further contributed to the decline of tourism, together with a diminishing reputation for hospitality. Tourists complained of a constant badgering from local carvers to buy their carvings and perceived a diminishing quality.[7] Had the disquiet brewing in the Trobriand Islands remained a local matter it might not have had such a marked affect on tourism. However, in 1973 riot police were flown in from the mainland and the Trobriand Islands made international news.

In the main, changes in the carving industry have occurred on Kiriwina Island where the impact of tourism has been most greatly felt. Carvers from the Kuboma district, originally the principal 'industrial' centre on Kiriwina Island, were no longer able to maintain their specialist edge. Once other Kiriwinans were encouraged to make money through the production of artefacts many other villages throughout northern Kiriwina began to 'specialise' in the production of specific articles. For example, the village of Okaiboma located on the east coast of Kiriwina Island now specialises in bowls shaped like fish, turtles and crocodiles, while the villages of Kwaibwaga, north of Omarakana, and Kabwaku, south of Omarakana, specialise in carving walking sticks.

Trobriand response to sustained demands from a European market, together with the opportunity to acquire cash, heralded an inevitable increase in the number of carvers involved in the industry. While at the turn of the century there were two distinct classes of carvers, these have increasingly become less differentiated, resulting in the position of the *tokabitam* becoming devalued.[8] Kuboma district carvers and *tokataraki* are now commissioned to carve yam house boards, prow and splashboards. While the changed status of Kiriwinan artists is related to a decreased demand for their work within the local community, other factors contributed to this situation. Their relationship to the production of tourist art, the increasing number of non-*kabitam* carvers, as well as other changes in the industry (for example, the disappearance of suitable wood and, in particular, the availability of ebony), are also responsible for their devalued status.

The leader of the Kabisawali movement, John Kasaipwalova, recognised the diminishing status of artists in the Trobriands and lamented a distinct drop in the quality of carvings (1975b: 6). To arrest this trend, Kasaipwalova made plans in 1974 for a revival of the arts in the Trobriands. Kabisawali supporters began to clear a site near Yalumgwa village (north-east coast of Kiriwina) for a Sopi Arts centre. It was intended that Trobriand artists could come to the centre to develop their skills in the graphic arts, drama, creative writing and music. The centre itself was never completed, but a village, Mwadauwosi, was built as a cultural centre in honour of 'Chief' Nalubutau in the late 1990s.

European influence on the carving industry was not felt equally by all carving communities within the Trobriand Islands. Geographic proximity to areas where tourists tended to go affected the degree to which various communities engaged in carving for Europeans. In those communities furthest away, professional carvers continued to carve primarily for local consumption, particularly in the carving of canoe boards and yam house decorations.

On Vakuta Island, carvers belong to the *tokabitam* class. There are no craftsmen such as those from Kuboma district. Like other communities in the group, Vakutans had to travel to the Kuboma villages to obtain the artefacts taken on kula voyages for trade and initiatory kula gifts. There are, however, *tokataraki* carvers on Vakuta, who either assist the *tokabitam* on major projects such as the carving of yam house boards, or who work alone on commission. But if they do take on a commission they are faced with the same dilemma as *tokataraki* working on Kiriwina Island a century ago. Their work is always considered second rate to that of the master carvers.

In the past master carvers were responsible for maintaining a repertoire of five to six different kinds of lime spatula designs (see also Beran 1988; Vargyas 1980). They claimed to be the only ones to 'know' how to carve these. The other styles did not belong to the *tokabitam* repertoire and were carved by the craftsmen of the Kuboma district. Today the *tokabitam* artists on Vakuta are principally commissioned to do boards for yam house decoration and boards for the kula outrigger canoe. For Vakutans, by far the most important of these are the prow and splashboards of the canoe.

Master carvers are differentiated from *tokataraki* carvers by title, economic reward and by ideology. Vakutans say that whereas a *tokataraki* carves with his eyes, a *tokabitam* carver works through his mind. Master carvers are considered essential members of the community because they have the 'knowledge' enabling them to execute the designs on the boards of a kula canoe. Unlike the master carvers on Kiriwina, the Vakutan artists had less incentive to become involved in the artefact industry. Cash was not flowing into the community in anything like the volume experienced by Kiriwinan villages during the 1960s and early 1970s. Because of their comparative isolation from events occurring on Kiriwina, few if any tourists visited Vakuta Island, thus restricting the concentration of buyers to Kiriwina. Vakutan master carvers continue to carve the boards for which they received acclaim from within their community in the past. The sharp distinction between artist and craftsman has been retained on Vakuta as artists continued to concentrate on the traditional repertoire. In this way, the profession of *tokabitam* artists has remained intact and their status high in the Vakutan community.

–3–

The Making of a Carver[1]

In the previous chapter a distinction was drawn between the Kuboma craftsman and the *tokabitam* artists of the remaining districts. This distinction is based on the quality of 'knowledge' each has access to. The craftsmen of Kuboma are trained at an early age in the practical execution of their special industry without the need for magic. An apprentice to the class of master carver, however, is given magic to prepare him for the receipt and processing of 'knowledge'. This sets a master carver apart from his contemporaries. If successful in his apprenticeship he will achieve prestige and social status within his community.

Within the four villages of the Vakutan community there are seven master carvers. These carvers are principally commissioned to produce the carvings associated with kula. Occasionally they are also commissioned to carve special classes of lime spatulae belonging to the particular repertoire of the master carver, as well as yam house decorations. In this chapter the process by which an apprentice becomes a master carver, and his role within the Vakutan community, will be explored in detail. However, to facilitate this a little groundwork is required to assist in our understanding of the nature of 'knowledge' as it is applied in Vakutan society.

For Vakutans knowledge is not accessible to everyone as a simple consequence of possessing a suitable mental faculty. Vakutans differentiate their knowledge into discrete categories which individuals compete for. The range of people able to qualify for certain categories of knowledge narrows according to the form of knowledge in question. Generally speaking, there are three forms of knowledge. The verb -*nukwari* corresponds closely to our usage of 'to know'. This verb denotes that the speaker 'knows' that something is a fact or a condition of what is being referred to. Another verb, -*kateta*, refers to a 'sharpening' of the 'knowing' that is encompassed in the verb -*nukwari*. -*Kateta* implies knowledge more profound than simply knowing something in the -*nukwari* sense. For example, I may know (-*nukwari*) that the fruit of a banana plant is generally classified as a banana, but a Vakutan adult would know (-*kateta*) the range, shape, colour and growing habits of particular varieties of banana. The first two forms of knowledge are thus differentiated by degrees of knowledge from general to specific. The word *kabitam* is used to differentiate the third form of knowledge. But let's not get ahead of ourselves – the way in which knowledge is differentiated needs further exploration.

Knowledge encompassed by the first form includes the entire range of activities and behaviour that normal individuals should have mastered by the time they reach adulthood. Some of this knowledge is differentiated by gender. For example, knowledge concerned with the growth of yams is the province of men and is taught to young boys as soon as they can help their fathers. Other examples include the knowledge of how to construct a house and how to thatch roofs with sago fronds. On the other hand, the construction of mats is a process that female children should acquire as they grow up. Similarly, skirt-making is a skill that every girl must learn. Skirts are not simply essential items of clothing, but also represent women's most important exchange item. Young girls acquire the knowledge of skirt construction while working alongside their female relatives. The example of skirt-making and yam cultivation, however, while illustrating the genre of general knowledge incorporated in the first form, *-nukwari*, can become more restricted. There is a transition from generalised knowledge to more personal applications of that knowledge. The degree to which this knowledge becomes personalised increases its value to the owner.

Many people possess their own specialised body of knowledge to assist them in certain tasks. This knowledge can be in the form of magic or a particular technique related to a variety of economic, health related and ritual endeavours. As such, this knowledge is specified by the individual ownership of magical spells, charms, potions or technical skills unique to that which is otherwise commonly known. Highly prized love magic, healing concoctions, birth control potions and spells all belong to this specialised body of knowledge.

Personalised knowledge, while a commodity held widely throughout the community, affords its owners a degree of prestige marking them off from others. In an essentially egalitarian society one's specialised knowledge, particularly if its application demonstrates to the wider community a desirable efficacy, creates a degree of social differentiation. For example, while immobilised by a swollen leg, I had the opportunity to observe the display of this personalised knowledge and the degree of competition that existed between various members of the community claiming to own a particularly effective remedy for my ailment. During my confinement these individuals came separately to administer medications. Each demonstrated a unique style and cure for my swollen leg and each competed with the previous individuals for the effectiveness of their personal cure. The woman who administered the last medication prior to the gradual decrease in the size of my leg received public recognition, both in directed conversation and in general village gossip, for owning the most efficacious knowledge for curing swollen legs. Whether the swelling in my leg subsided as a result of her ministrations or the natural outcome of whatever ailed me is not relevant here. She was the last person to attend me and apparently cured me. In a subsequent case of swollen limbs she was consulted as the authority. Others challenged her knowledge by administering their specific remedies, each confident that he or she owned the most effective knowledge. Those individuals who own particularly valuable knowledge, such as the means of effectively procuring an abortion or a potent love concoction, may be widely solicited, claiming significant remuneration for their services.

Although this genre of knowledge is secretly owned by individuals, nearly every adult has his or her own store of personal knowledge which is usually passed down from parent to child or from grandparent to grandchild, although it can also move through other relationships. Sometimes the recipient of the knowledge has given a series of gifts (*pokala*) to solicit this knowledge. *Pokala* is particularly appropriate if the recipient desires knowledge held by anyone other than a parent. Knowledge that is transferred as a matter of course from parent to child is usually given without undue solicitation. There may, however, be competition between siblings. *Pokala* is a useful means of attracting a parent's favour away from other siblings. These arrangements are generally private and between the individuals concerned.

Knowledge belonging to the third form consists of specialised knowledge highly valued by the community. Knowledge of magic systems (such as gardening magic, rain magic, war magic, kula magic and fishing magic), myths, astronomy, traditional songs and dances, the making of banana-leaf skirts, canoe building and carving fall into this category (see also Hutchins n.d.: 3). Because these skills are highly valued, the knowledge associated with these activities provides those who possess it with special status. These individuals are differentiated in name and maintain control over the transmission of their knowledge. These individuals are given the title *tokabitam* or 'man with knowledge'.[2]

Each type of knowledge at this level is distinct and does not necessarily have any relationship with other types of knowledge. The system of garden magic,[3] for example, is self-contained and does not share any components with the system of rain magic. Likewise, a person who owns the system of garden magic does not necessarily own, or even know the system of rain magic. He would have to refer to someone who owned rain magic in order to coordinate his goals for a given purpose. Similarly, someone who owns the knowledge of canoe building does not necessarily own carving knowledge and vice versa. Further, in any one community there may or may not be owners of any of the possible forms of knowledge at this level. For example, in the late 1970s there was only one man on Vakuta Island who owned the knowledge of rain magic. Although individual Vakutans have their private forms of 'knowledge' about a range of things, no one at the time owned a system of garden magic,[4] war magic or fishing magic at the level of *tokabitam*. For expertise in these areas of knowledge Vakutans needed to commission somebody who owned this knowledge from another community on Kitava, Kiriwina or Dobu islands. There were seven men on Vakuta, however, who owned carving knowledge and several others who owned canoe-building knowledge.

These men were sometimes commissioned by northern Kiriwinan villagers to employ their knowledge towards the building of a canoe or to carve the canoe boards.

Whereas the other two forms of knowledge are more or less evenly distributed throughout the community, in that acquisition of the first is expected of all fully functioning adults and the second, although private, is widely held throughout the community, the third form of knowledge is limited to only a few known members of the community at any one time. Restricted access to this body of knowledge is maintained principally by those already in possession of the knowledge for purposes of maintaining their control over it as a resource. The economic implications inherent in soliciting access to this knowledge are very high.

The means whereby initiates are given this knowledge further differentiates it from other forms of knowledge. Those who have succeeded in apprenticing themselves to a *tokabitam* must undergo a series of initiation rites accompanied by magical spells and substances to make them receptive to the acquisition of the knowledge they seek. Following the completion of these preparatory rites, apprentices are ready for practical instruction.

Whereas knowledge consistent with the first two forms is utilised by individuals to benefit or hinder other individuals, knowledge at the *kabitam* level is manipulated by individuals to affect the community as a whole. Someone who owns the system of garden magic is commissioned to perform the relevant activities for the benefit of the entire community. The person who knows rain magic utilises it for the benefit of the community or withholds it at some cost to the community. The person in charge of fishing magic generally performs his spells for community fishing activities. Although individuals may commission those in possession of specialised knowledge to perform their services for private benefit, this is not the principal and publicly sanctioned function of *kabitam* owners.

Kabitam distinguishes the most highly valued body of knowledge. All of the magic, techniques and technical information of outrigger canoe construction, for example, collapse into what is known as *kabitam masawa*, the knowledge of kula canoes. All knowledge necessary to the execution of carvings for kula canoes is called *kabitam ginigini*, or the knowledge of carving. Usage of the word *kabitam* also implies an acquired impulse to exercise the knowledge at any given time. This means that anyone who has received special knowledge of the *kabitam* order is by implication somewhat driven by that knowledge. That is, the magic has an additional impact on the initiate who takes it. *Kabitam* magic is thought to have a life of its own through the initiate, the latter merely being the vehicle through which the magic is expressed. In other words, a *tokabitam* is 'called' by the magic to employ his knowledge. In this sense, the *kabitam* magic is thought to be a separate power that is not only used by the owner but also, to some extent, uses the owner. For example, it is thought that a *kabitam* carver can become overwhelmed by his knowledge, the internalised *kabitam* magic compelling him to carve. The carver prepares his wood and the *kabitam* magic guides his hand. When something is said to be *kabitam*, or the result of *kabitam* magic, reference is being made to this power, or the force of the knowledge directing its owner to release its expression. Something produced without *kabitam*, but which may duplicate it exactly (a carving for instance), cannot equal that which is produced with *kabitam* magic because the former does not 'come from the mind' of an owner of *kabitam*. Hence, as well as *kabitam* knowledge, an apprentice also acquires the magical force related to his or her specific knowledge. In this way, the execution of *kabitam* always implies the utilisation and unleashing of associated magic. A *tokabitam* is the 'patient', passively responding to the flow of knowledge through his mind.

The prestige of a person in possession of a specific body of *kabitam* knowledge is not entirely due to his or her specialisation. A prerequisite of becoming an owner of *kabitam* is the 'clearing of the initiate's mind'. It is thought that this predisposes him or her to clear thinking on any given issue, although he or she can only claim expertise for the *kabitam* received. Thus an owner of *kabitam* receives renown for his or her specialisation but is also highly respected within the community for the condition enabling *kabitam* to be received.

Men are the main recipients of *kabitam* because it is principally those activities that are normally performed by men that fall within the *kabitam* body of knowledge: war magic, fishing magic and canoe construction. Women, however, have their own specialisation on Vakuta requiring *kabitam* knowledge. This is in the construction of banana-leaf skirts (*debumwoya*), which are highly valued exchange articles in mortuary distributions.[5] On occasion, women have been given *kabitam* magic for one of the *kabitam* systems by a father or grandfather when there have been no suitable boys to apprentice. In these cases a woman is not allowed to exercise her knowledge in the specialised system other than in the making of skirts. Instead, she 'holds' the knowledge until a suitable apprentice gives her *pokala*. She then initiates his magical purification and commences his instruction.

A person who owns *kabitam* receives acknowledgement of his or her position by being referred to as a *tokabitam*. This title denotes the person's possession of the specific knowledge owned, as well as a general capacity to think clearly. In relation to carving, a *tokabitam ginigini*, or master carver, possesses knowledge of the specific rules and patterns characteristic of Vakutan carvings for kula canoes. He also knows the 'animals' associated with the artistic tradition that he represents, their *kabitam* associations and designs, as well as the conventions of being a *tokabitam ginigini vis-à-vis* other owners of *kabitam* and the rest of the community.

The remainder of this chapter will focus on the carving profession practised on Vakuta. The process by which a young man becomes apprenticed to a *tokabitam ginigini*, together with the rules of etiquette and specific conventions influencing a master carver's behaviour in the execution of his carvings, will be examined.

Firstly, however, it is necessary to differentiate between those who 'carve through their eye' and those who 'carve through their mind'. These phrases are directly translated from what Vakutans say about the distinction, and represent the perceived differences between a master carver and a carver.

The Tokabitam Ginigini

Talent in the execution of carving is not the exclusive possession of a *tokabitam ginigini*. On the other hand, not all of those who can carve possess the essential knowledge to produce *kabitam* carvings. There are men on Vakuta who demonstrate a good deal of talent in carving yet do not own any carving knowledge. The word differentiating these men from *tokabitam* carvers was introduced in the previous chapter. There is a perception that *tokataraki* may be able to copy, or 'carve with their eyes', but they do so without knowledge. These carvers usually confine their work to the embellishment of lime spatulae, house boards, bowls or other items receiving aesthetic embellishment. Without the proper preparation to enable the flow of knowledge to move through his mind, a *tokataraki* must 'copy' a *tokabitam*'s work if he were enlisted to carve boards exclusively the prerogative of master carvers. A latent potential for a *tokataraki* to be accused of 'stealing' the designs of a master carver is usually enough to keep his talents directed towards mundane objects. On the rare occasion that a *tokataraki* is commissioned to carve a prowboard by someone unwilling to pay the high fees demanded by a *tokabitam*, the *tokataraki* is compelled to 'copy' the *kabitam* patterns. To do otherwise negates the efficacy of the boards as vehicles towards achieving successful kula. He does so, however, at great risk, as the owner of the *kabitam* designs has the right to smash the offending boards unless the *tokataraki* makes suitable payment to him as the owner of the designs. A *tokabitam* has invested considerable resources and personal sacrifices to achieve his knowledge and status. His knowledge is an economic and social asset that he guards carefully. People who copy his designs do not go unchallenged.

Reference has been made to the 'possession' of *kabitam*. This is quite in keeping with the general understanding of *kabitam* amongst Vakutans and corresponds closely to how Vakutans regard this asset and rights over its use.[6] A *tokabitam* owns his knowledge until he dies. Consequently an apprentice does not own the knowledge of carving until the death of the master carver. The possession of *kabitam* status gives the entire rights of use and distribution to the owner. He chooses whether to carve on commission and to whom he will give access to his knowledge. If he wishes never to transmit his knowledge, he is entitled to withhold it. Owners of carving knowledge use this resource as a means of adding to their economic status. A carver with *kabitam* status is regarded as a specialist with very clear expectations applied to his work. These are focused on the appropriate representation of the 'animals' as well as to the way in which they are executed. The magical and technical preparation of an initiate are thought to secure both the knowledge of the 'animals' and the aesthetic expression of these on the carvings.

A master carver is sought by anyone who needs his knowledge to execute the carving of canoe boards or yam-house carvings. It is said that the remuneration a *tokabitam* could demand in the past was more substantial than it is today. Prior to carving the four boards of a kula outrigger canoe, for example, in the past a *tokabitam* could expect a kula shell valuable to solicit 'his mind'. The quality of this valuable indicated to him the client's intention to pay well upon the completion of the boards. While carving, the *tokabitam* received cooked food, betelnut and tobacco from his client. These 'sweeteners' were meant to 'keep his mind clear', and hence facilitate the smooth flow of knowledge. The full payment for the completed work included a pig, kula shell valuables and a yam house full of yams at harvest. In the late 1970s money was part of the payment and I could see little indication of diminished reward. A *tokabitam* can anticipate further economic advantage through aspiring apprentices soliciting his knowledge. Young hopefuls initiate a sequence of gifts (*pokala*). A master carver may have several young men, in the hopes of being successful in acquiring *kabitam* knowledge, giving him *pokala* throughout his career. Many will become apprenticed, but only one will succeed in the final acquisition of knowledge.[7]

Vakutan carving knowledge is divided into specific styles, or schools, of carving. These are defined in terms of the magic one imbues. It is thought that the knowledge of a style, or school, is contained within the magic. There are four separate schools represented on Vakuta: *Sopila* Kitava, *Sopila* Kaileuna, *Sopila* Gawa, and *Sopila* Vakuta.[8] As is implied by their names, these schools represent magic from four geographic locations in the northern Massim. The word *sopi* refers to the magically impregnated substance, aesthetic style or school of carving. Reference is also made to the knowledge associated with a particular school and the specific representation of *kabitam* 'animals' associated with each school. Although the carving of canoe prow and splashboards has definite rules in relation to motifs, their patterning and placement, there are certain areas on a board where the rules allow for the 'signature' of the artist and his particular school. As a result people are able to identify what school a carving comes from and thereby the artist who is (at any given time) the representative of that school. Further, specific designs associated with the school and artist act in much the same way as copyright and patent, lending value to a design because of its unique association with a carver and the school he represents. To protect each carver's unique design patterning a master carver should give his knowledge to only one apprentice. Serious problems occur if this convention is not followed. To illustrate the difficulties resulting from a master carver shirking this convention, a conflict inevitably resulting in the collision of two carvers claiming to possess knowledge of the same school was inadvertently caused by me.

In Vakuta village there were five men sharing the same carving knowledge (*Sopila* Vakuta) in 1978. All five were given their knowledge by the master carver, Tauboda Kilivila, who was deceased at the time of this incident. Of the five men, three did not carve. They said that they were not given the full magic and could therefore not be owners. Perhaps, at a time when the other two have passed away, one of them will claim ownership and commence carving. The two practising carvers, however, both claimed to have been given the complete magic and disputed the other's ownership of *Sopila* Vakuta. As long as neither of them carved a prow or splashboard no real confrontation could arise. However, I commissioned the two to carve both a prow and splashboard each. My motivation for this commission, enlisting two carvers sharing the same *sopi*, was to ascertain whether, in fact, there was a specific style prescribed for each school. If so, I could expect the carvings from each master carver to be identical. Alternatively, each carver might have developed his own style. My experience of kula carvings until this point indicated that all the carvings looked markedly different from each other, regardless of whether they came from the same school or not (compare Plates 10 and 11). At this time I did not fully appreciate the ramifications of my 'experiment'.

The first carver, Rurupa, completed his set and when he had finished, the second carver, Kaitotu, who had inadvertently seen Rurupa's splashboard, said that his rival had carved incorrectly. Kaitotu claimed that his was the 'true' *sopi*, and he would carve the correct designs of *Sopila* Vakuta. He began to carve the next set. When he had finished his carvings, the first carver came to me loudly proclaiming that he had been copied and the second carver had stolen his designs. He threatened to break the other's splashboard. Breaking the offensive board is the sanctioned way an owner would receive justice for the theft of his designs and thus reinstate his exclusive ownership. In this instance, a public hearing was demanded by both carvers so that they could settle the question of ownership once and for all. During the public airing of grievances both proclaimed exclusive ownership of the *sopi*, making a reasoned case for their claims. Older men, particularly the carvers, were called upon to state the conventions of *kabitam* carving and so help in the arbitration. One well-respected master carver recalled how he had become a *tokabitam ginigini*:

> My 'father' gave me my *sopi*, and my 'father' and I carved alike. While my 'father' was alive, anything I received in payment for my carving I gave to my 'father' because he was the owner of the *sopi*. When my 'father' died, the *sopi* belonged to me. (Ruguna, Kuweiwa hamlet, Vakuta Village)

In his statement, Ruguna affirmed that if both disputants had the same *sopi*, it could be expected that they would carve alike, using the same designs. He also confirmed the convention restricting ownership to one carver. It was up to those assembled to decide which of the two was the rightful owner, given that both had been given the same *sopi* by Tauboda Kilivila. The case was decided according to the conventions of matrilineal descent and inheritance adhered to by Vakutans. Tauboda Kilivila was obliged to give the full *sopi* to a sister's son. It was determined that in this dispute Rurupa must be the true owner of *Sopila* Vakuta because the magic had been given to Tauboda Kilivila (a *Lukuba* clan man) by a *Malasi* man (his father), and that Tauboda Kilivila had, therefore, rightly returned the magic to a *Malasi* man, Rurupa.

Kaitotu, however, is also a *Malasi* man. It is here that the conventions prescribing *dala*, or sub-clan inheritance, become clearer. The difference between Rurupa and Kaitotu is that the former belongs to the same *dala* as the man who gave Tauboda Kilivila the *sopi*, while the latter belongs to a different *dala* altogether. Kaitotu was given the *sopi* because his father was a *Lukuba* man and belonged to the same *dala* as Tauboda Kilivila. They were, indeed, 'brothers'. As such, Kaitotu called Tauboda Kilivila 'father'. The only acceptable solution to the dispute, once it had been confronted within the public forum, was to adhere to preferred inheritance conventions, favouring the control and transfer of valuable assets within the *dala*. However, following the public's affirmation of *dala* priority, gossip exchanged on the verandas over the succeeding nights gave Kaitotu 'true' ownership over the *sopi*. The matter was clearly a case of a 'father's' preference for his son over *dala* privilege. However, publicly, and in protection of *dala* rights, it had to be given to Rurupa following *dala* inheritance rights. Further, it was clear to all that Tauboda Kilivila had committed an error in judgement by giving this knowledge to more than one initiate. Although only one of the five could claim ownership, they were all considered to be *tokabitam* – all five had been imbibed with magic. The title of *tokabitam ginigini*, however, only receives public usage if a *tokabitam* actually carves. While the three who did not carve were considered *minakabitam*, they were not officially *minakabitam ginigini*.[9] As the two carvers in the case described above both carved, they received public recognition as *minakabitam ginigini*. Following this confrontation, however, Kaitotu had to relinquish his carving status and remain a *tokabitam* without profession until the death of Rurupa. However, his status was still conditional on Rurupa not giving the *sopi* to another initiate.

Becoming a Tokabitam Ginigini

A young boy of approximately 8 to 10 years of age is either encouraged by his family, or has the desire himself to become a master carver. To achieve this goal, however, he must receive the magic and formal training necessary for him to accomplish this specialisation. He must become apprenticed to a master carver. He does this by initiating a *pokala* exchange with the master carver of his choice.

Although the boy continues to lavish gifts of specially cooked food, pieces of pork, fish, betelnut, tobacco and valuables (if he is able to acquire them) upon the master carver, his reward is delayed. Throughout this stage of the exchange the boy simply takes the gifts to the master carver and gives them without saying a word and without attracting public attention. Part of the etiquette of the exchange between a master carver and a potential apprentice prescribes a minimum of communication between them. It is not only considered bad etiquette to say what the gifts are for, but it is also thought to be disadvantageous to the outcome. The master carver may refuse the gifts if it is clear what payment is required. The objective of the boy is to create a substantial obligation so that the master carver cannot refuse to take him on as an apprentice. It may be that there are several young men eagerly competing for the knowledge owned by a master carver, in which case it is essential for each to strive to create the greatest obligation so that the only equitable response from the master carver is to relinquish the knowledge he owns. For those who do not succeed in becoming apprenticed, the master carver repays their *pokala* with a valuable considered by him to be equal to the amount of solicitory gifts. When the young man considers he has built up a suitable debt, he takes a particularly fine gift to the master carver and finally communicates his desire to become an apprentice under him. If the master carver accepts this final gift the young man becomes apprenticed and the master carver begins to prepare the boy for the receipt of carving knowledge.

Once a master carver has chosen an apprentice, the young initiate must begin to observe certain food taboos incumbent on anyone wishing to become a *tokabitam ginigini*. The taboos are concerned with the avoidance of those foods, that, although delicacies, display certain characteristics representing the antithesis of carving aesthetics and the smooth transference of knowledge. For example, an initiate cannot eat the head nor the intestines of fish or pig because their visual qualities reflect unwanted characteristics in the initiate. Brains and intestines are seen as twisted, knotted and tight. If an initiate were to eat either of these his mind would likewise become twisted, knotted and tight. His mind would no longer have the ability to remain clear, straight and untangled; essential qualities for the free flow of *kabitam* thought. An initiate cannot eat the tail of a fish because this part of the fish functions to propel it in the water by use of a wagging motion. If an initiate ate the tail of a fish his hand would likewise waggle. Thus afflicted, he would not be able to hold his carving hand steady so as to produce straight, clean lines. Nor is an initiate allowed to eat the bottom or the surface portion of a pot containing *mona*, a delicacy of pounded taro, yams or pumpkin mixed with coconut milk. The substance at the bottom of the pot closest to the heat has a glutinous consistency while the surface of the pudding forms a skin that is thick and sticky. If a carver were to eat the pudding from either part, his mind would likewise become sticky and tenacious, hampering the free flow of clear thought characteristic of *tokabitam*.

While the food restrictions are generally lifted after the initiate becomes a fully fledged carver, there are many other rules a carver must observe throughout his career. Most of them have to do with etiquette. One rule, perhaps the most important governing a carver, is that he must never copy another carver's designs. There are discernible differences between each carver's rendition of similar designs (although these may escape untutored eyes) and these remain the exclusive property of the carver. Another rule applies to a new carver working on his first commission. The client must bring cooked or uncooked food, tobacco and betelnut daily to the carver. This food is called by its exchange name *vakapula*. A new carver receiving *vakapula* for the first time must not eat any of the cooked food given. He can only eat food given privately to his wife in its raw state and later cooked by her. Nor can he chew any of the betelnut brought as *vakapula*. Should he break this rule, he loses his knowledge and ability to carve. After a carver has completed his first commission this rule is no longer applied. However, other rules continue to govern his behaviour. If a carver is working and receiving *vakapula*, other *kabitam* carvers are forbidden to consume any of it. Every day a carver works on a commission the client must bring *vakapula*. If the *vakapula* is brought publicly to the veranda where the carver is working neither he nor his family can consume it. Passers by are able to eat the *vakapula*. If, on the other hand, the food goes into the house, the carver and his family eat it in private. In this way, a distinction is made between the public and private receipt of *vakapula*. All carving must take place in the open, in full public view, so as not to hide the expression of *kabitam* magic. *Kabitam* is a public concern. The breaking of any of these rules will, according to convention, result in the loss of *kabitam* and the ability to carve.

As the young initiate continues to maintain a restricted diet, he is drawn closer and closer to the time when he is given the magic that will instil in him the essence of carving knowledge. Ideally there are three stages in the administration of the full complement of magic. However, today two of these stages are often omitted. *Kabitam* is internalised by drinking a magical concoction imbued with the essence of the specific knowledge one seeks to learn. The essence of *kabitam*, incorporated in this magical substance and absorbed by the initiate, enables him to attain the ability and command of the knowledge for his use at any given time, provided specific taboos are not broken which would otherwise destroy the efficacy of the magic. Among its meanings then, *kabitam* heralds a predisposition that enables specific knowledge to be utilised whenever necessary.

The way in which *kabitam* is imbued is through a specially concocted substance generically referred to as *sopi*. *Sopi* literally refers to any water or liquid-like substance, but it also has special usage in reference to specific forms of knowledge.

In the case of carving magic, the concoction is prepared and given by a master carver. Its use as a means of identifying particular styles or 'schools' of carving has already been noted. Choice of the term *sopi* to refer to magic is not entirely haphazard, nor made because of some kind of real likeness between magic and water. The usage of *sopi* is connected to major aesthetic attributions of water, as these are conceived by Vakutans (as well as other Trobriand islanders and Gawans; see Beier 1974, 1978; Kasaipwalova 1975b; Munn 1986; Nalubutau 1975). Water has the virtue of free flow, conceptually unhampered by obstacles. In a similar way, it is desirable for *kabitam*, or knowledge, to flow unhindered in the mind of a *tokabitam*. Water is used as a metaphor in many discussions about Vakutan aesthetics, differentiating such characteristics as clarity, precision, depth and straightness in contrast to cloudy, haphazard, shallow, bent or crooked (Campbell 2001). The latter are thought to be obstacles to clear thought and wisdom. The aesthetic quality of *sopi* will be revisited as the stages of transmission are described below.

The first stage of imparting carving knowledge to an initiate is probably the most important and most efficacious. This stage must take place for an initiate to become a *tokabitam ginigini* today. It is the one people refer to when talking about carving *sopi*. The master carver begins by crushing betelnut in a mortar and pestle or in the betelnut shell itself, adding the necessary lime and betel-pepper (see also Austen 1945: 194–195). He grinds the betelnut mixture until it forms a smooth consistency and is the classic bright red, characteristic of the betel, lime and pepper combination. The master carver speaks magic over the betelnut, imparting to it specific aesthetic qualities, knowledge of the animals and the designs of his particular school of *sopi*. He also impregnates the substance with the free-flowing predisposition for knowledge acquisition. This is done quietly with the betelnut mixture held close to the mouth of the master carver.[10] When he is satisfied that the substance has been infused with the essence of his *kabitam ginigini*, he paints the magical substance on the initiate. Two marks are put on the forehead, two marks on the chest, two on each shoulder, two on each elbow and two on each wrist. In this way the magic is placed strategically on those areas essential to a carver's ability to work in the accepted *kabitam* fashion. The forehead and the chest are the areas where knowledge is stored and from whence knowledge, when needed, is to flow smoothly and cleanly.[11] The chest is the centre of a person's desire and emotion. It is the storehouse for knowledge. The forehead is thought to be connected to the chest. It mediates between knowledge and the state of desire held in the chest. The forehead forces the external expression of these conditions. The wrist, elbow and shoulder are the joints that enable the external expression of knowledge. Once these body parts are touched magically by the transmitting medium of betelnut, the initiate is given the substance to 'drink', or, more precisely, to chew and swallow. In this way, the substance is transmitted from the master carver to the initiate who internalises the knowledge. That night the initiate dreams of the animals associated with his school of carving.

The second stage of transmitting carving knowledge takes place at the beach on the 'ocean side' of the island.[12] Here the master carver and young initiate go to the water's edge where the incoming wave dissipates into foam before retreating back to the swell. The master carver scratches a hole in the sand, damming one end so as to retain some of the foaming water (*yeluyelu*). A branch from a particular tree is placed into the hole with the *yeluyelu*. Magic is spoken over the water. Two trees chosen for this are *yolalala* and *katitareka*. *Yolalala* is chosen by one school because the inner tissues are made up of cells which appear perfectly round to the eyes. In this case, the quality of roundness is desirable. The *katitareka*'s branches, when held or touched, easily break from the main trunk. It is thought that this characteristic gives the carver an ability to see things that are aesthetically acceptable. The connection here is between the ease and rapidity with which the branch breaks and the comparative quickness with which carving knowledge should enter the mind of the initiate. It is thought that his senses will imitate the sharp snapping of the branch and quickly learn the designs, shapes and forms.

The initiate puts his hand in the *yeluyelu* and, lifting it to his mouth, licks the impregnated water from it thereby internalising the magical essence of *kabitam*. The dam is broken and the water rushes back to the sea. It is said that the initiate sees this and, by seeing, absorbs the image of a fast and clear line carved in the sand by the *yeluyelu* as it recedes to the sea. It is thought that the initiate's mind will likewise take on this characteristic and be quick and clear. Informants often remark upon the value of the water as something 'good to look at'. That night the initiate again dreams of the designs that represent the animals in his school of carving.

The third stage of initiation takes place on the opposite side of the island towards the mangrove swamp near the lagoon (*wa pasa*). Here a special snake resides called *kaisipu*, known to be wise (*nakabitam*). This snake's knowledge is connected to its particularly slippery nature. It is said that this snake easily gets away on account of its slippery qualities. The master carver locates one of its holes in the early morning and waits for it to emerge. When the snake comes up it is caught and its tail cut. Some of the blood is allowed to drip into a coconut bowl. After the initiate drinks the blood the snake is allowed to go its way. Magic spells may or may not be spoken over the blood, depending upon the school of carving. The blood of the *kaisipu* is thought to contain the very essence of its *kabitam*. In drinking its blood, the initiate partakes of this essence. In so doing, he retains the slippery quality of the snake. This quality is said to allow the initiate's head to be cleared and slippery like the snake, enabling him to learn the designs as they 'slip' into his mind. This characteristic also applies to the way the designs 'slip' through his body and onto the carving. After drinking the blood, a hole is made in the bottom of the bowl and it is put on a fire to burn. Without a hole in the bottom of the bowl, smoke would be trapped inside and the initiate's mind would likewise become cloudy rather than clear. That night the initiate dreams of his designs.

Of all the stages, the first is the most essential. People said that it is always performed, whereas there was disagreement as to whether the second and third stages need to take place. To become a *tokabitam* of any specialisation it is essential to clear the initiate's mind so that the knowledge of the particular specialisation can flow unimpeded. Therefore, much of the magic spoken over the betelnut substance concerns this clearing of the mind. More specific incantations may be added according to the type of knowledge being imparted.

The symbolism inherent in the three stages can be seen to contrast with significant spaces in Vakutan thought and to highlight the importance of water-like substances. Firstly, the *yeluyelu* of the sea is contrasted with the 'water' of the snake living near the lagoon. Both the sea and lagoon represent mediating spaces between land and water, but they are also thought to represent important contrasts. The lagoon is calm and non-threatening while the sea is rough and unpredictable. Several aspects of Vakutan life highlight this differentiation. Fishing in the lagoon requires specific technology and skills, while on the sea other skills are necessary (see also Malinowski 1922, 1948b). Fish caught in the lagoon are different from fish caught in the sea and different vegetation is found on the ocean beaches from that found on the shores of the lagoon. Men have to cross over seas to engage in kula while no kula is undertaken within the lagoon.

It is significant that the transmission of magic is via liquid substances. The carving action of a *tokabitam ginigini* is said to model the flow of water. Of note, too, are the associations with colour. The white of the *yeluyelu* contrasts with the dark red of the *kaisipu*, while the water of betelnut, being clear or 'white' initially, is transformed into red with the addition of lime (see Chapter 6 for a discussion of colour symbolism).

By outlining the three stages ideally performed in the initiation of a new *tokabitam ginigini*, a closer understanding of the qualities Vakutans consider necessary for the successful transmission of carving knowledge is possible. The essence of *kabitam*, incorporated into *sopi* and absorbed by the initiate enables him to acquire the ability and command of the knowledge. An apprentice does not begin to carve in earnest for between three and four years after receiving magic. In the intervening period he gains the aesthetic and practical instruction for his chosen specialisation. He learns the various magical formulae associated with carving and the empowering of his carvings for kula. He is shown the correct trees to use for particular carvings and learns the process of drying and seasoning wood. He learns the manner in which lines are carved into wood, the lore of the specific *kabitam* animals and their graphic representations. This period takes many years of instruction as the initiate listens to and watches the master carver work.

In the intervening period between the magical inception of *kabitam* and the time when the apprentice begins to carve he must learn how to make and repair the tools of his specialisation. Today these consist of several kinds of screwdrivers and nails, together with other iron implements to suit the purpose (*kaiwawaiya*). These are beaten on the ends to produce a variety of sharp edges. The most used edge is a long, flat one to cut long straight lines. Often a carver will use this for all lines, but may have other tools for more specific line construction. A wooden paddle or hammer (*kaigilagela*) is used to hit the nail and thus force it into and along the wood. A small hand knife (*kipoum*) is now used to dig out the lines to make them deep and clean, ready to receive and 'hold' the paint. For shaping, the carver uses an axe (*kema*) and an adze (*rigogo*). To smooth off the finished carving, a carver uses the skin of a stingray (*vai*) or a special leaf with a hard, rough surface rather like sandpaper.

The initiate is taught the qualities of various types of wood, where to find the desirable species for canoe prowboards, how to cut a piece from root-buttress and how to judge the dimensions required for size and strength. The art of seasoning wood is also important to learn. If the wood is not properly seasoned the apprentice may find that halfway through carving a canoe prowboard it splits and he has to begin again.

Throughout this period emphasis is on learning the designs: their character, form, placement and patterning. The apprentice has to learn the animals represented by the designs and the reasons for selecting certain animals. He also learns which animal designs are important, always needing to be represented in particular places on the boards. Finally, the young apprentice is told the rules of conduct and etiquette expected of a *tokabitam ginigini*.

When the master carver considers that the initiate is ready to apply all that he has learned to its physical execution on wood, he directs the boy to begin carving. The prescribed procedure is that the apprentice carves a succession of six splash-boards (*lagim*) and six prowboards (*tabuya*). The boards are not life-size. They are reduced in size to give the young carver experience with carving in wood and in making the necessary designs. The carving process should take place inside the house (this process is called *kavasaku*), in contrast to carving in the open like a *tokabitam ginigini*. During this work the master carver inspects the carving regularly and gives appropriate instruction. He looks for the correct design patterning and positioning, making sure that each area of the board has the correct designs represented. The master carver also checks that the lines are straight, clear and deep. He looks for the character of the line to ensure they convey 'animation' and 'spring'. Following the completion of each board the master carver gives the young carver criticism and instructs him to burn the board and try again on a new one. People said that six *lagim* and six *tabuya* are carved by the initiate and burned. When the master carver inspects the seventh completed board he finds it perfect, and tells the young carver that he is now a *tokabitam ginigini*. His period of initiation and instruction is over and his *pokala* has been repaid.

Sopi is an instrument understood by Vakutans to be a means of infusing certain qualities into a young person. To be a *tokabitam ginigini* a man must have had specific qualities 'added' to his person. This is done through *sopi*. The ability to carve in the *kabitam* style is thought to be derived from a clear and open mind from which knowledge is able to flow. This uninhibited flow allows for the successful transmission of other qualities necessary to make a carver a *tokabitam*. The connection between the mediators of *sopi* (crushed betelnut, fast-flowing ocean water and the slippery smoothness of the snake) and their desired effect is straightforward. All three mediators are believed to impart their essence into the mind of the initiate. Once this is achieved, other important qualities and abilities become increasingly possible. For example, the simplicity of designs, lines and colour arrangements are qualities obtainable only through the clearing of the mind through *sopi*. The quickness and clarity of designs coming to the hand of the carver are also dependent upon a clear and freely flowing mind. The ability to recall the designs from the repertoire as well as the urge to refine and perfect the designs are all characteristics of a carver who has imbibed the essence of *sopi* and become a *tokabitam ginigini*.

Part II
The Art

–4–

The *Kabitam* Form

[I]f someone makes an image of something he has experienced, he can choose how much of the shape he wishes to include . . . When a person who has been asked what a winding staircase looks like describes with his finger a rising spiral, he is not giving the outline but the characteristic main axis, actually non-existent in the object. Thus the shape of an object is depicted by the spatial features that are considered essential. (Arnheim 1974: 47–48)

Our visual experience of the environment around us is conditioned by the way we are genetically programmed to see it. However, our view of the environment is also heavily defined by another kind of programming. From birth we are taught how to 'see' our environment, our vision seeking the key elements that make any 'scene' culturally meaningful. Our ability to make sense of what we see is constrained by our knowledge of the image and is ultimately constructed by our sociocultural conditioning. This makes the way in which artists share their view of the world interesting; their depictions, while often a reaffirmation of our own, are sometimes challenging. Artists, particularly in the Western tradition, regularly upset established conventions of representation, forcing the viewing public to apply more than a glancing appreciation of their work. They draw us in and engage us in a kind of discourse, often conducted solely between the individual and the artwork itself. When conventions are broken, we are forced to interrogate the piece, trying to make sense of the apparent discord and in this way come to a clearer understanding of what we expect to see. In many other artistic traditions, however, artists are far more careful to apply their skills in ways that conform to expected representational formulae. In these 'traditions' it seems to be more important for artists to reproduce faithfully shared cultural perceptions of the world around them. This is not to deny change and innovation in non-Western artistic 'traditions'. To the contrary, there is considerable evidence of change over time from around the world (Barnes 1992; Berlo 1999; Cohodas 1999; Layton 1992; Niessen 1999; Silverman 1999; Thomas 1991). However, the art produced in these societies for local consumption continues to contain within it those culturally defined elements of representation that Arnheim has argued are essential features of representation. Although Arnheim's example draws a connection between a shape and spatial features not actually in the form represented, one could equally invoke an example whereby the shape recalls an emotion, mental image or epistemological 'truth'. Indeed, this is precisely what Vakutans represent in their construction of form. They represent 'imagined' characteristics, aesthetic concepts and states of being in the forms they carve into their decorative boards. In this way, they are not necessarily replicating images that they physically see, but are engaged in a representation of what they 'know' about the world.[1]

In his seminal discussion of art, style and culture, Gell observed that the attention anthropologists once lavished on the formal analysis of art had lapsed in favour of what he considered a misplaced focus on art as a 'grammar' akin to languages (1998). I wish to resurrect the formal analysis of an artistic system, using this approach to art as a stepping stone towards understanding the ways in which Vakutans represent what they see. In order to understand representation – that is, how ideas find expression in the relationship between things – we must begin by a formal examination of those basic elements used to delineate that which is represented.

An analysis of form in any artistic system is a valuable means of providing insight into the ways people perceive their environment, how they break it down into simple line and shape to capture the formal properties of a shared cultural code in a meaningful world. In Vakutan carved art, for example, the egret (*Egretta alba*) is regularly represented by a single form exaggerating a long, curved beak with an elongated head and neck. In fact, the egret has a long, straight beak with only a very slight curve. Why then should Vakutans conceptualise and then represent the egret with a long, curved beak? Indeed, why choose this bird from all the possible species available to them with curved beaks? When asked, their matter-of-fact response was invariably, '*naminabwoita tagisa*' ('she is a beautiful animal to see'). This seemingly simple reply belies the complexity of meanings motivating its representation. It is not merely the perceived beauty found in the curved beak and neck that is important to represent in the carved lines. The form itself highlights the importance of the head and mouth (beak) as well as the relationship of the form to other carved forms around it. While these representations are explored later (see Chapters 5 and 7), it is the significance of form and its ability to delineate meaning that will be examined here.

One important outcome to an analysis of form is that it helps us to identify style.[2] A particular artistic style can be distinguished from others through visibly discernible differences in the shape, contour, emphasis, depth and quality of line. For example, there is a marked difference between the utilisation of the line by Northwest Coast Native Americans and that used by Massim artists. Although both styles utilise curvilinear form to encode meaning, Massim artists tend to interlock lines so as to form continuous spirals and volutes while Northwest Coast American artists prefer to isolate their lines into separate design units: curves within curves and circles within circles (Boas 1927; Holm 1965; F. Morphy 1977). While we can see the discernible differences between these two art styles, a formal analysis helps to articulate what those differences are and suggests distinct cultural approaches to representation. It may also help us to understand the way people think about themselves and the world they live in. For example, one could argue that the interlocking scrolls that are an identifiable element of the Massim style highlight a preoccupation amongst the cultures of this area with the interdependence between island communities. Robert Thompson argued that the quality of a line in Yoruba sculpture is more than a mark of Yoruba style, drawing aesthetic comment from consumers. Through his analysis of Yoruba sculpture he found a more pervasive relationship between lineal images and Yoruba philosophical reflections on their civilisation and its 'historical' development (1973). However, inferring deeper intellectual constructions from style opens up a precarious abyss towards which one must tread carefully.

The Massim style appears superficially homogeneous, but in fact it incorporates a number of sub-styles differentiated on the basis of formal characteristics. Each sub-style is unique, corresponding to discrete cultural regions such as the Trobriand Islands, the Marshall Bennett Islands, the Amphlett Islands, and so on. Further differentiation exists within these groups. Indeed, this level of differentiation is made by people themselves on the basis of often very minor formal differences. Taking the Trobriand Islands as an example, people differentiate sub-styles from different districts. Thus Trobrianders can identify the 'Kuboma district style', the 'Kitavan style' and the 'Vakutan style' of design utilisation. Finally, within these districts further differentiation identifies different 'schools' (*sopi*) and the individual carvers who represent these. Therefore, within the Massim style we can differentiate between discrete sub-styles that become increasingly specific to groups of people. Although there is generally a shared corpus of form utilisation between these discrete areas, ultimately linking them within an identifiable Massim style, the encoding of meaning applied to the designs may not, likewise, apply across group boundaries. Apparently similar sub-styles may have very different meanings associated with the individual components, even when used in different contexts within the same group.[3]

Anthropological interest in non-Western art formed part of the earliest investigations of so-called 'primitive' peoples. Indeed, the collection of material culture was considered an essential component of anthropological method, supplying Western museums with rich collections of peoples' artistic tradition (O'Hanlon and Welsch 2000; Price 1989; Thomas 1991). As well as the collection of representative pieces of material culture, considerable interest was directed towards the analysis, classification and comparison of form (Boas 1927; Edge-Partington 1969; Firth 1936; Haddon 1894, 1895; Reichard 1933). This analysis, however, is not so much concerned with stylistic differentiation for its own sake.[4] Instead, the focus is on the ways in which form may reflect particular methods of encoding meaning. It is to this end that our direction now turns. In the following discussion

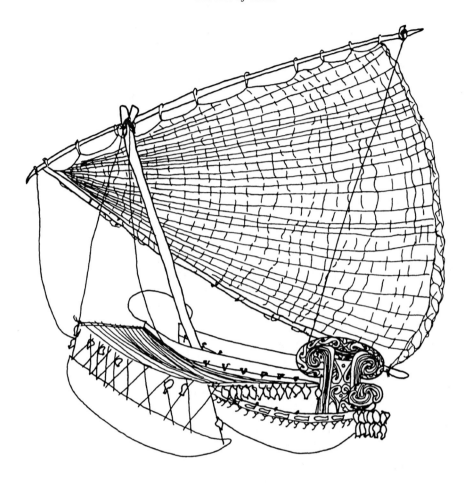

Figure 4.1 Vakutan *masawa*

attention is directed specifically towards those forms that delineate the carvings made for kula. These include the prow and splashboard as well as the forms carved and painted along the sides of the outrigger canoe (Figure 4.1, Plate 1).

Kula Carvings

In the Massim area there are two styles of outrigger canoe. These are distinguished by Vakutans as the *masawa* and the *nagega*. The *masawa* is thought to have originated from Dobu, while the *nagega* is said to have come from Muyuw. Vakutans claim that they once constructed the *nagega* but decided that the *masawa* suited them better and so began to make these exclusively. The *nagega* is a much larger and heavier sea craft, while the *masawa* is smaller and lighter (Damon 1990; Haddon and Hornell 1938; Munn 1977, 1986). Both styles, however, utilise only one outrigger, resulting in neither a fixed bow nor a fixed stern. The performance of the outrigger canoe depends upon the positioning of the outrigger on the windward side of the canoe. Hence, the bow and stern of these boats change according to the direction of the wind. This means that the two ends of an outrigger canoe must function as both a bow and a stern.

There are four boards, or two sets of splashboard (*lagim*) and prowboard (*tabuya*) carved for each *masawa*. Vakutans distinguish between the two sets linguistically, conceptually and physically. The set placed on the canoe with the outrigger on its left is the *dogina* end, while the set placed with the outrigger on its right is called the *uuna* end. These sets are distinguished further according to the directions they 'look' to. The *dogina* is said to 'go to Dobu first', while the *uuna* 'looks' towards Kitava (Plate 14). This distinction is connected to the actual wind directions considered necessary for a safe voyage in either direction. That is, when the south-westerly winds are blowing it is considered the best time to sail to Kitava Island, placing the outrigger on the right with the *uuna* facing the direction the fleet is heading. On the other hand, when they wish to sail to Dobu they wait until the north-westerly winds blow, positioning the outrigger on the left with the *dogina* facing Dobu. This distinction has further significance marking the relative difficulty of engaging in a kula expedition to Dobu as compared to one to Kitava. Kula with Dobu is considered to be fraught with dangers and unpredictable difficulties. Vakutans place much more emphasis on the *dogina* end of the *masawa*, as we shall see.[5]

Once the carver has selected the tree and cut four pieces from it, he roughly shapes them before carrying the boards to the village. There he further shapes the pieces to more closely resemble the prow and splashboards. A finer planing smoothes the boards and shapes them more precisely to his liking. Throughout this process the boards are left in the shade to dry out the wood slowly. Once the boards are finely adzed and planed to the carver's liking, he is ready to begin cutting the designs into the boards.

Each set is visually distinguishable from the other by physical markers. For the splashboard the larger 'loop' is always positioned on the side of the outrigger (Figure 4.2).

The *dogina* and *uuna* prowboards are distinguished by the occurrence of perforations along the bottom of the *uuna* and the absence of these in the *dogina*. A further distinguishing marker is the changed line of the *dogina* 'nose' (Figure 4.3).

The inclusion of specific forms located in particular areas is another means of distinguishing the sets. This is particularly so for the prowboard and will be discussed in greater detail as the analysis unfolds. Finally, the prow and splashboard

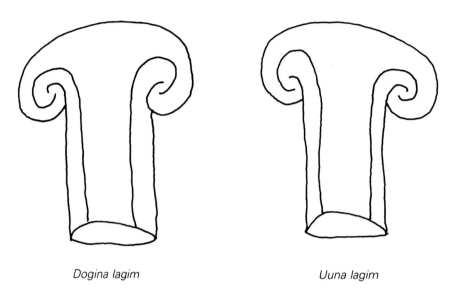

Dogina lagim   Uuna lagim

Figure 4.2 Visual distinction between *dogina* and *uuna lagim*

are internally divided into distinct sections (Figure 4.4). This division corresponds to the way Vakutan carvers organise their work and further facilitates descriptive and analytic convenience for the purpose of exploring the encoded meanings. When carving and talking about the designs, carvers distinguish these sections by using body-part names.

Although each carver works in his own way, there is a general order in which the boards are carved. For the splashboard, section 1 (see Figure 4.4) is first divided from the rest of the board and the basic orientation of the central designs in this section are lightly marked so as to establish the basic delineation of all the designs.

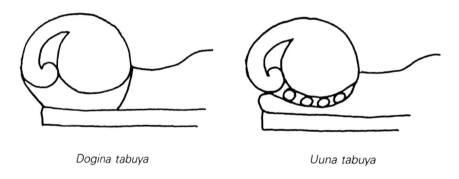

Dogina tabuya   Uuna tabuya

Figure 4.3 Visual distinction between *dogina* and *uuna tabuya*

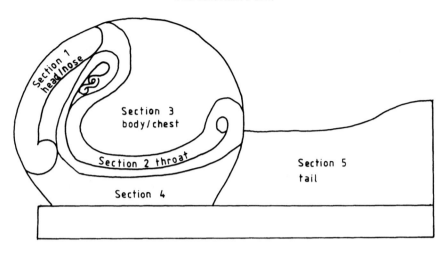

Tabuya

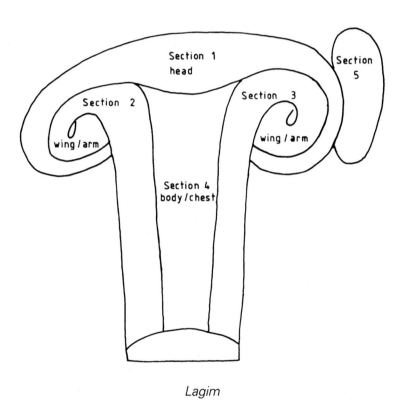

Lagim

Figure 4.4 Division into sections for the *tabuya* and *lagim,* showing body-part associations

Following this, the lines dividing sections 2 and 3 from section 4 are cut. In this way the sections are clearly distinguished. The details within each section are then given greater attention. For the prowboard, carvers generally begin by delineating section 1 by means of digging out the perforation between sections 1 and 2. Following this, either section 3 or 4 may be carved, but again major sections are first differentiated, followed by the carving of internal details within sections. Section 5 on the prowboard is usually completed last. Some designs may be carved in conjunction with the same designs on the other side. In other words, a carver may work on the central design in section 3 of a prowboard, periodically turning the board over during the operation to complete the design on the other side.

A Formal Analysis of Form

Form evokes an aesthetic appraisal from Vakutans who are particularly concerned about the appearance of line. Lines carved into wood should be 'clean', 'strong', 'unwavering' and 'balanced'. The relationship between lines should provide a sense of balanced interaction, avoiding an overall feel of fussiness. Vakutans react to an overly worked board with disdain, claiming that it appears 'tangled' (*'nugwenigwe'*), or 'confused' and 'cluttered' (*'pitupitu'*).[6] When the discrete forms are in balance Vakutans say the effect is *'katuvi'* ('clean cut'). Other aesthetic judgements draw attention to the 'tension' of a line; it must not be too tight or too loose, but must give the correct amount of 'spring' to the lines (Nalubutau 1975, 1979). Lines should always be simple and clear, yet bold and strong. The quality of a line is an important marker of good *kabitam* carving (see also Beier 1974; Nalubutau 1975, 1979). When a work is completed the quality of a carving (and by implication the quality of a carver's magic) is judged by these criteria. Indeed, the more significant details informally discussed and judged by the public are the quality of line construction, the correct arrangement of representational elements and the correct 'paths' for the colours. It is to this first quality, line construction, that we now turn.

The formal arrangement of lines can be grouped into three categories: category A, category B and category C forms. This differentiation is based upon the formal properties that distinguish them in their spatial orientation. For example, some forms appear to be the principal markers between sections. Indeed, they seem to be the primary design units defining the sections. Other forms are contained within these while still others appear around and between them. The formal system constitutes a hierarchy with some forms seeming to dominate the spaces while others provide emphasis. Prior to a discussion of the structural relationship between these three categories, however, the forms need introduction. The sections in which various forms occur are referred to regularly, therefore Figure 4.4 should be consulted in conjunction with the presentation of the formal repertoire. Reference to Plates 6 to 13 will also be helpful.

Category A includes those forms generally operating as the main designs in their respective sections. There are five distinct forms, each having three or more variations (Figure 4.5).

A1 forms are distinguished by their orientation and axis on the boards. Form A1.1 is differentiated from the other two by the elongation of one end. This form occurs only on section 2 of the prowboard. Indeed, it constitutes the boundary delineating section 2. Form A1.2 encloses the upper portion of the splashboard, containing two directionally opposing forms (A4):

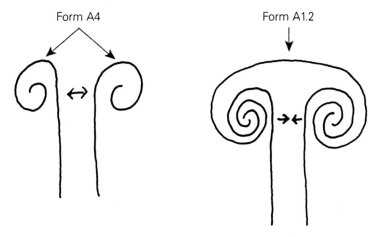

Form A4   Form A1.2

While this form has no name or label it probably plays the most important structural role on the splashboard. It binds, or holds together the entire composition, creating a 'tension' in the overall feel of the board. These are aesthetic terms often discussed among 'critics' (see also Beier 1974; Mosuwadoga 1978; Nalubutau 1975, 1979). When the splashboard is decorated with white cowry shells attached along the entire length of this form, its shape is greatly emphasised. Form A1.2 contains within it other forms (A3.1, A5 and C6). Form A1.3, like A1.1, is open at the top (opposite to form A1.2). When this form occurs it is placed in section 4 of the splashboard and contains circles (B1.2 or B1.3) within it. It is associated with a particular school, *Sopila* Kitava (Plate 13).

There are three variations for form A2. All variations are based upon a volute with one end almost continuing into a coil, while the other is left uncoiled or straight. The distinctions between these variations are based upon the relationship of the coiled end to the whole form: the kind of 'tail', or stem, whether it is curved or straight and the orientation of these on the boards. Form A2.1 delineates section 1 of the prowboard. Form A2.2 sometimes occurs in section 5 of the *uuna* prowboard with the coiled end directed downwards (Plate 9). It is never carved

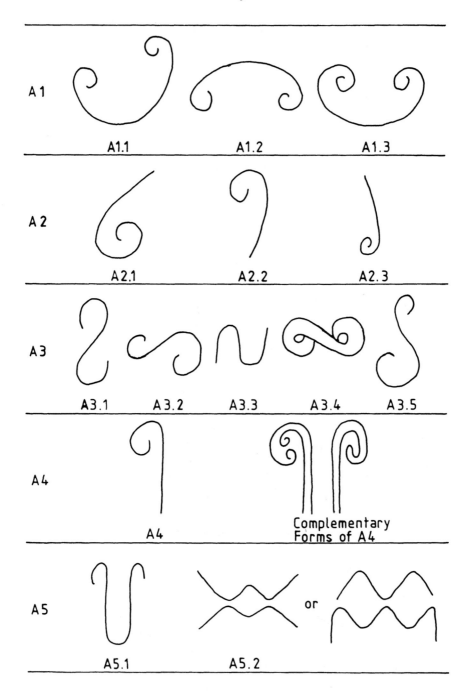

Figure 4.5 Category A forms

on the *dogina* prowboard in section 5. This form may also be carved in section 4 of the splashboard depending upon the carver's school or personal attempts at innovation (compare Plates 10–13). Form A2.3 is placed on the outrigger side of the splashboard (section 5). It is not always carved. Its inclusion on a particular board depends upon the carver and his inclinations.

Form A3 is related to form A2 except that the end that remains uncoiled on A2 is coiled in A3. The coil, however, is in the opposite direction from its counterpart in the design. Hence, the form more or less resembles the letter S in our alphabet. The distinctions made in this analysis between the various manifestations of this basic form are based upon the differing relationship each has to the other forms, as well as to the formal properties that dictate their diverse orientation on the boards. For example, form A3.1 is repeated to form a linked 'chain' around the structural outline delineated by form A1.2 on the splashboard (section 1). However, form A3.2 is also located in section 1 of the splashboard. It is distinguished from A3.1 by the differing tension of its two coils; one coil is tight while the other is loosened. This form is placed at the end of the 'chain' incorporating form A3.1 and visually occupies the centre of the upper splashboard (Plates 10–13). Form A3.2 makes a break in the 'chain', thus emphasising form A5.2 in the centre of the splashboard. Form A3.3, like A3.1 and A3.2, is situated at the top of the splashboard in association with section 1. It is, however, located outside this section and placed on top of form A1.2. This form is not usually carved on Vakuta because it is a Kitavan innovation. Form A3.4 has tightly coiled ends, closely resembling the links in a chain. The coils actually meet the bar that joins them. This convergence creates two inner circles. The form has no specific location as it often occurs at the ends of various forms in category A. Form A3.5 is featured in section 5 of the *dogina* prowboard and is part of the design complex identifying the *dogina* from the *uuna* prowboard. It is similar to form A3.2 in that one of the coils is larger than the other. The two forms have a different orientation, however, as well as a differing board association. Form A3.2 is placed on the horizontal axis, while form A3.5 is vertically oriented (Plates 6, 7 and 8).

Forms in category A4 are complementary rather than variations. These forms are always associated with sections 2 and 3 on the splashboard. Unlike the forms of A2, these contain the coil at virtual right angles to the stem. The stem gives no indication that it may end in a coil. These complementary forms are differentiated according to the section in which they occur. They are also marked by the diversity of coil endings. One ending is only associated with section 2, while the other distinguishes section 3 on the splashboard (compare Plates 10–13).

The basic line of form A5 finishes in two loops at each end, with the stem dropping away before rising again to end in the other loop. Form A5.1 occurs in section 4 of the splashboard. However, it is a specific design belonging to the Kitavan school and is therefore only included by a carver who owns *Sopila* Kitava

(Plate 13).[7] Form A5.2 is utilised in various configurations to outline the basic shape of the human figure always featured in section 1 of the splashboard (Plates 10–13).

Category B includes those forms usually located within the boundaries of category A forms. Unlike the forms in the previous category, they are not specifically associated to sections or boards. Instead, they occur anywhere. There are four basic forms, each having two or more variations (Figure 4.6).

Form B1 is immediately identifiable as the circle. The variations of this basic form include a single circle (B1.1), a double circle (B1.2) and a triple circle (B1.3). The single circle is always white and occurs against a black background within category C forms. Alternatively, the form is located in a white background in association with category A forms. In this position the white-on-white design stands out because of the carved line encircling form B1.1. Although commercial paint is available, lime continues to be used as white paint on Vakuta Island when the expense of commercial paint is prohibitive. As it dries out it becomes powdery because the bonding agent consists primarily of oil and water. Hence its cohesion to the surface of the wood is not enduring, allowing the natural colour of wood to emerge. Carvers get around this by carving deep incisions (category B forms) into the designated white areas consisting predominately of category A forms. These incisions are said to 'hold the lime paint' and thus retain a semblance of white after the majority of the paint has washed away. The effect leaves these forms deeply etched into the A forms and highlighted as white visual fields against the natural colour of the wood (see Plates 1, 6 and 10). In this way form B1.1 is visually effective as a white-on-white design. Form B1.2 has two colours; the outer circle is white while the inner circle is black. Its placement is more restricted than B1.1 as it occurs only in section 4 of the splashboard in the Kitavan school. The triple circle (B1.3) is also more restricted than B1.1, occurring only in section 4 of the splashboard and section 4 of an *uuna* prowboard. The outer circle is white, the middle circle is red and the inner circle is black. Cross-sections of the B1 forms may help to illustrate their differentiation:

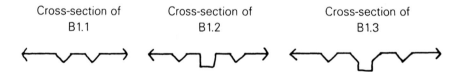

| Cross-section of B1.1 | Cross-section of B1.2 | Cross-section of B1.3 |

Form B2 incorporates the half-circle. Variations of this form are based upon an open half-circle (B2.1), a less open half-circle (B2.2) and an elongated, narrow half-circle (B2.3). Forms B2 occur only within category A forms and visually intensify the forms they are associated with. In accordance with this, these forms

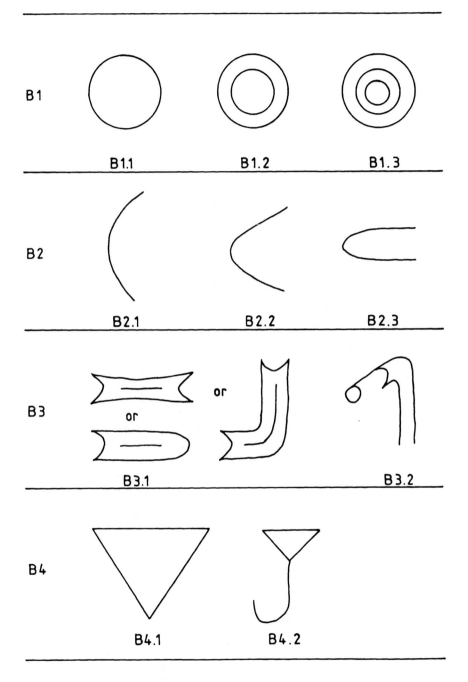

Figure 4.6 Category B forms

tend to occur in repeating sequences, emphasising the curved lines of other forms. For example:

In essence, form B3 has two variations. Within these variations, however, there are further elaborations. The form is based on a bar that is made up of either curved-in or curved-out ends. It can be straight or bent to fit into category A forms or can have a circle (B1.1) attached to it (B3.2).

Form B4 is based upon a triangular form and has two variations that are differentiated by the presence of a 'tail' on form B4.2. These forms again occur within the boundaries of category A forms. B4.2, however, is also associated with the sides of the canoe where the form is strung together in a line along the hull (see Figure 4.1).

Category C comprises forms that are located between and around category A forms. These forms are all associated with the colour black, although two are also represented in red. There are ten distinct forms within this category, none of which have variations except for those unspecified differences in form associated with individual carvers (Figure 4.7).

Form C1 is carved only on the *dogina* prowboard. That is, according to the rules of *kabitam* this form must be represented in section 5 of all *dogina* prowboards. It is, however, sometimes carved on *uuna* prowboards as a matter of individual artistic preference (Plates 6–8).

Form C2 is found on the top rim of the dugout canoe, immediately below where the first longitudinal board is attached (Figure 4.1, Plate 1). This form is repeated along the entire length of the hull. When the boat is in the water this design skims along the water's surface as flying fish and dolphins do. When in a continuous line along the hull the form is alternatively painted black–red–black–red along a white background.

Form C3 is carved only in section 3 on all prowboards. The form takes on various stylistic modifications according to an individual carver's interpretation and design implementation. It is also governed by the amount of space available on each prowboard. The basic form, however, is always present. The form is painted black and often has white circles (form B1.1) to set off the rather large areas of black incorporated within this form (Plates 6–9).

Forms C4 and C5 are often found in section 4 of the splashboard. Their presence depends upon the choice of designs an artist makes in accordance with his school of carving. Again, the colour associated with these forms is invariably black.

Form C6 is carved and coloured in alternating red and black in section 1 of the splashboard. It may also appear in section 4 of the splashboard and in various sections of the prowboard along with forms from category A. If so, the colour association is only black.

Forms C7, C8, and C9 primarily occur in section 4 of the splashboard. Sometimes these also occur in section 5 of the splashboard but their presence here depends upon the carver's design choices for this section. Black is always the colour given to these forms. On occasion form C7 is repeated thus:

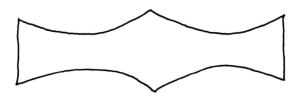

This repetition, however, is dependent upon the use of category A forms.

Form C10, although visually similar to C9, is carved only on the prowboard in section 5 (Plate 9). As with the other forms in this category the colour associated with this form is black. It occurs between and below category A forms chosen for this section.

At various points on the splashboard and prowboard there are perforations through the wood. Many of these are structurally important, particularly for the binding of the splashboard to the canoe's prow. Holes for attaching white cowry shells to decorate the *lagim* are also considered necessary for practical reasons. They are essential to the boards because they allow the waves to pass through rather than smash upon the surface of the boards, thereby guarding against potential breakage. All but one set of perforations, however, correspond to the forms actually incised on the boards as designs. Forms B1.1, C6, C7, and C8 are carved straight through the board. On the splashboard these occur primarily in section 1 where form C6 runs along the inner edge of the area outlined by form A3.1 (Plates 10–13). These perforations are used to fasten the cowry shells to the top of the splashboard (Plate 15). The perforations around forms A5.1 and 2 are always carved in the top/centre of section 1 and cannot be said to conform to any of the designs. These spaces are not consistent between boards because the spatial relationships between the other forms in this area vary according to the carver's spacing of the design elements.

Sections 2 and 3 of the splashboard also have perforations. Both sections have a hole through the body of the board where the splashboard is lashed to the canoe's prow. This hole is called *kosobu* and corresponds to form C8. Section 2 has a new

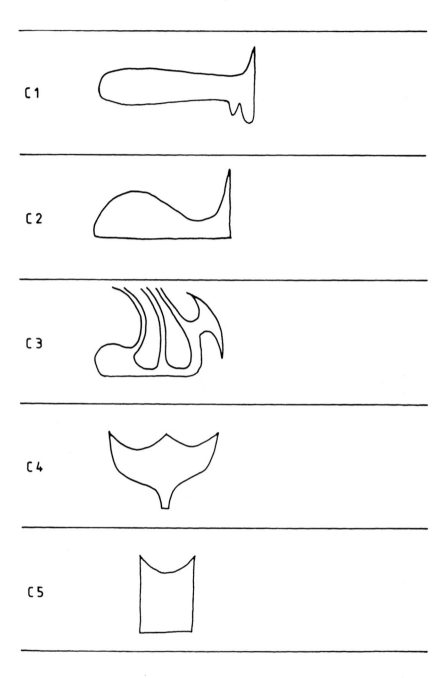

Figure 4.7 Category C forms

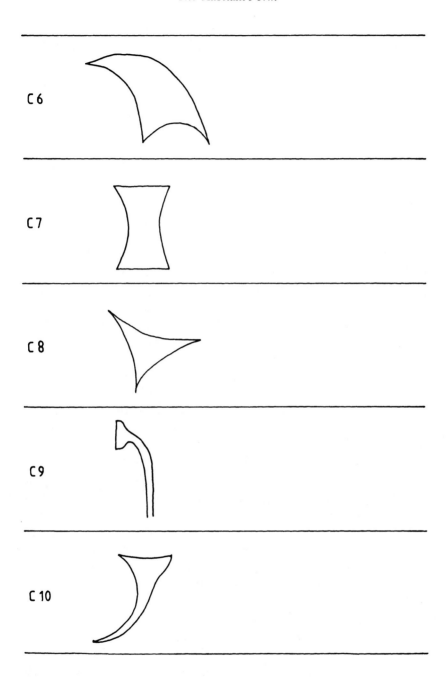

Figure 4.7 Category C forms *(continued)*

shape in its centre where the red lines turn in on themselves to meet the black lines. The form that is perforated through the board is created thus:

In section 3 the perforations in the centre of the section correspond to form B1.1 except that, unlike the carved forms related to B1, they are not perceived as white. A perforation is perceived as black. This is in accordance with the physical placement of black forms generally as they are the most deeply incised forms.

The prowboard also has perforations occurring in sections 1, 2 and 4. The perforation associated with section 1 is in fact between it and section 2. It is usually the first thing to be cut and shaped on the prowboard after completion of its outer shaping. Each school has different conventions on how large this perforation should be. Section 2 has the 'tear-drop' form also found in section 2 of the splashboard, as well as a perforation corresponding to form C6. Further, section 2 has small circular holes at the end of form A1.3. Perforations in section 4 of the prowboard identify the board as an *uuna* prowboard. *Dogina* prowboards have no perforations in this section (compare Plates 6 and 9 with the *dogina tabuya* in Plates 7 and 8). Depending upon what design complex a carver chooses to incorporate in this section the perforation may correspond to forms B1.1, C6, C7, C8, and so on. Those forms in the C category from C5 onwards may all emerge depending upon other forms utilised. Perforations are not given any special linguistic marker. They are simply referred to as holes (*pwanana*) and are principally conceived as structural aids in the wear and tear of the boards, as well as handy spaces to attach decorations.

The shapes of the boards correspond closely to form A4 identified above. The splashboard can be seen as a folded-out prowboard. If we visualise the prowboard placed upon its end and split along the top, it falls open to form a shape similar in outline to a splashboard. The design complex utilised on the prowboard, however, is not related to that carved on the splashboard. The splashboard has an informal line running from top to bottom along the centre, one side essentially mirroring the other as if it were opened outwards along a central axis (cf. Plates 10–13). Vakutans do not talk this way about the boards, however. Indeed, they are usually at great pains to demonstrate the differences between the two sides of the splashboard. It is interesting, though, that there are strong visual similarities distinct from very specific formal differences. Looking for difference amongst a sea of similarity is a recurring theme in Vakutan thinking.

The Significance of the Formal Categories

The formal components utilised by *tokabitam* carvers to produce kula art provide a significant point of departure for a comprehensive analysis of the boards. When broken down into discrete units of form, we can further examine the relationship between the formal components by focusing on their spatial positioning and orientation, as well as the dynamics that emerge between them.

One way of 'seeing' the relationship between these discrete units is by looking at the positive and negative images that emerge from the intentional delineation of certain forms. For example, it is inevitable that negative, or secondary forms will become manifest through the skilled hand of the carver in his shaping of positive, or primary forms. The former seem to float or recede, depending upon the execution of primary forms. The identification of the three categories has inadvertently separated the discrete forms into positive and negative groupings. The positive, or primary, forms correspond closely to those grouped into category A, while category C forms, with the exception of C2, are secondary forms resulting from the carving of category A forms. Category B forms, however, are carved in both category A and C forms to emphasise, repeat or highlight those forms around them. As a result, a hierarchy seems to emerge with some designs delineating and apparently dominating the available spaces on the boards while others emphasise, repeat or emerge from them.

Given that the emergence of negative forms is coincidental to the intentional delineation of positive forms, one could be tempted to eliminate the negative forms from further analysis. However, such a move may prove too premature. There is a danger in assuming that forms manifestly born of others are therefore meaningless. As we move further through the analysis, particularly when examining the representational nature of the system, a more inclusive approach to the treatment of all forms as potentially valuable is supported.

Another way of thinking about the formal components of kula carvings is by focusing on the relative frequency with which discrete forms appear. Category A forms are more versatile in their placement, frequency and orientation than those of the other two categories.[8] These forms seem to generate other forms, being the positive images on the boards. This versatility can also be demonstrated by the greater range of variations possible for each of the basic forms discussed above. Perhaps it is not surprising that these forms carry the greatest density of meaning in the system. Further, as we shall see, the frequency and versatility of the forms in this category suggest that the meanings associated with them vary depending upon their positions on the boards. The relationship of these forms to those of the other two categories is primary. They not only generate the forms in category C, they also restrict the occurrence of forms in category B.

While category A forms can be described as 'versatile', an appropriate descriptive term for category B forms is 'restricted'. These forms occur within the boundaries outlined by the forms of category A. The only exception to this is form B1.1. However, its placement is inside category C forms, thus it remains restricted within other forms. None of these forms are contained within each other. Instead they either emphasise others of this group or intensify the versatile forms within which they are bound.

Category C forms can be considered less versatile and more 'fixed'. The execution of these forms is largely dependent upon the versatile forms used. These forms can be seen as the negative responses to category A forms. They occur around and between the versatile forms and emerge from them. This does not, however, necessarily decrease their representational significance. Indeed, forms C1, C2 and C3 are very important when they are associated with particular representations. These forms are the only ones of the fixed group given 'animal' names (see Chapter 5). There are no variations to any of these forms apart from carvers' specific styles.

The formal distinction between versatile and fixed, or positive and negative forms is further supported by the depth of incision made in their execution. A carved board has five levels, or four differential incisions. Firstly, there is, of course, the surface and it is this level which is occupied by the versatile A forms. Secondly, there is a deep, but narrow incision made within the boundaries of the versatile forms of category A. These incisions are said to hold the lime paint. This level belongs to the restricted B forms. The third level is carved at an angle and can be argued to form a transition between the white, upper level, and the deeper, black level. This third level is always painted red and generally echoes the lines of the white versatile forms located on the surface. The fourth level is deeper than the second level and much broader. Indeed, the cutting away of the wood to create this level can be seen as the opposite of the upper surface level. It is not left at an angle, nor roughly cut, but smoothed flat, like the surface. Whereas the surface is painted white, this deeper level is painted black. The breadth of this level corresponds to the fixed forms of category C. These four levels can be shown in cross-section to illustrate the varying relationships:

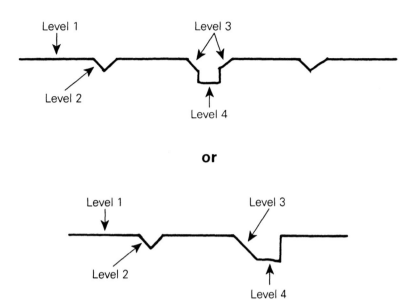

or

The fifth level is in fact the absence of wood. The perforations made through the wood are functional. These differentially carved levels correspond to the colour patterning of the boards. Colour plays an important part in the aesthetics of Vakutan life, conveying layers of meaning about people's well-being. Throughout the discussion of form it has been impossible to isolate form from colour entirely; indeed form and colour are closely associated in Vakutan thinking. Further, there is a general correspondence with colour and the differentiation of the formal categories. The versatile forms are by and large white with further emphasis in red. The fixed forms are all black. The restricted forms of category B are mostly assoc-iated with white, being contained within white versatile forms. As colour evokes considerable semantic reference, an entire chapter is devoted to a discussion of the use and meaning of colour (Chapter 6). In this chapter the forms adorning kula outrigger canoes have been isolated. Meaning has been omitted from this formal investigation. It is to the exploration of meaning that the next chapter turns.

–5–

The *Kabitam* 'Animals'

This chapter will examine the repertoire of representations and the meanings that are associated with the forms examined in the previous chapter. The repertoire consists of several kinds of birds, a mollusc, a shellfish, an insect, two mammals, a variety of plants, the moon and an assortment of mythical creatures. The designs, however, are not merely the representations of those things with which they share a name. Although there is, in most cases, an iconic component to the relationship between a *kabitam* design and the named animal it represents, the relationship is far more complex than a mere labelling based on iconic features suggests. Rather than representing the animal as an end in itself, the system encodes attributes of the animal relevant to a Vakutan rationale for idealising certain animals, or, more specifically, certain *features* of animals in association with the aims of kula. Vakutans accord value to certain characteristics possessed by chosen animals as models worthy of emulation rather than idolising the animal as a whole, although a few animals featured in the repertoire do receive near idolatrous attention. This system identifies relevant characteristics that convey qualities of motion, aesthetics and behaviours considered successful to kula. There are some forms, however, with no iconic relationship to their namesakes in the natural environment. The relationship between these forms and the animals they are derived from is schematic. Their importance to the system is related to specific symbolic assoc-iations that will be examined in this and the remaining chapters.

All forms and colours associated with the boards and outrigger canoe are referred to by using the noun classifier -*na*-. This linguistically places all members of the *kabitam* repertoire within the animal classification, regardless of whether their natural counterparts are similarly classified. For example, in everyday speech plants and wood are identified by using different classifiers than -*na*-. Including them within the animal classification effectively separates them from their namesakes. Further, the classifier -*na*- is used to distinguish female from male. Thus all women are identified by use of the classifier -*na*-.[1] Although the design elements are discussed by using the noun *mauna* (animal), incorporating the -*na*-classifier to specify the 'animal' nature of these elements implicitly associates them with women, as distinct from men. This reference to women on the boards, the association with women while sailing on kula expeditions, together with the symbolic relationship women have to the actual kula transactions will become increasingly apparent.

The *kabitam* 'animals' are chosen because they are thought to impart certain beneficial features to the enterprise concerned with successful kula. Their powers are considered benevolent as long as they are constrained within the boundaries of the boards. Magic is the constraining force and this is effected by the utterance of various spells by either the carver or the owner of the canoe, depending upon who knows the magic. As well as their beneficial association, the 'animals' have a negative side. Should the outrigger canoe be capsized or shipwrecked it is thought that the magic constraining them dissolves, releasing the 'animals' to engage in more malignant behaviour. Together with the flying witches, *mulukwausa*, believed to rush to the scene of an endangered craft, the 'animals' feed on the flesh and internal organs of kula men. During this feast the 'animals' are explicitly equated with flying witches. Another noun used to refer to the flying witches is *vivila*, the generic term for women.[2] Vakutans use this word more often than *mulukwausa* because the latter reference is thought to draw the attention of these dreaded women. To avoid attracting them they use a euphemism and refer to women in general. Flying witches represent the very essence of all that is feared and potentially uncontrollable in the feminine gender; a theme that is examined further in Chapters 8 and 9.

There are several other ways of referring to the formal components of the system besides by their animal representations. One of these is the use of the second-form possessive. There are three possessive forms of address in the Kilivila language,[3] each denoting degrees of closeness to ego. The first possessive form is used to indicate that which is inalienable to an individual (*-la*; third person singular possessive suffix). Nouns included in this possessive form are body parts and kin. The second possessive form refers to items that are in some circumstances alienable while in others inalienable (*kala*; third person singular). For instance, food comes into this category. Prior to food being ingested it is alienable; once eaten, however, the food becomes a part of the person and therefore inalienable. Implements associated with food and nourishment, body decoration and clothing are denoted by this possessive form. While the second possessive form retains a certain degree of intimacy with ego, the third loses all intimacy and is ultimately alienable (*la*; third person singular). Examples of items that take the third possessive form are houses, land, spears, gardens, yams earmarked for exchange, husbands and wives. It is important to note that the use of these possessive forms is entirely contextual. I may give someone my yams (third possessive form, first person singular, *ula taitu*) in an exchange. The recipient refers to these yams using the second possessive form, *kagu taitu* (first person singular). If he then decides to cook them and give them to someone, perhaps even back to me, he uses the third form possessive while the recipient uses the second.

The design components are grouped in the second possessive category with food, cooking utensils, body decoration and clothing. Their association with body decoration and clothing is not surprising given that at one level the designs are thought of as the decorations of the prow and splashboards. Indeed, the prow and splashboard take on the second (*kala*) possessive form when spoken of in relation to the canoe: the canoe's prow and splashboard (*kala tabuya e lagim*). The owner of the canoe, however, uses the third form possessive in reference to the prow and splashboard; they do not decorate or 'clothe' the owner, they decorate the canoe.

Although the association with body decoration and clothing seems obvious, there is a corresponding relationship to food that is not entirely haphazard. As indicated above, if a boat is endangered, resulting in a shipwreck, the magic restraining the 'animals' dissolves and their uncontrollable and destructive nature reverts to a feast of human flesh. In other words, the human members of the *masawa* become food for the *kabitam* repertoire. As one of the master carvers put it: '*Kasi kawelu matausina usagelu*' ('Their [the *kabitam* animals] food, those men, the [human] crew'; Youwa, Wakwega hamlet, Vakuta village). Thus, when talking about the forms and their 'animal' and colour associations by using the second possessive *kala* or *kasi* (third person plural), reference is explicitly directed towards the decorative nature of the designs for the canoe, with an implicit reference to food; perhaps an unconscious reminder of the inherent dangers of embarking upon kula expeditions across untamed seas.

The use of body-part terminology is another way in which Vakutans refer to the forms carved on the kula ensemble. The purpose of this terminology is to isolate, and thereby emphasise, the various characteristics of the 'animals' thought to enhance the objectives of successful kula. The head (*dabila*) and 'mind' (*nanoula*) are body parts commonly referred to by Vakutans when discussing the *kabitam* 'animals'. The *dabila* is located in the forepart of the head roughly corresponding to the brain, while *nanoula* is centred in the upper chest. These two areas of the body are conceptually contrasted by Vakutans. The *dabila* is where human thought and intelligence generates the first and second levels of knowledge discussed in Chapter 3. The chest, or *nanoula*, is where creativity, wisdom, and knowledge of the *kabitam* order resides. More will be said of these distinctions later.

Teeth (*kudila*) are another body part frequently referred to. Teeth are conceptually attributed with the ability to capture and grip prey. This behaviour is especially useful on kula expeditions where shell valuables may be more elusive than one would like. The beak (*kabulu*) of a bird and the mouth (*wadila*), more generally, are also seen as important in capturing prey. Vision, on the other hand, is considered necessary for perception and knowledge. Wisdom is made possible through sight, making the eye (*matila*) a significant body part to receive attention in the *kabitam* repertoire. The eye is also the focus of desire, particularly sexual desire. This is not without meaning in kula, as we shall see.

The throat, *kaiyau*, is where taste and memory of taste are stored. When some-one is hungry for a special delicacy, Vakutans say that it is the throat that stimulates desire as it remembers the taste of something. This has reference to the desire for kula shell valuables, especially the large and famous ones. The motivation to embark on kula expeditions is sometimes expressed in terms of the throat wanting to make kula. Further, the throat is perceived as a long, tubular organ resembling the vagina. The length of the throat is talked about as a desirable attribute, while the throat and vagina are thought to be connected in women. One version of Trobriand conception beliefs tells of the spirit child entering the head of a woman and from there travelling to her womb via the throat. When the foetus has reached full size it enters the narrow passage of the vagina and from there is born (see also Malinowski 1927c, 1932: 148).[4] In *The Sexual Lives of the Savages*, Malinowski cites the belief that 'the throat is a long passage like the *wila* (cunnus) and the two attract each other. A man who has a beautiful voice will like women very much and they will like him' (1932: 478).

Reference is often made to the 'face' (*migila*) of the boards. Facial features are said to communicate inner feelings and receive considerable aesthetic attention. If a man is blessed with a beautiful face, he will be able to attract women and shell valuables. It is important for the face of the splashboard to be beautiful so that it, too, will attract the attention of kula partners who will want to 'throw' their shell valuables towards the canoe, bespelled by the beautiful 'face' of the lagim.

Finally, arms (*lamila*) and wings (*pinipanela*) are important body parts for motion and thus find representation on the boards. In discussing the 'body parts' of the boards, the face, arms/wings, chest/mind and the head are used to refer to different sections. The face, for example, refers to the entire carved surface of the prow and splashboards. Those areas referred to as arms or wings are positioned in the two lobes (sections 2 and 3; see Figure 4.4 for their locations) on either side of the splashboard, while the chest and mind are located in the centre of section 4 on the splashboard. The head of the splashboard is, not surprisingly, located in the centre of section 1.

Structural Terminology

Some of the 'animals' in the *kabitam* repertoire are important to the spatial and structural organisation of the boards. These 'animals' delineate whole areas on the boards and contain within their boundaries other 'animals'. There are two 'animals' who perform this task: beba and doka.

The *beba* (butterfly) is located on either side of the splashboard, corresponding with the entire area of sections 2 and 3. While these are referred to as *beba*, other 'animals' reside within these sections:

beba

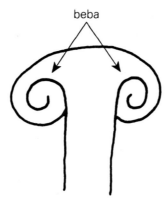

Vakutans chose *beba* because they value the characteristic flight of butterflies. Vakutans say that the butterfly moves effortlessly upon the currents of the wind and it is this ability that they hope will be emulated by the outrigger canoe. The structural form of these two sections is said to correspond to the wings (*pinipanela*) of the butterfly. One person expressed an opinion that the form of the butterfly on the splashboard looked more like the outline of antennae (*gogosu*) on its natural counterpart:

Although the relationship between the butterfly's wings and those carved on the splashboard is of primary significance because flight, particularly that of the butterfly, is a significant attribute desired by a kula crew, the relationship to the antennae of a butterfly is also relevant. Antennae are considered an important part of the butterfly's flying apparatus, as well as being instrumental to its intelligence (particularly in relation to flight). Further, the shape of the antennae is reminiscent of one of the main forms in the system (A4). Hence it is not surprising that a butterfly's antennae are also related to the delineation of sections 2 and 3 on the splashboard.

The butterfly is thought to have mastered the knowledge of flying technique and ability, hence displaying qualities of wisdom. It appears to flutter effortlessly through the air. When a *masawa* is so far ahead of the others in a fleet, resulting in its appearance as a mere speck in the distance, Vakutans say, '*Bogwa imila beba*', or 'already the canoe has the face of/has become a butterfly'. The *masawa* is equated with the small, easy flight of the butterfly.

The *doka* is another 'animal' important to the spatial and structural organisation of the prow and splashboard. Carvers use this 'animal' form to divide space, particularly on the splashboard. The main *doka* is placed at the top of the splashboard (section 1) on either side of the human figure:

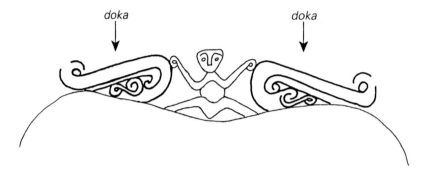

Other *doka* occur elsewhere as extensions of the principal *doka*. One is found in both sections 2 and 3 of the splashboard:

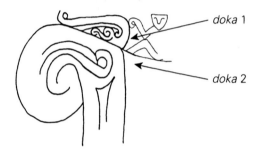

The *kabitam* carvers incise the primary *doka* (*doka* 1, section 1) before any other design on the *lagim*. It is said that it marks the 'path' (*keda*) for the other designs, acting as a standard of measure to set out the main spatial division of the splashboard. Once carved, the lines dividing sections 2 and 3 from section 4 can be struck down the length of the splashboard:

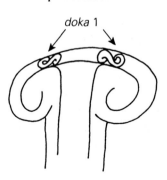

'If the *doka* is carved correctly the rest of the "animals" will fall into place. If not, the splashboard will be ruined' (Ruguna, Kuweiwa hamlet, Vakuta village). This statement, like many others expressed by carvers and ordinary members of the Vakutan community, places emphasis on the importance of the *doka* to the structure of the splashboard. Another master carver said that, 'If a person can carve the *doka*'s eyes, mouth and other features, people will say he is a real *tokabitam*, if not, then he is not a real carver' (Youwa, Wakwega hamlet, Vakuta village). In this respect the *doka* governs the spatial domains of the other 'animals', and only a true master carver will be able to accomplish this balance.

The *doka* is also represented on the prowboard. The main *doka* resides at the head of section 2:

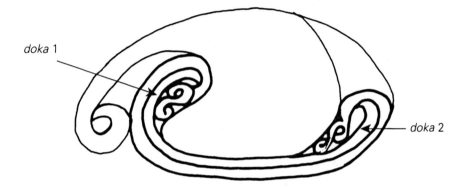

Haddon thought this design was a representation of the frigate bird because of its curved beak (1893, 1894, 1895). However, the frigate bird is not represented in the *kabitam* repertoire on Vakuta.

The *doka* does not have any counterpart in the natural world; it is an imaginary 'animal'. Some people said that the *doka* is a flying 'animal' with the head of a bird and the body of a snake. Others said it lives at sea, while there were those who claimed the *doka* is really human, but one that can fly: '*Manana tomota makawala yokwa, yaegu, taga bilola e biyoyouwa*' (This animal [is] people like you and I, but it will walk and it will fly'; Ruguna, Kuweiwa hamlet, Vakuta village). All agree, however, that the *doka* is exceedingly wise. In this respect the *doka* is related to those carvers who possess knowledge. Conceptually, the *doka* and the carver go hand in hand to produce the correct carving of the *tokabitam ginigini*. The carver utilises the *doka* to organise the design components into the prescribed system, thus representing the expression of his knowledge of *kabitam*.

The *beba* and *doka* are terms that isolate important structural spaces in *kabitam* carving.[5] The areas delineated by these terms contain many of the other *kabitam* 'animals' and are not necessarily designs in themselves. They emphasise, however, important aesthetic and conceptual forms that exist in the natural world. Although the two are not conceptualised as single designs, they are thought to carry the designs that are placed within their boundaries. For example, the *beba* is not a distinct design unit found within sections 2 or 3. Instead, it *demarcates* section 2 and 3 and contains within it the appropriate 'animals' for these sections.

Animal and Plant Terminology

The animal and plant terminology comprises the most extensive range of components in the system. As members of the *kabitam* repertoire, their purpose is to extend the 'valuable' characteristics associated with these particular animals to the success of the kula expedition. The 'animals' are presented alphabetically according to their vernacular names so as to avoid imposing at this stage a hierarchical structure on the repertoire. In general, the importance of one 'animal' over another is a contextual matter. Later, an examination of the relative significance of the 'animals' within their various contexts is considered (Chapter 7).

The *boi*, or egret (*Egretta alba*) occurs repeatedly on the boards. On the splashboard the egret is found in section 1 on either side of the human figure and shares the same form as *doka*. Indeed, *boi* is the second name for *doka* so that the form has both a conceptual reference as well as an 'animal' namesake. The egret is also found in sections 2 and 3, directly below the *doka/boi* of section 1. Its long neck and curved beak form the whole of sections 2 and 3 (Plates 10–13). On the prowboard, the *boi* is again synonymous with the *doka* in section 2. The *boi*, together with the human figure, are the 'animal' captains of the *masawa*. These two are thought to instruct all the other 'animals' to eat the human crew should the latter capsize or in any other way endanger the *masawa* (Campbell 2001, 2002, n.d.[c]).

The egret is itself considered a 'wise' animal (*nakabitam*) in its natural habitat. Vakutans see the egret standing still in the shallows waiting for the right moment to strike for fish. The egret is thought to have its own magic (*kaimwasila* – magic that involves parts of plants or trees for its success), and, when its fishing is poor, the egret goes into the forest to perform this magic. Once performed, the egret returns to the lagoon and proceeds to catch fish with improved precision.

Unlike the *boi/doka*, who must rely upon the performance of its magic to succeed in fishing, the *buribwari* (osprey, Malinowski's 'fish-hawk') is magic personified. The relationship between the *buribwari*, on the one hand, and the *boi/doka*, on the other, represents an important distinction between wisdom that is not attainable (symbolised by the *buribwari*) and wisdom that is attainable by human actors (symbolised by the *boi/doka*). This distinction receives further elaboration in Chapter 7.

The osprey is an invariable and extremely important member of the repertoire, always occurring in section 1 of the prowboard:

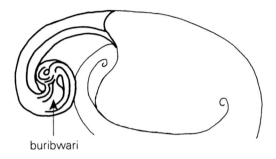

buribwari

It is carved on both the *dogina* and *uuna* prowboard, but its most important position is on the *dogina* end. The *dogina* of a *masawa* conceptually 'goes to Dobu first'. A common Vakutan sentiment amongst kula men is captured in the following statement: 'people in Dobu see the *dogina buribwari* first and are afraid because of its power' (Kunabu, Kuweiwa hamlet, Vakuta village). When landing the *masawa*, it must be turned around so that the *dogina* end with the *buribwari* lands first and is seen first, regardless of the wind-determined end that led the boat to its destination.

In many respects the *buribwari* is thought to *be* the prowboard (see also Malinowski 1935 Vol. 2: 301). With it rests the success of the kula expedition in procuring a large quantity of kula shell valuables. Vakutans say that, 'When Dobuans see the *buribwari* they will want to throw their kula shell valuables at the crew because his magic is so strong.' When placing the *dogina* prowboard into position on the outrigger canoe a small packet of herbs (*kaimwasila*), which has had magic spoken into it, is placed under the nose of the *buribwari*. Although the packet is hidden, the crew is reassured by the knowledge of its presence. The magic of *kaimwasila* is said to act upon the minds of the kula hosts, surreptitiously delivering its potency upon them and unleashing their desire to give up their shell valuables easily.

The osprey receives this special attention because it is thought to be extraordinarily 'wise'. It sits at the tops of trees watching the movement of the water below. Suddenly it swoops down, without hesitation, to a seemingly inconspicuous spot on the surface of the water. It strikes quickly and grabs its fish:

> The *buribwari* always catches its prey, it does not simply strike here and there hoping to take a fish. That is why the *buribwari* always lands first in kula because it will never fail to get all the *vaiguwa* and *mwari* [kula shell valuables]. The Kitavans and Dobuans will see the *buribwari* and throw away the *vaiguwa* and *mwari*. (Youwa, Wakwega hamlet, Vakuta village)

Malinowski, in *Argonauts of the Western Pacific*, lists a spell for the prowboard in which the osprey is invoked:

Moruborogu, Mosilava'u!
Fish-hawk,[6] fall on thy prey, catch it.
My prow-board, O fish-hawk, fall on thy prey, catch it.
I shall kula, I shall rob my kula (1922: 343)

Unlike the *boi* and *buribwari*, the *dodoleta* is believed to be less important to the success or failure of the kula expedition, yet this 'animal' appears more frequently on the boards. *Dodoleta* is often used to refer to all the carving within the boundaries of white forms. However, in its narrower sense it refers to sequences of curved lines:

The purpose of the *dodoleta* is simply to 'hold' the lime in place so that when the paint dries and turns into a powdery substance the *dodoleta* incisions within the white forms hold the powder, thus retaining the overall colour scheme.

Dodoleta in the natural world makes reference to a particular shrub with fleshy foliage. Although it is said that the plant and design only share the same name, the shrub, or its leaf to be more precise, has a distant link to kula. A favourite pastime of children is to make a sail of the leaf and, holding it on the water, allow it to catch the wind. Held thus the leaf 'sails very quickly across the sea' (Isaac, Kumwageiya hamlet, Kitava Island). A *masawa* that has caught the wind in full sail invokes praise from kula men; 'Oh *dodoleta*', they cry, referring to the children's idle pastime in making 'sails' with the leaf:

Part of the carving magic given to an initiate invokes the action of carving, or digging out the *dodoleta* designs. The magic calls on the initiate to make the lines deep and clean.

The *duduwa*, a small, round and light-green snail living in the gardens, shares its name with a member of the *kabitam* repertoire because its shape is thought to exemplify perfect roundness.[7] This garden snail's membership in the *kabitam* repertoire is based upon the form of its shell and not due to any inherent wisdom in the mollusc itself. Its 'wisdom' emanates from its shape, which is carved on the splashboard of Kitavan *sopi* in section 4 (Plate 13) and sometimes in section 3 of the *uuna* prowboard.

Another animal, the *ginareu*, is a small hermit crab living on the reef sands. As the representational system continued to develop, it attracted the attention of old master carvers.[8] It is not considered inherently wise, but when these crabs walk across the sand their legs leave little 'drawings' which, it is said, moved the master carvers to repeat these lines in their carvings:

Together with *dodoleta*, the *ginareu* designs are carved within white forms to hold the lime. The *ginareu* design is also used to emphasise other curved lines. Illustrated below is the adaptation of the hermit crab's 'footprints' in carving:

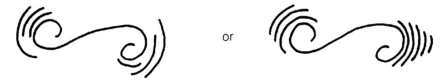

or

Kaidada is another 'animal' carved exclusively within white forms. *Kaidada* also refers to any horizontal piece of wood. The purpose of the *kaidada* design is again to hold the lime and thus retain the white pigment against the black and red pigments on either side:

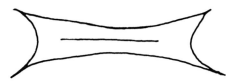

In other contexts, reference to *kaidada* is found in association with the front boards of a yam house platform upon which people hoist themselves for relaxation. This board, together with the *kamkokola* posts, is removed at the death of the yam house owner and given to the senior man of the deceased's *dala*. These boards are meant to represent the deceased and to remind people of his name and his place in society. Although the actual objects referenced by the noun *kaidada* in the natural world are not animal (indeed, the noun classifier used to refer to these is -*kai*- and includes all tree/wood-like objects) their membership within the *kabitam* repertoire transforms their classification into 'animal' by use of the classifier -*na*-. This is a good example of the corporate identity these design forms become associated with regardless of their classification outside of the carving context.

The *kapaiyauwa* refers to a bat, one of the more important 'animals' in the repertoire. Its significance is closely related to the value Vakutans place upon this mammal. People remark upon the perfect blackness of the bat, considered an aesthetic quality unparalleled in the natural world. Further, bats demonstrate a particularly desirable flight pattern that Vakutans claim is exactly the way the kula outrigger canoe should perform on the open sea. At dusk bats dart about in the skies, darkening the village. Their movement demonstrates great speed and agility. This characteristic is a desirable trait for the *masawa* on a kula expedition, particularly when having to negotiate the seas in the dark. As exemplified by the *kapaiyauwa*, Vakutans want their *masawa* to dart easily and speedily over the waves, avoiding all the dangers lurking below and above. It is this agile characteristic that makes the *kapaiyauwa* an ideal candidate for the *kabitam* repertoire.

The *kapaiyauwa* sometimes features on the splashboard, depending on the school of the carver and in correspondence with the rules of *sopi* ownership. When carved it is placed in the central area of section 4 and is always in black. An example of an adaptation of a design from the real animal is exemplified by the *kapaiyauwa* on the splashboard. 'The ancestors chose the *kapaiyauwa* because its chest looked good' (Youwa, Wakwega hamlet, Vakuta village; Plate 13):

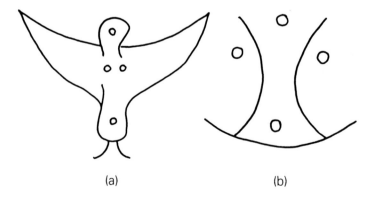

(a) (b)

While sitting with Youwa discussing his bat design I made a drawing similar to that displayed above (a). He looked at my drawing and said, 'Already it is true. We will see this animal (a), it will fly and its head is above its body. But, this animal [pointing to b] we will carve' ('*Bogwa mokwita. Batagisa manana* (a), *biyoyouwa e dabala biorakina. Taga, manawena* (b) *bataginigini*'). The drawing (a) corresponds to the view of a bat from below, the most usual vantage point for the terrestrial humans. The mammal's chest, appearing black against the twilight, is revealed when its wings are spread in flight. The drawing on the left depicts, in simple form, what a bat is perceived to look like from below. The drawing on the right is how a Vakutan carver 'transforms' the perceived form into *kabitam* graphic form. Youwa noted how the head is distorted and brought down to fit into the structure formed by the exaggerated wings in his carving.

While its appearance on the splashboard is dependent upon the school and inclination of the carver, the *kapaiyauwa*, in a different form, is always carved on the prowboard and features in section 3:

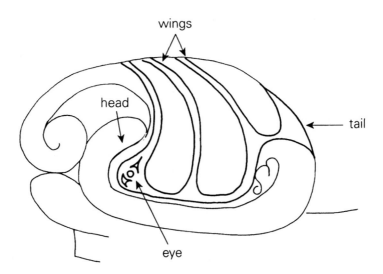

In this schematic representation the wings, head and tail are depicted from a side-on view. Although the design is not actually carved over the top of the prowboard and onto the other side, it gives the appearance of 'falling' down the other side. This form is the only one in the corpus that seems unfinished at the top of the prowboard, lacking the curvilinear flow prevalent in the other forms.

The *karawa*, or fern, is represented by a curved form representing the line of an unfurling fern frond. The design itself gets its inspiration from the gentle curve of the frond that Vakutans said motivated old master carvers to incorporate the form into their repertoire:

When it is carved on a board, it receives the colour red only. This 'animal', how-ever, belongs to a particular *sopi* (*Sopila* Kaileuna) and cannot feature on boards carved by artists of other *sopi*.

   'The *minutoula* is not an animal that we can see, it does not fly, swim, or walk. It is only a name' (Kunabu, Kuweiwa hamlet, Vakuta village). Vakutans insist that their ancestors created the design and called it *minutoula*. The word could mean 'the people of Vakuta who go first'.[9] The design is primarily associated with the side of an outrigger canoe and is carved along the entire length of the canoe (Figure 4.1):

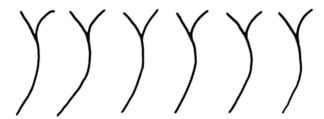

   While the *minutoula* always features along the side of the canoe, it sometimes embellishes section 5 of the *uuna* prowboard. Here the 'Y' form delineates the top while an extra curved line descends from it to swing down and form a C:

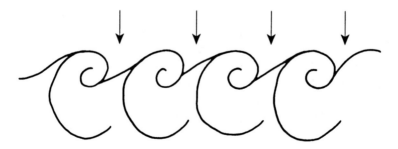

The snake, *mwata*, is another member of the *kabitam* repertoire and is depicted in many forms on the splashboard.[10] If it is incorporated into a carving, it is only carved in section 5. The snake is associated with power, particularly the power of shedding old skin for new, attractive and 'young' skin. In some of the kula-related myths, heroes shed their old skin for new skin, allowing them to attract the kula shell valuables. The snake is also associated with beauty magic. This, and the ability to regenerate, is very important in Vakutan thought: a concept that will be explored in more detail later. The snake's valuable characteristics are related to its smooth, slippery skin. Recall that in the past, young initiates drank the blood of a certain snake so as to acquire this desirable quality, and thereby enable the smooth and slippery passage of *kabitam* knowledge to flow through their bodies.

The *papa* is another imaginary 'animal'. It is said to 'belong' in the ocean, but no one could say any more about its characteristics. The word is also a noun for 'wall'. The *papa* design is found running along the length of the outrigger canoe or the 'wall' just below the attached side planks, making the craft seaworthy. Its colour alternates black and red on white (see also Figure 4.1, Plate 1):

The *sawila*, or sandpiper, is only carved on the top of a splashboard. It belongs exclusively to the Kitavan school (Plate 15).[11] It is a fairly recent innovation, having begun within the living memory of Vakutans (see also Scoditti 1977). Vakutans do not know why Kitavan master carvers chose to include the *sawila*. They say only that it is a 'lucky animal'.[12]

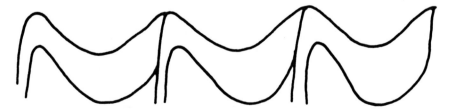

Taregesi are shellfish that attach themselves to the trunk of a sago palm.[13] In the past women collected the shell to use as a tool to split leaves for skirt making.

Carvers said that the design called *taregesi* is reminiscent of the formation made by these shellfish as they are lined up along a sago palm trunk. The design is located within the white forms and embellishes other major designs:

The *tokwalu* represents humanity. He stands for all men, women and children. This design is always placed in the middle of section 1 of the splashboard between the two *boildoka*. Sometimes he is represented by only one human figure, sometimes by two. There seems to be no significance in the number of figures carved. It is entirely up to the carver as to whether he carves one or two figures (Campbell n.d.[c]; Scoditti 1980):

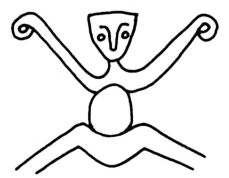

The word includes two morphemes: *to-* and *-kwalu*. *To-* is a noun classifier for the male gender when a distinction is required between male and female. *To-* is also used to incorporate all human beings, regardless of gender and age, when a distinction between human and non-human is needed. *Kwalu* may be a transformation of *kwabu*, or 'image'. Idiomatically, *tokwalu* refers to something that is an image of something else; a reflection or a photograph, for instance.

Although *tokwalu* can be said to represent humanity, and carries in its word structure a male classifier (*-to-*), when referred to without use of the noun, the classifier *-na-* is invoked. For instance, a grammatically acceptable sentence would be:

| *Manana* | *tokwalu, iyamata* | *usagelu.* |
| That [female/animal] | *tokwalu*, it looks after | the crew. |

In this sentence there is an inherent contradiction in the corresponding words *manana*, specifying that the *tokwalu* is, in this context, a female/non-human thing, and the word *tokwalu* which carries in it a male/human specification. Indeed, as this analysis develops it will become apparent that the relationship between male and female is a central theme in kula and the art that is produced to facilitate its success. This apparent contradiction warns of the complex networking of information operating within the system of kula art. Further exploration is required before beginning to disentangle some of these complexities.

Another 'animal' in the repertoire is the *ubwara*. It is described as perfectly round and is signified schematically by three concentric circles:

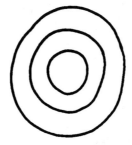

Ubwara shares its name with an uncultivated yam growing in the gardens and surrounding forest. It is not generally eaten because of its bitter flavour.[14] However, it is considered good for the soil and is often left in the garden plots to grow alongside the cultivated yams, although it receives no attention whatsoever. It is the internal property of this yam that is said to be aesthetically appealing and thus receives artistic expression. In cross-section perfect concentric circles can be seen in the flesh. Malinowski describes the yam as consistent with 'long white tubers' (1935 Vol. 2: 154).

This form corresponds to what Nalubutau (1975) named *susawiwi*, and is carved on Kiriwinan splashboards. Vakutans do not include *susawiwi* within their repertoire. However, the iconic relationship between the form and *susawiwi*, on the one hand, and *ubwara* (or *duduwa*, see above), on the other, appears to be similarly conceived in both systems. It is the shape of the 'animal' which inspires Trobriand aesthetics; roundness with an internal order consisting of a spiral (as in the case of the snails) or concentric circles (as in the case of the wild yam). This example illustrates the level at which the labelling system operates. It is not that Vakutans (or Kiriwinans) are concerned to represent a wild yam or garden snail. Rather, they are focused upon representing a particular attribute. It does not matter whether they call a circular form a snail or wild yam. It does matter, however, that their naming system encodes specific aesthetic and conceptual information. In this context, the wild yam or snail must have the necessary characteristics. The representational system is a cultural construct. Vakutans are not merely represent-ing things in the natural world. That is not their aim. What Vakutans hope to achieve is a propitious transfer of valuable characteristics perceived to enhance their kula aspirations.

The final 'animal' regularly occurring in the design repertoire is the *weku*. Although some people claim to have heard it, no one has ever seen it. People disagreed about what kind of animal it is. Some said the *weku* is a small black bird who lives in the forest, while others asserted that it lived at sea and was a fish. All remarked upon its beautiful voice beckoning listeners to find it (see also Scoditti 1977, 1980). However, no one has been lucky enough to see the source of this beautiful voice. The 'animal' is represented in the *kabitam* repertoire as a complex design in black, red and white. Its prime position is in section 5 of the *dogina* prowboard, where it must be carved:

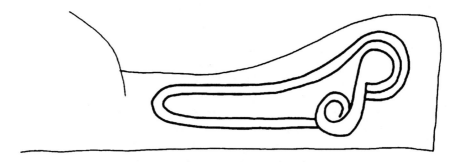

This completes the list of major 'animals' recruited to make up the *kabitam* repertoire. The set of *kabitam* 'animals' introduced above is the one most commonly agreed upon by the carvers on Vakuta today. These 'animals' are said to have an important function in the desire to secure kula shells. There are, however, other 'animals' who sometimes feature on the boards, but only in cameo appearances, attesting to some degree of flexibility in the representational system. Individual carvers will occasionally add to the above set of 'animals' when pointing out design configurations on their own carvings, particularly within section 4 of the splashboard. It is significant that it is in this section that individual creativity is allowed expression. This area is the 'chest' of the splashboard. It is in the chest of human beings that knowledge and creativity reside. Other sections on both the splashboard and prowboard are more restricted, the choice of the *kabitam* designs considerably limited.

The way in which natural phenomena are selected and finally incorporated into the graphic system is inherently complex. There is no *a priori* relationship between the natural and graphic 'animal'. In a system such as this, features of the 'animals' are selected, isolated, compared and finally combined to create a system of meaning that, though built from the natural order, remains independent of it. In this way, the graphic system is culturally specific in the sense that a person not socialised into Vakutan culture would find it difficult to interpret the meanings encoded in the designs with access only to their names. Perhaps this is why Malinowski, in his response to a letter from A. C. Haddon, complained that, 'there is no getting beyond the disconnected agglomeration of unrelated motives [*sic*]' (Haddon n.d.). As we have seen in the preceding discussion, Trobrianders do indeed have names for their designs. But simply learning the labels for the graphic system reveals little else other than the design's natural or mythical counterpart. One must explore more extensively the relationships between the labels, the colours and the representational choices made by Vakutans to gain any insight into their intent.

–6–

The *Kabitam* Colours

The use of colour by *kabitam* carvers in the execution of kula carvings is a further medium through which meaning is conveyed. In one sense colour is the most important aspect of the carvings. The bold patterning of white, black and red gives a visual impact to the boards not achieved by the incisions. Vakutans do not consider the boards complete until the paint has been applied and reapplied prior to each kula expedition. Paint is often taken on an expedition so as to renew any parts of the boards or boat that have had paint washed off on the outgoing trip. Touching up is done again before the return home.

It is not so much the neatness with which Vakutans apply the paint that is of major concern. More importantly, it is the correct patterning of the three colours that is vital to the impact and ultimate influence the boards may have (Plate 1).[1] In this respect, the carving underneath the paint becomes insignificant.[2] When it comes time to paint the boards, Vakutans are uninterested in the obliterated designs painstakingly carved by the *tokabitam*. European paint may be used today. The dense consistency and relative longevity of this paint effectively covers the detailed incisions made to hold the less invasive lime paint. I asked why they still carved out the lines that hold the white paint when European paint adequately adhered to the surface. People insisted that the incisions were still necessary to ensure the paint adhered to the surface. This suggests that although the carved lines are said to be insignificant when it comes time to apply paint, carvers' persistence in meticulously carving these lines indicates otherwise. It is clear from other contexts, too, that the carving process and the associations imparted into the carved lines are important in the process of imbuing power into the boards. In other words, the wood acquires the power of the encoded meanings by being carved with the designs of the graphic system. While many forms have a functional role, this does not interfere with their significance to the encoded meanings associated with them.

The painting of the prow, splashboard and canoe adds another layer of meaning independent of the labelling applied to the *kabitam* designs. Vakutans point to and name *kala kaimalaka* (red), *kala kaivau* (black) and *kala kaipwaka* (white). Note the *kala* possessive (second form, third person singular) used here to direct attention to 'its' (the prow and splashboards') red, black or white colour. In the same way Vakutans speak of the designs and the representations as belonging to the boards by invoking the second possessive form, colour too is part of this process of focusing possessive qualities to the kula boards. Finally, reference to the colour paths is yet another way of labelling the designs made on the kula carvings. In this case, however, the designs are delineated by colour rather than incised lines.

Colour Terminology

The Kilivila language only distinguishes three basic colours. This places the language at the lower end of a scale developed by Berlin and Kay (1969) to measure languages and, by implication, cultures according to the development and extension of colour terminology. However, this model is of limited value when we take into account other ways so-called 'primitive' colour terminologies distinguish the coloured world around speakers. For example, the Berlin and Kay model does not recognise words describing the density or gloss of colour.[3] Although many societies utilise only a few colour terms according to the criteria established by Berlin and Kay, several analyses have established that these languages employ other means of denoting the quality of colours. In particular, further investigations have established a range of terms isolating various properties of colour considered by the speakers to be far more important than terms that simply distinguish colours from one another. Kilivilan, likewise, uses terms that identify other qualities than the three basic colours. These are used to indicate saturation, gloss, pigment and hue.

The three basic colours are black *(bwabwau)*, white *(pupwakau)* and red *(bweyani)*. *Bwabwau* and *pupwakau* are not monomorphic. A breakdown of these into smaller linguistic units reveals the incorporation of specific nouns epitomising the colour. For example, *bwau* is the noun referring to black rain clouds, while *pwaka* is the word for bleached coral. When baked and crushed, the powder forms the white lime used as paint. This lime is also used as one of the essential ingredients to betelnut chewing. Only *bweyani* seems to be monomorphic and does not, to my knowledge, have any meaning other than denoting red.[4]

Digadegila is perhaps a fourth 'colour' term used on Vakuta and generally identifies yellow objects. On occasion it is also used to refer to green. Sometimes brown objects are said to be *digadegila* if they contain enough yellow in them. Unlike the other three colour terms, however, this term is a noun referring specifically to the crest of the sulphur-crested cockatoo *(Cacatua galerita)*. The word is also morphologically linked in this context to the noun *dagila*, meaning feather. Further, *digadegila* differs from the other three colour terms in that it has not become a standardised term for yellow. People know what is meant when it is used as a colour term because the word refers to the sulphur crest of the cockatoo and, by implication, yellow. However, there are other words that can equally be used to describe yellow, green and brown objects. These are *geguda/matua* unripe/ripe and *genata/menu* (raw/cooked). The use of these not only evokes the colour but also the texture and consistency of the objects referred to. For example, the use of *genata* to refer to yellow things focuses attention on a raw state when objects are thought of as hard and dense. These are conceptualised as green even though their actual colour may not be green according to Western colour classification. Use of the words *genata* (raw) and *geguda* (unripe) infers a colour association with green, while things that are *mwenogu* (ripe) or *menu* (cooked) are conceptualised as yellow. These latter terms imply the textural attribution of cooked or ripe things as soft and mushy. A corpse is sometimes referred to as *mwenogu*. Reference is made to its colour, conceptualised as yellow, and to its consistency, thought to be soft and mushy.[5] An unripe yam is described as *geguda* (unripe) and conceptually likened to green and hard objects although it is not, in fact, green. When yams mature *(matua)* they are described as *mwenogu* (ripe), in which case yellow and soft attributions are invoked even though a mature yam is neither yellow nor soft. Briefly then, the use of terms referring to ripe/unripe and cooked/raw states implies conceptual categories linking perceived colour and texture (Table 6.1).

Table 6.1 Conceptual categories implied by unripe/raw and ripe/cooked

State	Colour	Consistency
Unripe/raw	Green	Hard, dense
Ripe/cooked	Yellow	Soft, mushy

The practice of interchanging the use of these terms to refer to colour, on the one hand, and the state of matter, on the other, extends beyond objects that are edible. Grass, for example, is described as *genata* (green/raw). We have no problem identifying grass as green, but the word *genata* simultaneously implies the condition of the object for Vakutans. In this case, grass is equated with a raw, hard and dense consistency. When coconut fronds are freshly plaited and still green they are described as *genata*. However, as they dry they are described as *matua*. To our eye we would say they were brown, but for Vakutans the term draws reference to other objects that are yellow (or brown), ripe, soft and mushy. Although dried coconut fronds are not mushy, but brittle, this is not the key inference important to Vakutans. Instead, people are referring to the draining of life, the decomposed state of the leaf. Describing it as *matua* simultaneously draws together perceived relations between yellow/brown, mature, soft and mushy.

Colour terms not only identify discrete colours and the condition of matter, they also refer to the degree of saturation. For example, blue (for which there is no term) is classified with black *(bwabwau)*, but Vakutans put a condition on this classification by saying '*pikekita bwabwau*' ('a little bit black') because they say blue does not achieve a full intensity of saturation comparable to black. Vakutans value the intensity, or full saturation of colour. It is this condition that they strive to reproduce in paint and dyes. Correspondingly, there are several ways in which Vakutans describe the saturation of these colours. When, for example, red is of a desired saturation it is said to be 'sharp', or *kakata*. In judging a colour to be 'sharp', Vakutans are focused on its perfection, as they see it, and its proximity to the desired degree of saturation. If the saturation level does not meet with approval, people will say that it is either without colour *(bulebula)*, or it has too much colour and is therefore black *(bwabwau)*.

This raises an ambiguity in the evaluation of black. While primarily conveying negative values, as will be discussed later, black can be positively valued when it is of the desired saturation. At this level of distinction two other descriptive terms need introduction. These are concerned with the gloss, or brightness (*sigala*), as opposed to the dullness (*dudubila*) of colour. If a colour becomes too saturated it loses its sheen. The colour is blurred, resulting in a dark or dull effect. In this state it is described as *dudubila* or *bwabwau*. Colour with too little saturation is likened to water and described as *bulebula*, without colour. However, colours that retain the correct amount of saturation remain 'sharp' *(kakata)* and 'glossy' *(sigala)*.

Pigment Terminology

In the context of painting, white, black and red are given other terms that are derived from the pigments used to produce them. While these pigment terms are synonymous with the colour terms in the context of carvings, they are not in other contexts. For instance, *kala kaimalaka* is synonymous with *bweyani* in describing the colour red on a carving. It is not, however, appropriate to refer to someone's betel-reddened mouth by saying *kala kaimalaka*. Instead, *bweyani* is used. When talking about colour on the prow and splashboards Vakutans predominantly use pigment terms.

Pigment terms are derivatives of their source. Vakutans have two sources for red pigments, *malaka* and *noku*. *Malaka* is the red ochre obtained from the D'Entrecasteaux Islands. Red pigment is also obtained from a locally growing plant that produces red seeds *(Bixa orellana*; Paijmans 1976). When these are crushed they produce a red pigment suitable for use as paint. This plant is known as *malaka*. *Noku* is a root used to produce a red pigment suitable for dyeing the fibres of banana and coconut leaves for skirt making. Generally, *noku* is used by women, while *malaka* is used by men as the source for their red dye.

There are two sources from which white pigment is obtained. *Pwaka* refers to coral suitable for rendering into lime. In its powdered form it is also used for betelnut

Plate 1 The art of kula

Plates 2a and 2b *Mwari* washed and prepared for display; the kula crew are ready to return home

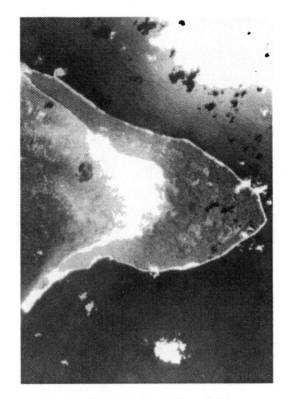

Plate 3 Aerial view of Vakuta Island

Plate 4 A selection of early carvings for tourists

Plate 5 Youwa carving a *tabuya*

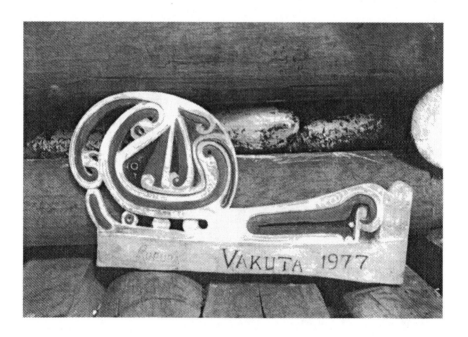

Plate 6 Rurupa's *uuna tabuya*, *Sopila* Vakuta

Plate 7 Kaitotu's *dogina tabuya, Sopila* Vakuta

Plate 8 Gigimwa's *dogina tabuya, Sopila* Kitava

Plate 9 Youwa's *uuna tabuya, Sopila* Kitava

Plate 10 Rurupa's *uuna lagim, Sopila* Vakuta

Plate 11 Kaitotu's *dogina lagim, Sopila* Vakuta

Plate 12 Gigimwa's *dogina lagim, Sopila* Kitava

Plate 13 Youwa's *uuna lagim*, *Sopila* Kitava

Plate 14 *Masawa* en route to Kitava for kula

Plate 15 *Masawa* moored on Kitava

Plate 16 *Kavatam* poles 'planted' in the garden

Plate 17 Roboti of Giribwa village wears Nanoula, a high-ranking armshell that was circulating in the early part of the last century (Malinowski 1922: 504). He also wears the necklace, Kasanai, given to him by a Dobuan hoping to lure Nanoula away from him

Plate 18 Washing *mwari* on a secluded beach off the Vakutan lagoon before returning to the village after a kula expedition to Kitava

chewing. When water is added to the lime powder a white pigment is produced and is used for face painting *(soba)* and for filling incisions on carvings. *Lilau* is a white, sticky clay said to be collected from the foot of the reef along the ocean floor. This pigment is used to paint yam house boards and is said to smell very strongly of decaying fish. The pigment is considered dangerous because its smell is thought to attract flying witches. It is often used in painting yam house boards but rarely for kula carvings. Attracting flying witches to a kula canoe would be foolhardy. It is valued, however, because of its density and thick consistency.

Finally, there are three pigment terms for black. These are *vau, budakola* and *pwanasi. Vau* is the name of the fluid ejected from the squid *(suwoiya)* or octopus *(kwita)* when disturbed. The substance is highly valued as a pigment for painting canoe boards. When asked why the squid and octopus were so valued when other sources of black pigment are more easily obtainable, the characteristic behaviours of the squid and octopus were recounted several times by different people: 'They are very wise and can go forward or backward with ease.' This has particular implications for kula outrigger canoes that are designed to go backwards or forwards without turning around. Although the black pigment obtained from the squid or octopus is highly valued, so much so that the black lines on the boards are named after this pigment, the more common source of black pigment is *budakola.* A mixture of charred coconut flesh and coconut oil makes this a dense paint. *Pokiyou* refers to the ashes and charcoal of a wood fire. These are scraped and mixed with water or oil to form a black pigment called *pwanasi. Pwanasi* is used for face paint, and for body paint during mourning.

Pigment terms are derived directly from the nouns that signify the source (Table 6.2).

Table 6.2 Pigment terms and sources

Pigment source	Colour
Ochre or plant (*malaka*) Root (*noku*)	Red (*bweyani*)
Crushed lime (*pwaka*) Coral 'clay' (*lilau*)	White (*pupwakau*)
Octopus/squid 'ink' (*vau*) Charred coconut flesh mixed with oil (*budakola*) Charcoal mixed with coconut oil (*pwanasi*)	Black (*bwabwau*)

When asking for the names of forms delineated by the three colours the terms *kala kaivau, kala kaipwaka* and *kala kaimalaka* are invoked. The use of this form of reference is of interest because the linguistic construction of these terms implies further layers of associations.

While the *-malaka*, *-vau* and *-pwaka* segments of these terms refer simply to the names of the pigments, the *kai-* prefix is a classifier specifying trees, objects in tree-like shapes or wood in a tree-like shape. For example, a pen, although not made of wood, receives the classifier *-kai-* in the phrase '*makaina penna*' ('that tree-like pen'). On the other hand, while a boat receives the classifier *-kai-*, a wooden table does not. The latter's shape being so odd and inconsistent with trees that it warrants inclusion in a category specified by the classifier *-kwai-*. The boat, however, retains a tree-like shape and so remains within the *-kai-* classification. The design components on the prow and splashboard do not all have a tree-like appearance, yet all receive the *-kai-* specification through the pigment term. A relevant question here queries the significance of *kai-* in the words *kaimalaka*, *kaipwaka* and *kaivau*.

The morphology of the tree is used to symbolise major themes in Vakutan thinking. In particular, it is relevant to the symbolism of kula and its related art. The ends of a tree, the bole and tip, are classified according to a female/male opposition *(uuna/dogina* respectively). This opposition, as symbolised by the opposing ends of a tree, is used in the various contexts of kula to express fundamental issues concerning gender relationships in Vakutan society. In the remaining three chapters this will become increasingly clear as we return again and again to the symbolic significance of the opposing ends of a tree. With this in mind, it seems plausible that the *kai*-segment in the colour terminology used for kula carvings is connected to the symbolism of a tree. To my knowledge this classifier is not involved in any other contexts where pigment terms are used.

Applying the Pigments

Before colour is applied to the canoe and its decorative boards, magic is spoken into the pigments. Once these have been mixed to the desired saturation a man who owns pigment magic, often a master carver, holds the mixture close to his mouth so that the magic contained in his breath is imbued into the pigment. All three colours receive this attention. The spells for each colour, however, differ in their content as each colour evokes different associations. While images of purity are part of the spell for white paint, sexual imagery – including notions of desire and attraction – is called upon in the spell for red paint. The magic for black paint includes imagery of malevolent powers, such as those possessed by flying witches and sorcerers. The different spells for each colour, however, have in common the invocation of certain qualities. These include the adhesiveness of the paint to the boards so that the colour does not wash away before it has had the desired effect upon the kula hosts. There is, likewise, a call for brilliance and shine to be imparted into the paint, giving the colours their 'sharp' edge so as to ensure the adoration of kula partners.

While Vakutans and Kiriwinans perform magic over all three colours, Gawans seem only to bespell the red paint. Munn, in contrasting her Gawan material with Malinowski's data from the Trobriands, argues that red is the 'power' colour in Gawan evaluation and colour symbolism because it is the colour 'with the strongest sexual connotations' (1977: 49, and 1986). In contrast, Malinowski claimed that black was the most important colour in Trobriand colour symbolism (1922: 140). For Vakutans both red and black are 'power' colours. But the 'power' evoked by each is substantially different. Neither of these colours has supreme importance over the other except within specific contexts where they are contrasted. For example, in contexts where the power of physical attraction predominates (symbolised by red), black receives less attention and becomes subordinate. However, when the power of knowledge gained through the process of maturity and experience is paramount (symbolised by black), red receives peripheral attention.

Each colour has its specific placement on the boards and canoe. No deviation from this pattern is tolerated, particularly as the application of colour complements the forms covering the surface of the boards (Plate 1). In this way colour is superimposed on form, in some cases obliterating specific forms. Colour does not, however, overlap or cut across the major spatial divisions.

It was noted in Chapter 4 that there are several levels, or layers carved into the boards. These correspond to the application of the three colours. While I argued that there were five levels on the boards, ranging from the surface to the perforations, there are only three levels in the context of colour. The first (surface) level and the last (perforations) level described previously are subsumed within two of the colours, white and black respectively.

White is applied to the surface and first shallow incision. These incisions 'hold' the white pigment:

Red is applied to the carved angle linking white to the black level:

Black pigment is applied to the deepest level on the boards:

In applying the three colours, each is set against the others in contrasting contexts. Each colour physically occupies exclusive spaces on the boards. This spatial differentiation is complementary to other contexts where colour symbolically distinguishes the physiological life cycle of organisms. The meanings of many Vakutan epistemological constructions derive from a preoccupation with the temporal movement between birth, death and the time in between.

Colour Symbolism

In many societies colour receives considerable symbolic attention. Whereas in some societies colours represent bodily functions such as breast milk, semen, blood and excrement, the part played by colour in Vakutan thought is concerned overwhelmingly with the stages of the life cycle: a trajectory from birth to youth, age and, inevitably, death. This trajectory, however, is not lineal in the Vakutan model of the biological process. As elsewhere in the Trobriand Islands, Vakutans believe in reincarnation (Malinowski 1922, 1932, 1948a: 216–220, 1948c: 126–138; Weiner 1977). This is reflected in the cyclical association of the colour triad as well as in the movement of the sun and moon. White is associated with day, black is associated with night, while red represents the transitions between them: day to night, and night to day (white to red to black to red to white, and so on). However, treating red as a transition between white and black, on the one hand, and day and night, on the other, is too simplistic. Indeed, all of the colours in Vakutan thinking could be said to be transitional – one merging into the other.

The life cycle begins with birth and is associated with the colour white. This stage is epitomised most succinctly by the newborn child, who is said to be 'clean' and 'pure'. A baby has not yet built up a life experience that is gradually and accumulatively 'contaminating'. It is significant that white is applied to the surface of the boards, as this space is the one least worked. The colour red symbolises the gradual process of maturing, the time between being newborn and 'clean' to becoming mature and 'unclean'. It is significant that red physically defines the space between white forms and the deeply set black forms. The space it occupies is carved at an angle between these and expresses the gradual process of physical (and social) growth towards maturity. Black occupies the deepest set spaces. These are correspondingly the most worked surfaces on the boards. Much effort goes into the gouging, shaping and finishing of these areas. This has relevance to the symbolism of black in general and corresponds to physical age and social maturity. In short, the contextual juxtaposition of the colours sets white on the surface where it 'emerges' from a more deliberate carving of the red and black forms. In their application to the boards, the physical relationship of the three colours echoes Vakutan conceptions of the life cycle. In this respect, organisms pass through a developmental process beginning with being new, clean and uncontaminated to becoming old, unclean and decayed.

White conveys images incorporating the state of being new; a kind of purity that only new things can claim. White is associated with cleanliness, both physically and metaphorically. When things are white as opposed to black or red they are clean, new and uncontaminated. Further, when things are 'clean' they are in the open (public) and thus are not dangerous. For example, a white kula armshell (*mwari*) is considered clean and uncontaminated both physically and metaphorically. Its clean and 'glossy forehead' displays no history of kula desire and intrigue. In this state it is considered uncontaminated by the dirty tricks that accompany kula and the desire to possess shells. According to Vakutan conceptualisation, a white *mwari* has not yet been associated with incidents involving jealousies, desires, manipulations and the death of men. It is said that with increasing age a *mwari* acquires 'colour' as it begins to accumulate its 'history'. *Mwari* with 'histories' are considered to be dangerous as they cause further competition between men in their desire to possess them. Ultimately, the competitive tactics utilised to acquire an 'old' *mwari* include death. A white *mwari*, although undesirable to a kula man in search of prestige and fame, is desirable from the perspective of its guaranteed safety. Less ambitious men are content to handle only white *mwari*. As it becomes more experienced in the hands of kula men and begins to colour, however, its status changes, with more competitive desires making it a more dangerous shell to acquire (Campbell 1983b).

This theme is carried into other spheres of Vakutan social life. The whiteness attributed to a woman in her first pregnancy (*igavau*; see also Malinowski 1932: 179–196), and to all newly born babies, again symbolises newness and cleanliness. They have not yet begun the process of accumulating life's experiences. A woman becomes socially recognised across generations through her biological productivity. At one level, this is a woman's prime social value. Until she has given birth for the first time, a woman is not an active generator of social 'history'. With her first offspring she begets a child to the *dala* and assures her role in the future of her *dala*, while simultaneously, in the act of her first labour, marking a point in the history of the *dala*. Generations later she will be recalled as the source of *dala* solidarity. During a woman's first pregnancy several ceremonies are performed where the colour white predominates (Malinowski 1932: 179–196; Tambiah 1968: 203). The emphasis is on making her skin as white as the infant she is carrying. Symbolically she is equating her newness (in pregnancy) with the regeneration of *dala* in the form of a new being. It is as though she, too, were experiencing rebirth, this time of her own social position rather than her physical emergence. She subsequently generates her own 'history' and that of her offspring, ensuring a social and spiritual future for herself and her brothers. Together they form a unique branch of the sub-clan. Her newborn is likewise conceptually associated with white. A baby has no 'history'. The reincarnated ancestor awaits rebirth, having sloughed all past associations on entering the world of the dead. In its newborn state a baby is innocent of the impurities generated through growth and the gradual accumulation of experience fraught with jealousies, contention and competition.

Although white is presented in the above as a positive value, it sometimes assumes a negative connotation. The kula armshell offers a good example. While the white *mwari* is considered pure and free of 'historical' contamination, it remains low in value and unsought by experienced kula participants. The ambiguity accruing to this dual evaluation of white stems from the very characteristics that generate its positive, ahistorical associations. People with light skin are said to be more desirable partners because the 'whiteness' of their skin is said to be a sign of their 'safe' character, devoid of ambitions that might attract foul play and the jealousies of others. People with darker skins, on the other hand, while dangerous, excite greater sexual response because they seem more erotic. White, although pure and uncontaminated, evokes feelings of security, but in so doing seems less exciting.

According to the Vakutan perception of colour as it reflects organic processes, white is not a permanent state. People inevitably change from 'white' to 'red' and then 'black'. To avert the accumulation of life experiences is impossible. Using colour as a symbolic code for the human life cycle, a child, from birth, gradually darkens in colour, becoming 'redder' upon entering youth. On Vakuta there are no age grades or initiation ceremonies based upon the achievement of certain ages. When a child becomes sexually active he or she can no longer be considered a child (*gwadi*). Sexually active adolescents instead become *nakubukwabuya* (female youth) or *toulatile* (male youth). Red is the colour associated with sexual allurement and excitement (see also Tambiah 1968; Munn 1977). Red is used symbolically to represent attraction and sexual desire. It is not then surprising that red is associated with sexually active youth. The red mouth of a *nakubukwabuya* or a *toulatile* produced by the continuous chewing of betelnut is seen in the context of sexuality. Young unmarried women who are sexually available wear very short red skirts to attract partners. The abundance of red in these skirts advertises their availability and willingness to accept small gifts as solicitory tribute prior to sexual adventure. Contrary to the attire of young unmarried girls, married women, except on special occasions, wear only drab-coloured skirts at knee length. A red skirt would not be worn by a married woman as daily attire. To do so would indicate one of two things: either she deliberately advertises an inappropriate desire for sexual encounters or she is in a severe state of mental deterioration. During the final stages of the mortuary cycle, when women come to the foreground of the public arena and display their wealth and social position *vis-à-vis* other women (Campbell 1989; Weiner 1977), married and unmarried women alike dress in the attire of young, sexually active adolescent girls in the prime of their sexual vitality.

Very short skirts full of red colour set off reddened mouths, red hibiscus flowers and mature betelnut strung together in long strands and draped around the body.[6] These combine in the attire of women who are displaying their wealth and social position, as well as celebrating their sexual powers of attraction and the procreative powers of their respective *dala*. A widow, at the end of her mourning restrictions, is ritually cleansed of the combined dirt and black mourning pigments. She is given a new red skirt cut short to symbolise her regained 'youth' and her licence to participate in the competition for sexual partners.

In the classification of shell valuables, red is the colour associated with the highest ranking and most desirable pieces. Although the redness of the *mwari* and the *vaiguwa* (kula necklace) are measurements of quite different criteria at one level (Campbell 1983b), the consensus is that all shell valuables should be red. While *mwari* are described as male, *vaiguwa* are thought of as female.[7] When a successful kula path (*keda*) is operating, the opening transaction (attractor/*vaga*) and closing transaction (attracted/*kudu*) are described as married (Campbell 1983a). During their 'marriage' the redness (high rank) of one is continually attracting the redness (high rank) of the other, and between them they are attracting more shell valuables into their path. When the 'marriage' is broken, it is conceptually attributed to one of the shell valuable's attraction to another's redness. In this respect there is a conflation of high rank and sexual attraction in the classification of kula shell valuables. When shells of either the armshell or necklace type begin in kula circulation they are conceptually 'white'. As they gain 'history' and desirability they also gain rank and become conceptually linked with an accumulating redness. This is particularly true of the highest ranking *mwarikau*. It seems that the shells used to make *mwari* (*conidae*), once they have had the epidermis removed, begin to form red striations and a patina on the surface as they age through handling. These striations are called *ureri* by Vakutans. New, non-striated shells entering into the classification system are placed into categories at the lower end of the hierarchy. As they age and develop red striations, they are revalued into the upper ranks as people's desire for them increases. Although *spondylus* and *chama* shells do not 'gain' colour as they age, they do occur in variations of colour ranging from white-pink to a reddish-brown.[8] The red shells are the most valued shells and reach the higher ranks of the classification system with an accumulation of exchange history.

Youth is thought to be an invigorating time of life for Vakutans. This period in one's life conveys a special power: the power of sexuality and sexual attractiveness. Vakutans value these qualities very highly. In many of the kula myths old men are unable to attract kula shell valuables to themselves until they shed their wrinkled, blackened skin for glossy red skin; thus making their sexuality so compelling that the kula shell valuables are 'thrown' their way by stunned and adoring kula partners (Fortune 1932; Malinowski 1922, 1948c: 126–128; Young

1983a). However, as with the contextual ambiguity in the value of white, red, too, has a shadow cast over its positive qualities. It is the old men of the myths who, having achieved the knowledge enabling them to shed their blackened skins, in the end get the best shell valuables, leaving their sons and sisters' sons, adorned in the red skin of youth, with only the 'white', low-ranking shells. While youth displays the shiny red power of attraction, resplendent in their physical beauty, mature men have the advantage of experience and knowledge. With these they are able, through internalised power, to circumvent the physical power of youth. Weiner makes a similar point:

> Each infant only becomes a social being as it claims ties with others beyond *dala* identity . . . In life this process continues as the locus of power shifts through time from the power of one's physical self – the power of youth – to objects external to one's self. After marriage, the display of objects becomes more important and denotes a wider range of relationships than did the display of self. As one ages, one's own private individual power, such as knowledge of magic and land grows inside one's body. (1977: 225–226)

Munn found similar distinctions between surface/youth and 'interiorised/age' as these were connected by Gawans to the symbolism of the canoe:

> Whereas youths can impart vitality and light to the surface of the canoe, because the surfaces of their own bodies are "beautiful", a senior man can animate the canoe through verbal spells and associated operations, knowledge of which is thought to be stored inside the body. This *interiorised* knowledge gives the prowboards their *exteriorised mobile* attachments.
>
> In this respect we may note that it is senior men, not the young, who have influence in kula exchange, and perform the main kula spells. Just as their power derives from *interiorised* sources, so it *extends further out in space* than the power of the young. (1977: 50)

While youth are admired for their external beauty, a feature they 'wear on their skin', they nevertheless lack the experience and accumulated internalisation of power which marks the 'skin of maturity'.

Red is conceptually a transient colour between white and black. This is particularly expressed in the colour patterning on the outrigger canoe and its decorative boards. Generally there are no specific forms identified with red. Red pigment is placed on 'paths' emphasising the white forms. The only exception to this predominance of white and black forms is the *karawa*, or 'fern frond'. However, it is not an essential design. It only occurs in section 4 of the splashboard or section 5 of the *uuna* prowboard (see Figure 4.4). Both areas are relatively unrestricted in design content, their inclusion relying upon the whim of the master carver. When this form does occur, however, it is always painted red. It is significant that where red has a specific connection to a unique form its representation is of the young fern frond said to be beautiful to look at, its mere form a delight to the eye: 'It stands up straight all on its own showing its beauty. It is uncurled, but not yet weeping. It is at the height of strength.'[9]

All three colours have ambiguous evaluations. While white and red on the whole symbolically evoke positive values, they also encode negative associations. Black, likewise, is associated with positive and negative ambiguity. An example will serve to illustrate the nature of this ambiguity and relates notably to something that has exchange as well as subsistence value.

Malinowski observed that gardeners described a diseased yam as *bwabwau*, or black (1935 Vol. 2: 102). A white yam, on the other hand, was synonymous with a healthy yam. This assessment of the yam's health is based upon its surface appearance; a 'black' skinned yam is diseased while a 'white' skinned yam is healthy. However, when Vakutans are judging the maturity, or 'ripeness' of the yam, black is invoked as a positive quality. Malinowski made a similar observation when, in a particular ceremony performed by the garden magician to ripen the harvest, *tum* magic makes reference to the inside of the tubers becoming 'black': 'The same word 'black' we have met in other contexts . . . as 'bad', 'diseased' [yams] as against *pupwka'u*, 'white', 'good', 'healthy' [yams]. In the one case the adjective refers to the surface of the [yam], in the other to its inside' (1935: Vol. 2: 171).

When the inside of a yam is 'black' it is ripe for harvest and can be transformed into food or circulated in intra-community exchange. However, the blackened skin of a yam indicates disease and decay, providing no further use value to the tuber. The ambiguity associated with the colour black in the context of yams spills over into other contexts where black on the surface, as opposed to an internalised black, reflects equally distinct judgements of health and disease. However, even in the more negative evaluations associated with black there is an inherent value attributed to it. While black is associated with the negative connotations of age, disease and death, in other contexts it is positively valued for its representation of maturity, the possession of knowledge and the power associated with knowledge.

As one moves through the life cycle and grows older, the body is thought to become 'blacker' – an observation made about the surface of a person's ageing body. There was a time when old people were able to relieve themselves of their blackened skin, sloughing it for new glossy 'red' skin. However, the knowledge required to achieve such a rejuvenation was lost according to myth (see also Malinowski 1948c: 127). There is a correlation here between the 'blackened' skin of mature yams and the blackened skin of old people; the implication being that like the blackened skin of the yam, age brings with it disease, decay and death. However, if people can exchange their skin for the red, vigorous skin of youth they can avert this process. For men in a matrilineal society, death represents the end of their use value whereas women's use value is evaluated against their progeny and the regeneration of *dala*.

The accumulation of black internally is also thought to cause disease, illness and death. Sorcerers *(bwagau)* and witches *(mulukwausi)* are the source of sickness and death in others. As their knowledge is stored internally, making them 'black' on the inside (as all forms of knowledge do), their malevolent deeds likewise cause their victims to decay from the inside. But there is also a natural accumulation of black within people caused by their ageing and accumulated knowledge. As people age they are said gradually to become contaminated by a lifetime of experience. Contentious relationships, lies, jealousies and unresolved rivalries slowly build up and darken the innards of mature people. This accumulates within and gradually leads to the decay of the individual. Because of their experiences, particularly those activities that lead a mature person to acquire wealth and high status within the community, the aged attract the jealousies of sorcerers and witches.

Death extends its contaminating effect to widowed persons because of their closeness to the deceased. Throughout the mourning period a widow/er smears her/his body with black to symbolise the continued relationship with the deceased. Widowed people, however, are not necessarily 'black' internally. Only their skins are marked with black. These are 'sloughed' at a cleansing ceremony marking the end of this particular period of the mortuary sequence. Released from their immediate association with the deceased, their skins become 'new' and 'desirable'. While not yet ready to embark on courtship, they are nevertheless cleansed of their blackened skin and symbolically released from their intense mourning responsibilities.

Black also finds symbolic representation in kula shell necklaces. There are a wide variety of hues naturally generated in the development of *spondylus* shells. Darker hues are associated with impurities and disease. They are said to be black and dull, lacking the desired lustre and gloss of the brighter hues found in the shells. The most highly valued shell necklaces are those with a majority of red discs. This provides the necklace with an overall red, lustrous impact (Campbell 1983b). Discerning kula men said that a necklace with a predominance of the darker red shell discs is 'black'. They said that the living shell, from which the discs were formed, was somehow diseased, creating an impure colour. The association is clearly linked back to the symbolism of the yam and its black surface being a sign of disease. This symbolism can be extended to human disease and illness. Disease can be caused by black blood accumulating within the body. Bloodletting of affected body parts is thought to release this impurity and thus restore health.

Returning to the image of the yam, however, and focusing on the internally accumulated maturity and ripeness represented by black, the ambiguous associations with this colour become apparent. In this context the symbolism counters the negative evaluation. While people negatively value the loss of one's youth, the accumulation of age, and with it the dulling and darkening of one's skin, is also a mark of one's social maturity. With age and social maturity one acquires knowledge, magic and social status. Although the power of sexual attraction is associated with a vigorous youthful body, heightened by the 'red' gloss worn on the skin, older people have gained the experience and knowledge to outwit the younger generation. Through their knowledge and use of magic older people can compel others to be attracted to them, giving off an illusion of 'beauty' and youth. This stage of social and physical development, while being negatively valued on the one hand, is highly valued for the accumulated powers that go with maturity. Finally, although darkened skin heralds the eventual loss of life because the power to rejuvenate was lost, death, according to tradition, is the prerequisite for entry to 'life' on Tuma where one's powers of attraction and sexuality are restored (Malinowski 1948a: 149–274). Red again becomes the prevalent condition on one's skin as *baloma*, the spirits of the dead, enjoy the pleasures of 'life' before rebirth heralds the white, uncontaminated flesh of the newborn.

It would be a mistake to reduce the relationship between the three colours as essentially a bipartite system, with one colour, red, transitional between white and black. As with the cyclical forces of life, the colour triad symbolises the transitional nature of each stage, passing inevitably through an eternal process of birth, death and rebirth. For Vakutans there is no prominence of one stage/colour over another, no beginning point moving relentlessly to an end point. The process is ongoing. There are positive and negative aspects of each colour just as each stage in the life cycle elicits desirable and undesirable elements.

–7–

The Meaning of *Kabitam*

In preceding chapters the meaning communicated by kula art remained a secondary consideration in the discussion while the more formal elements of the system were examined. As such, the analysis to this point has concentrated more on the details of components used, particularly in relation to the delineation of form, representation and colour, as a way of explaining how the system organises and encodes meaning. It is hoped that this approach adequately demonstrates the complex ways in which information is conveyed. It is now necessary to reintegrate the formal components and move towards a more comprehensive interpretation of the meanings encoded. This chapter begins by examining the themes found in each section of the prow and splashboards. By focusing on these we begin to see how ideas emerge from the kula boards, providing unique insight into ways Vakutans conceptualise their world and the role of kula in this scheme. The chapter concludes by suggesting how these themes reflect similar ones implicit in the activities associated with kula.

The meanings carved and painted into the boards are multidimensional. That is, meaning is not merely transmitted through the label or colour association attached to a simple design form. The lines worked into the carved surface of the prow and splashboard provide layers of meaning that are revealed by exploring the ways in which the formal components are organised in relation to each other: their specific orientations, colour associations and the multiple references encoded in the various representational components.

Visual symbolism is not structured to convey meaning in the same way that a simple sentence, made up of specific grammatical units, transmits meaning lineally through speech. Rather, meaning is built up using layer upon layer of associations that, on close examination, provide a cross-referencing between the layers. If one were to visualise this, it would look rather like a circuit board criss-crossed in a maze of wires. Although each wire has only two connections, it is the overall networking that enables the build up of connections between the points to generate energy, or meaning, as is our current concern. However, the analogy becomes less useful when we consider that a circuit board is a self-contained, bounded system. The art of kula, I suggest, is not closed. The interaction between the layers generates associations to the wider cultural field. This process, it seems, is expansive, leaving room for the system to reflect contemporary experiences and to situate these within a cultural context that makes sense to the participants at any given time. For example, the placement of form A3.2 in the central area of section 1 on a splashboard marks a structural guideline for the formal patterning of other forms:

As argued in Chapter 4, there is also an implied formal hierarchy in the relationship between this form and others with reference to their placement. When Vakutans link this form to the representation of an egret (*boi*), new meanings become possible, such as the ability to be successful and maintain a competitive edge. The form, however, is not a passive vehicle upon which these possibilities are conveyed. The form itself qualifies the representational potential by delineating the egret's head, with details of its eye and beak. These single out particular body parts and the beliefs about how these affect one's potential. The addition of colour further generates associations and interacts not only with the colours and forms that surround it on the boards but also suggests further reference to Vakutans' understanding of their world.

The extent to which people are able to interpret the communicative elements on the boards varies. While a few go to some lengths to engage in intellectual discourse about the meanings of the lines, others are content with more limited interpretations. In general, however, most people only partially understand what is communicated by the design elements, preferring to focus attention upon specific aspects of the carvings instead. The connections that draw together all the layers remain, by and large, unsolicited. Explanations identifying and connecting representation, form and colour are available for those people who ask. However, solicited information is not given unconditionally. Bits of information are offered casually, often imprecisely, so that one is obliged to inquire at frequent intervals. While this may appear to be a device for controlling the flow of information, and is perhaps a strategy to avoid any demystification of meaning, it may also be a means of measuring it out bit by bit, thus enabling sufficient time for reflection and assimilation of what is being communicated. While a general understanding of the meanings may be readily comprehended – that is, the carved and painted lines on the boards are about the successful acquisition of shell valuables in kula – the underlying messages are far more carefully constructed. To be able to grasp meaning at this level, however, requires cultural competence. For young people learning Vakutan natural history and indigenous taxonomy, this task is part of a growing awareness of the culture they live in. For them the interpretation and gradual decoding of the carvings is concurrent with their assimilation of other cultural codes. Adults are at an advantage with their wider experience. Nevertheless, only a few Vakutans have pursued at length the relationship between form, representation, colour association and meaning on the kula outrigger canoe's prow and splashboards. The majority are content that a few are sufficiently schooled to know the depth of meanings so that the boards are carved correctly.

It might be expected that master carvers are the most knowledgeable about the meanings they carve into the boards. This is not necessarily the case, however. The majority of Vakutan carvers could verbalise only a limited range of representational elements. Generally they professed to know only the superficial interpretations and were not interested in extrapolating these any further. One carver used only colour terminology to identify design elements. He was unwilling to offer representational labels because, as he said, he was uncertain of the names attached to form. Clearly, this is what Malinowski must have experienced when he endeavoured to find meaning in the designs. Of the non-carvers there were several people, principally men, who were able to give considerable exegesis for the range of meanings encoded on the carved boards, while others showed little knowledge. Most were only concerned that the boards were carved and painted correctly. With this knowledge they felt assured of the power of the boards and confident that these would compel Dobuans and Kitavans to give up kula shell valuables.

The following analysis of each board requires regular reference to Figures 7.1 and 7.2 to refresh one's memory of the forms, *kabitam* 'animals', body part and colour associations. We will start the analysis by examining the *tabuya* section by section.

An Analysis of the Prowboard (Figures 7.1a and 7.1b)

Section 1 of the prowboard contains specific reference to the *buribwari* (osprey, form A2.1). All other forms in this section are related to the body parts of this raptor (B2.1 and B3.1). The tiny hermit crab *(ginareu,* form B2.1) is used to emphasise the eye and is also carved along the neck of the *buribwari* to hold the white pigment (Plates 6–9). The significance of *kaidada* (form B3.1) in section 1 is related to its association with 'coming first' and may be connected to the competition between Vakutan men to 'come first' in kula by attaining the most valuables. At a more abstract level, the association of the *kamkokola* and *kaidada* with a deceased man has relevance to the promotion of men beyond their lifetime as individuals whose names are worth remembering. This is an important outcome for kula men.

Recall that *buribwari* is considered one of the most important 'animals' represented on the carvings, particularly its placement on the *dogina tabuya* (Chapter 5). This aerial hunter personifies qualities highly valued on Vakuta; it 'works' with

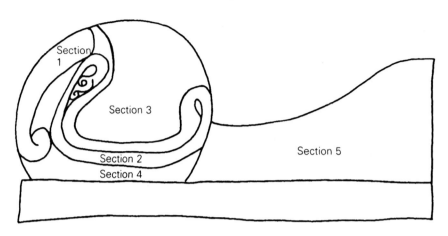

Figure 7.1a *Tabuya* sections

precision, it 'knows' the necessary behaviour for its livelihood and it strikes only at the right time. In this way it always succeeds in catching its prey. To Vakutans the *buribwari* is the embodiment of success. Although it is also represented on the *uuna tabuya*, its place on the *dogina tabuya* is the most significant. Emphasis is continually placed on the temporal and spatial position of the *dogina tabuya* with reference to *buribwari*. In every respect it 'goes first'. The *dogina tabuya* is the first board placed on the *masawa*. It lands first on the beach. It is perceived to be the first thing hosts see upon the arrival of the kula crew, and the *buribwari* will make it possible for the crew to be the ones who attract the most kula shells. This success will enable them to 'come first' in the intra-fleet rivalry.

It is no coincidence that the *dogina tabuya*, the board thought to embody the essence of the *buribwari*, is ritually anointed on the ocean beach, Kadabomato, prior to its insertion on the canoe.[1] The osprey is known to sit in the tops of trees (the *dogina* of the tree) along the ocean beach waiting for the right moment to fall upon its prey. The ocean beach is a transitional space between two opposing elements, land and sea. The ocean beach is contrasted with the lagoon beach at several levels, one of which associates the ocean beach with the transition between safe, domesticated space (land and lagoon) and dangerous, uncontrolled space (the open sea). This tripartite relationship is conceptual rather than actual. Most people neither leave nor enter the land from the sea via the ocean beach on Vakuta, preferring the calmer waters of the lagoon and the tidal creeks as watery pathways to the village.[2] In this sense the ocean beach is not generally a transitional space relevant to coming and going. Rather, the ocean beach represents the mediation between two opposing conceptual realms. The significance of this relationship will be discussed in greater detail in the following chapters.

Form		Colour	Body part	Animal
	 A1.1	white with red repetition	neck	*doka*
	 A2.1	white with red repetition	head, beak, and neck	*buribwari*
	 A2.2	white with red repetition	wings	*minutoula*
	 A3.4	white	head, beak, eye	*boi/doka*
	 A3.5	white		*weku*
	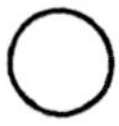 B1.1	white	eye	*duduwa*
	 B1.3	white, red, and black		*duduwa*
	 B2.1	white		*ginareu*
	 B2.2	white		*dodoleta*
	 B3.1	white		*kaidada*
	 C1	black	nose (penis)	
	 C3	black	head, wings, teeth, tail, chest	*kapaiyauwa*
	 C6	black		
	 C7	black		
	 C10	black		

Figure 7.1b Form, representation, colour and body-part terminology of the *tabuya*

The central theme of section 2 on the prowboard is the head. According to Vakutan thinking the head is that part of the body generating wisdom, knowledge and intelligence. The head is contrasted to the stomach/chest *(nanoula)*, thought to generate emotion, belief and volition. Intelligence is signified by the *doka* (form A3.4) and reinforced by the hermit crab design (B2.1). As in section 1, the body parts represented are all connected to the head (eye, beak and neck). One carver said, 'We carve the *doka* because it thinks, we carve its head. The rest of it [the form] is like a snake' (Youwa, Wakwega hamlet, Vakuta village). Even forms B2.1 and B3.1 become *doka* when combined around an 'eye' design thus:

This configuration is often called *doka* when connected to a *doka* 'head'. Unlike the representation of the *buribwari*'s head, thought to specify a particular kind of wisdom and embodied only in the osprey, the *doka* head represents achievable human intelligence and human rational knowledge. Whereas the *buribwari*'s wisdom is sustained by an internalised magic, human intelligence is achieved by an acquisitive mind. There is a conceptual difference here between wisdom or embodied magic on the one hand, and intelligence or acquired magic on the other.

Vakutans believe that the *buribwari*'s sagacious behaviour is sustained by his internalised knowledge and experience. The *buribwari* is beyond failure because he embodies the magic of perpetual success. Together with this perceived quality, his knowledge represents the ultimate goal of Vakutan men. Some men try to achieve this level of knowledge and wisdom by internalising *kabitam* magic. The substance of this magic is said to impart absolute knowledge to its recipient. Theoretically then, as with the *buribwari*, a master carver does not need to 'think' about the designs he will carve on the prowboards. As a consequence of the magic and the wisdom it imparts, a carver is said to be compelled to pick up his tools, allowing the designs, patterning and form to 'flow' from his mind through his hand and eye. The knowledge is thought to spill forth in unerring precision. In reality, however, master carvers do make mistakes. Likewise, observation suggests that some carvers are better than others. Carvers also admit that 'knowledge' does not always 'flow' readily, requiring them to resort to refresher magic in an effort to regain the 'flow'. This involves chewing magically prepared betelnut. Thus refreshed, the carver is able to return to his work. In contrast, the *buribwari* never needs to regain faltering knowledge. The *buribwari* is considered knowledge personified.

While men rarely achieve the wisdom of the *buribwari* they can reach a certain level of intelligence, this is represented by the *doka*. The word *doka* is morphologically similar to the verb *-doki*, to think. This relationship was suggested to me by one carver when I asked him about the meaning of the word. He told me that men think and assimilate experience and knowledge for future use. A man can think about the ways to attract a woman, make a successful garden or persuade a kula partner to give up a shell valuable. A man is able to calculate rationally the potential outcome of specific behaviour and modify his actions accordingly. Whereas man, as he is represented by the *doka*, must resort to all the knowledge gleaned through experience before he acts to achieve specific goals, the ideal, as represented by the *buribwari*, simply acts in response to internalised knowledge or wisdom. A Vakutan master carver told me, 'The *buribwari* doesn't think, it knows' ('*manana buribwari gala bidoki, manawena binukwari*'; Ruguna, Kuweiwa hamlet, Vakuta village). When we consider the relationship between sections 1 and 2 of the *tabuya*, a subtle, yet significant difference between the encoded messages emerges. *Doka* is not a real animal. It is the creation of a Vakutan desire to represent human intelligence, and, situated behind the ultimate representation of wisdom in section 1, it represents what is achievable by humans.

Forms B2.1 and B3.1 occur within the central area of section 2 and are carved to hold the lime. No doubt this is the practical function of these forms but their selection is not so random. There is a relationship between these secondary forms and the symbolic milieu they occupy. For example, the hermit crab (form B2.1) is not only an animal inhabiting the transitional space between land and sea, it is also a carnivorous scavenger, feeding upon decaying corpses; a characteristic shared with the greatly feared flying witches, who get more than a passing reference in the rituals of kula, to which we will return.

The animal represented in section 3 of the prowboard is the *kapaiyauwa,* or bat. An outsider examining this section on the prowboard may find it difficult to see a bat. A Vakutan, however, would have less difficulty (Plates 6–9). The ways in which we seek visual cues from design representation vary according to different values placed on those 'features' represented and how they are transposed onto a graphic schema. Tailored schematic forms are used by diverse conceptual frameworks to convey distinct cultural ideologies. From a Vakutan perspective, the schematic representation of a bat (that is, the abstraction of its 'real' form into a 'meaningful' graphic form) elucidates its significance according to a Vakutan system that values certain phenomena. On the prowboard it is the head, wings and tail that are given schematic representation. Any attempt to understand the meaning of this design must start by asking what is the value Vakutans place on these 'features'.

Like the *buribwari*, *kapaiyauwa* are thought to be exceedingly wise. This is exemplified by their nocturnal flight. They point to the evening sky and comment upon these aeronautic acrobats as they manoeuvre in the diminishing light. They move so fast that there simply is not enough time for them to 'think' about direction nor the avoidance of obstacles. Their flight pattern demonstrates internalised wisdom. Other nocturnal animals do not display the agility and speed of the *kapaiyauwa*. Other animals can fly, but they are aided by the light of day. They can *see* where they are going, whereas the bat is thought to *know*. Although it is classified with birds, insects and other animals that fly, this bat is recognised as having special skills. Not only does it have exceptional agility in flight, it bears and suckles live young and it prefers night to day for its hunting activity.

The colour of the *kapaiyauwa* is another quality much admired. Vakutan colour aesthetics places a positive evaluation on 'strong' colour. This does not simply mean that the saturation of a colour gives it its 'strength'. 'Strength' is also perceived in a spatially dominant colour. An area of colour should not, however, be too large. It must always be in correct proportion to the surrounding colours and forms. Nevertheless, when a colour is in perfect harmony within its graphic environment, yet is allowed a relatively large space, the aesthetic appreciation of the colour is regularly remarked upon. Several people commented on this section, specifically pointing out the positive effect the colour black has to the balance of the board. The black of the *kapaiyauwa* in graphic representation, however, has further meaning.

Whereas the *buribwari* carries the magic and associations of success in kula, the black of the *kapaiyauwa* could be said to represent malevolent magic: the magic that older men possess and the magic of sorcery (*bulubwalata*). A comparison of the colour scheme for sections 1 and 3 displays a marked contrast. Whereas white and red are the only colours associated with section 1, section 3 is predominantly black. Black is applied to the deepest-cut level (Plates 6–9).[3]

I argued in the previous chapter that red is the colour of youth, a colour that is 'visible' on the surface (skin) of youth. Black, on the other hand, is symbolically associated with age. Older men, during the process of maturation, accumulate and monopolise magic that affects society at large. This magic can be invoked for benevolent or malevolent purposes. For example, the magic of imparting speed to one's canoe also decreases the speed of others, while, in making one's yam garden more fertile, garden magic simultaneously inhibits the fertility of others. Knowing magic thought to affect rain, drought, winds and other elements can be used to ill effect. Sorcery, too, involves magic controlled by older men, who only acquire this kind of magic by also gaining age and social maturity while, at the same time, experiencing a reduction in the 'glossy red' of their bodies. The loss of visual beauty and its associated power heralds the onset of a condition that enables the accumulation of internalised power: ageing. In the form of knowledge, experience, 'history' and magic (other than love and beauty magic) older men lay claim to sources of power not available to young men. The colour of the *kapaiyauwa*, said to be an animal sometimes employed by sorcerers to administer their magic, is painted in the carved portion of the prowboard and represents the more malevolent associations of magic carried in kula. Its position in section 3, behind the *buribwari* and *doka*, helps to diffuse the full impact any association with malevolent magic (*bulubwalata*) has and thus avoids arousing recriminatory attacks by their hosts. It is carved behind the *buribwari* who is 'seen' first. The *kapaiyauwa* is tucked away behind the 'glossy' white and red representing the magic of attraction.[4]

Other forms in this section all relate to the bat, providing details of the body while reinforcing other body part designs (B2.1 and B3.1). Of particular note is the eye (form B1.1) carved in the main part (head) of the bat design. The eye is emphasised by curvilinear triangles thus:

While this is commonly said to be the bat's eye, it is alternatively referred to as its teeth. Eyes are considered the route by which experience and information are gained by the mind (intelligence) and the chest (emotion). Teeth, on the other hand, evoke notions of securing, fastening or clinching. These body parts, together with speech and beauty, are essential elements in achieving successful kula.

Section 4 is distinct from the others because carvers are allowed greater latitude to display their creative inclinations. Whereas in other sections the forms and their representational content must occur in prescribed patterns, the focus of section 4 is on the creative ability of each carver and/or the representation of his school of carving magic. Further, the symbolic associations linked to various forms in other sections become disassociated in section 4 so that the carver is relatively free to arrange the forms in his own way and represent what he likes (cf. Plates 6–9). Another significant aspect of this section is to differentiate the *uuna* from the *dogina*, a distinction accomplished by structural alterations to the boards. Perforations are made through the *uuna tabuya* while the *dogina tabuya* remains solid. Other forms that may feature in this section include forms A2.1, A3.5, many of the B forms, as well as forms C6 and C7.

Before leaving this section, it is important to note the area immediately below the head of the *buribwari* in section 1 of the *dogina tabuya* only:

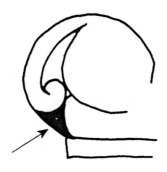

This area is always painted black and usually contains a circle (form B1.1) emphasised in white. There is no 'animal' name given to this area; it is simply referred to as 'its black pigment' (*kala kaivau*), and the white circle is its eye (*matala vau* or 'eye of the black'). The association may be with age and the systems of magic controlled by older men. Although I was told that the magical bundle of herbs placed under the 'nose' of the *dogina tabuya* is associated with the *buribwari*, it is no coincidence that this bundle is placed just below the black area of section 4, an unambiguous marker of the *dogina tabuya*.

As with section 4, section 5 of the prowboard is an area distinguishing the *dogina* from the *uuna tabuya*. Section 5, however, is not as unambiguous a marker as section 4. Whereas the distinguishing feature of section 4 is in its shaping, the differentiation between a *dogina* and *uuna tabuya* in section 5 is in the graphic design. On the *dogina tabuya* form C1 must be carved and painted. The corresponding section on the *uuna tabuya*, however, has freer associations depending upon the preference of the artist. Often form C1 is carved in section 5 of the *uuna tabuya*, but here it carries less significance than in its position on the *dogina tabuya*. If C1 is not carved in this section of the *uuna tabuya* the most usual forms found here are A2.2 (*minutoula*) and A3.4 (*doka*).

Although section 5 contains several heterogeneous forms, the entire complex of designs on the *dogina tabuya* is perceived by Vakutans as one unit. In other words, form C1 can be analysed as being, in a formal sense, made up of several distinct forms (distinct in that some of the forms have separate values in other contexts). On section 5 of the *dogina tabuya*, however, the value of these separate elements is combined to form a specific unit (C1)

The principal 'animal' in this section is the *weku*, a mythical animal. The central feature of this representation is the black form C1. This form is elaborated by the surrounding red and white, while another white form (A3.4) is added to the end. The entire complex is illustrated below:

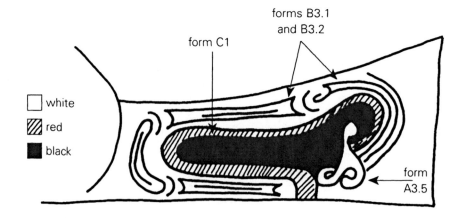

Much has already been said about the 'animal' representations associated with forms in the B category and the same applies to their representation in section 5. These designs are conceived as belonging to the white forms of category A, while their 'animal' representations relate to the specific behaviour or characteristics displayed by these animals in their natural habitat. For example, value is associated with roundness, bilateral half-circles and straight wood. The other two forms, however, do not occur in any other part of the kula carvings and are specifically confined to this section of the *dogina tabuya*

There is no 'animal' association specifically connected to form C1. When asked, people would generally say that it is only 'its black pigment' (*kala kaivau*). Occasionally *kala kwaisaru* ('its burnt coconut husk') would be offered as the label attached to this form, referring to the origin of the pigment. *Kwaisaru* is also used for face paint (*soba*), a cosmetic for beautifying the face.[5] The rounded end of the form is called 'its nose' (*kabulula*), which in some contexts is a euphemism for penis (*kwila*). The colour associated with form C1 is invariably black, although the design is echoed by the surrounding red and white 'layers'. It is the black, however, that Vakutans point out when discussing this design.

A mythological animal is represented at the far end of the prowboard (form A3.5). This animal is known as *weku* and is most often described as a small black bird. Although several people claimed that this animal really exists and that they had actually heard it calling in the bush, efforts to find it were always in vain, the bird disappearing before being spotted. The *weku* has thus remained unseen by anyone. Its 'work' is unknown and the reason for choosing it for representation in the *kabitam* repertoire is a mystery to those spoken to. Because of the scanty information concerning this animal, only a rudimentary interpretation can be attempted of its symbolic significance.

Although the animal is said by some to live at sea, its 'song' is heard in the forest whence people venture in the hopes of catching a glimpse. Either there is a contradiction here concerning the habitat of the animal or its realm is inclusive of sky, sea, trees and/or forest. It may be significant that its 'voice' is not only 'heard' but simultaneously entices its listener to seek it. A voice, if beautiful according to Vakutan standards, is associated with eroticism and the ability to entice the opposite sex. When asked what was important about *weku*, nearly all informants were ambiguous about its habitat, 'work' and colour, yet all spoke of the attraction of its voice. It would seem that the significance of the *weku* and its place within the *kabitam* repertoire stems from its voice. The quality and effect it has on people, particularly its ability to attract them to it, are desirable characteristics to be utilised by kula men (see also Scoditti 1977, 1990).

The colour patterning of section 5 is relevant to understanding the encoded meaning. Black is the innermost colour both two- and three-dimensionally; the black area is carved deeper into the wood than the surrounding red. Red pigment is applied to an area angled between the white and black levels. White is the surface colour, the colour with which people begin life after a period on Tuma. The colour patterning in section 5 corresponds to Vakutan conceptions of the temporal passage of things: from new to old, hard to soft, unripe to mature and innocence to all-knowing.

In summary, the *tabuya* features several representations that are concerned with success *(buribwari)*, flight *(kapaiyauwa)*, effective magic *(doka, kapaiyauwa* and *buribwari)*, the power of attraction *(weku)* and wisdom *(buribwari* and *doka)*. Other elements reinforcing these major themes include representations from spatial oppositions (land versus sea) and individual fame *(kaidada)*.

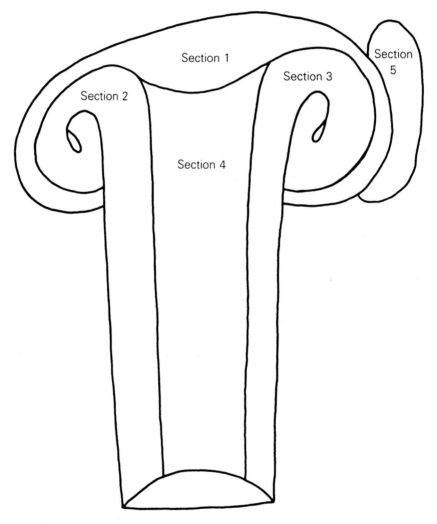

Figure 7.2a *Lagim* sections

Form		Colour	Body part	Animal
	A1.2	white with red repetition		
	A1.3	white with red repetition	mouth	
	A2.2	white with red repetition		*karawa*
	A3.1	white		*dodoleta*
	A3.2	white with red repetition	head with eye and beak	*boi/doka*
	A3.3	white	head/body eye and beak	*sawila*
	A3.4	white	head with eye and beak	*doka*
	A4	white, red, and black	head, neck, and beak – wing/arm	*beba, boi/doka*
	A5	white, red and black	entire body	*tokwalu*
	B1.1	white	eye	*duduwa*
	B1.2	white and red		*ubwara*
	B1.3	white, red and black		
	B2.1	white		*ginareu*
	B2.2	white		*dodoleta*
	B3.1	white		*kaidada*
	B3.2	white	head/eye	*boi, doka* or *weku*
	B4.1	white		*taregesi*
	C4	black		
	C5	black		
	C6	alternating black and red		
	C7	black		
	C8	black		
	C9	black		

Figure 7.2b Form, representation, colour and body-part terminology of the *lagim*

An Analysis of the Splashboard (Figures 7.2a and 7.2b)

Section 1 of the splashboard is contained within form A1.2.[6] The forms thus held may appear to be numerous (Plates 10–13). They are, however, limited and are arranged according to specific orientations. A single 'scroll' unit (A3.1) is linked to form a 'chain':

These are found curved around the two lobes, or *beba*:

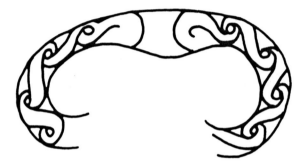

The background form emerging on either side of the 'scroll' is C6. Along the outer 'chain' these are usually coloured red,[7] while the inner 'chain's' secondary form is carved through leaving perforations. These are conceptually 'black'. Labels attached to form C6 include *kala kaivau* ('its black pigment') and *kala kaimalaka* ('its red pigment'). The main function of this area is to provide a structure upon which to fasten rows of *buna* shells *(ovula ovum*; Plate 15).

The most important 'animals' in section 1 are the *boi/doka* (form A3.2), *doka* (form A3.4) and the *tokwalu* figure (A5). These are located in the central area of section 1. The *tokwalu* bridges the gap between sections 2 and 3, complementing the tension created by the restraining form A1.2. Associated with this area are the head, eye and beak (mouth) of the *boi*. Under this 'animal's beak is the *doka* (form A3.4).

While the *buribwari* is the principal 'animal' of the prowboard, the *boi* together with the *tokwalu* assume the principal focus on the splashboard. There is a difference, however, between the derived 'power' of these two 'animals'. Whereas the *buribwari* stands perched alone on the prowboard, the *boi* is always associated with *doka* on the splashboard. The *boi* is considered a wise 'animal' but, unlike the *buribwari*, it needs to recharge its 'wisdom' through the use of magic. A recurring characterisation of this animal is that 'It strikes wisely and gets its fish.

However, when the *boi* misses, it goes into the forest and performs its *kaimwasila* magic. It then returns to the water and resumes fishing.'[8] In this regard, the *boi* is likened to men who also have to perform magic in order to succeed at their work. A *tokabitam* has to resort to 'refresher' magic if, when carving, he finds it hard for the designs to 'flow' from his mind and through his hands onto the wood. Like the *boi*, a carver thus afflicted goes off to the forest and prepares a particular *kaimwasila*. He swallows it and returns to the village to resume his work. The conceptual likeness between the *boi* and humans is given symbolic persuasion by their close proximity on the splashboard; both inhabit the upper, central space in section 1. The positions of 'mankind', represented by the *tokwalu*, and the *boi* are bolstered by the close proximity of the *doka* signifying wise thought. In a kind of ironic twist, these representations will turn against the crew and destroy them should the latter endanger the outrigger canoe.

The *tokwalu* figure represents humanity and is associated with the 'head' of the splashboard.[9] People would sometimes discuss the splashboard according to body parts, pointing to the '*tokwalu* in the head' of the splashboard. Based on reference to this area as 'the head', it is tempting to associate the reincarnation of *baloma* as *waiwaiya* (foetus) with the placement of *tokwalu* on the 'head' of the *lagim*. One version of Trobriand belief has the *waiwaiya* entering a woman's vagina via her head. Blood then rushes to her head and, upon this tide, the foetus is carried to the womb where it develops (Malinowski 1932: 149). As regards the *tokwalu*, it is possible that at one level the figure represents a reincarnated ancestor at the head of a *dala* woman waiting to be carried to the womb.[10] Since much of the symbolism of kula is concerned with men engaged in the reproduction of male wealth through their relationships with male partners, it would not be surprising if the representation of the *tokwalu* at the 'head' of the splashboard communicated these messages at some level, although Vakutans never articulated this.

The remaining forms of section 1 are often unseen owing to the decoration of *buna* shells. However, they must be there. The theme represented in these forms is connected to the human mind and the process of thinking which, not being infallible, must be reinforced by magic. Humans, throughout various mythological events, lost many of their previous powers: for example, the power of rejuvenation (Malinowski 1922: 307–311, 322–326; also Young 1983a: 383–394) and the knowledge of how to make a canoe fly (Malinowski 1922: 311–321). Trobriand Islanders recall in myth how these capacities were lost through human error. Section 1 of the splashboard recalls these 'mistakes' by way of an oblique reference to those times. In this sense, man remains innocent and vulnerable (white), devoid of the heroics of the mythological past which saw men rejuvenate, make their canoes fly and acquire all the wealth (red) of others. However, jealousies growing out of these heroics (black) resulted in the destruction of these heroes and the subsequent loss of their knowledge. White is the predominant colour of section 1, with a mere hint of red and black to balance the section both visually and metaphorically.

Sections 2 and 3 of the splashboard, although visually differentiated, are motivated by the same basic form. These two sections are both constrained by an external line with internal elaborations based upon the simple 'volute'. The internal representation focuses attention upon the *boi*, again the dominant 'animal', while other designs relate to it. This design is also called *doka*. While in section 1 all forms have individual labels, in sections 2 and 3 they tend to take on the name of the main design; in this case, that of the *boi/doka*.[11]

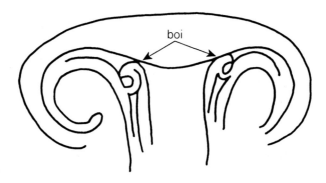

The designs of these sections are all associated with the head, eye and beak, reflecting the value Vakutans place on this region of the body. The face is the visual focus of beauty and the key to potential power; others cannot refuse the desires of someone with a beautiful face. It is said that beauty stuns, and in this way succeeds in attracting wealth, fame and immortality. Another important feature located in the head is the eye. Eyes are the windows of desire and the tools used to enchant one's partners. The mouth, too, is important, controlling the magic one possesses by either blocking or emitting magical utterances. Words are always spoken when *mwasila* magic is used (as opposed to *kaimwasila*, magic relying on ingested vegetable matter). Before a man dies he instructs his relatives to gag his mouth to stop the magic from coming out, thereby avoiding possible harm to the living.[12] The head is thought to contain all acquired knowledge and is the place where *kabitam* wisdom is formulated.[13]

Although these two sections on the splashboard are visually different, they are, on close examination, conceptually identical. The visual differentiation is created in the treatment of the central portion of the design (compare Plates 10–13). In section 2 the design orientation retains the forms associated with the upper, white level together with the series of forms that regularly feature here (category B forms). Section 3, on the other hand, replaces the white with a black form (reminiscent of form C7). This completely alters the visual impact of these two sections. As has been described for other large blocks of black pigment, section 3 of the splashboard provides an aesthetically pleasing design while at the same time recalling other symbolic associations with the colour black:

As well as the internal structuring and design patterning, the circumscribing form itself has meaning. The entire form is called *beba*, or butterfly. The larger lobe is called 'the big butterfly' (*beba kaiveka*), the smaller lobe 'the small butterfly' (*beba kaikekita*). With the butterfly in mind, Vakutans would talk about these sections in terms of the splashboard's 'wings' or 'arms'. Like the flight of the bat, butterfly aerodynamics represents a desirable characteristic for the ocean-going canoe. The lightness of the butterfly is a quality desired for the canoe.

Section 4 of the splashboard is unlike all other sections of the outrigger canoe carvings. There are no fixed design representations, nor any rules of design patterning. Although there is a set corpus of forms available for use in section 4, these can be organised in any way that suits the individual artist. Each carver organises the forms in such a way as to correspond with Vakutan aesthetics in general, but these are much less rigid than the patterning of forms in other sections. When an observer looks at various splashboards, he or she will encounter the different surfaces the carvings present. This is due to the variations allowed in section 4. As a general rule, the eye tends to ignore similarity and focuses instead on the differences between carvings. This is in keeping with Vakutan preoccupation with an individual's unique physical identity and the Trobriand perception that no one 'looks' like anyone else (cf. Malinowski 1932: 173–178).[14] When one carver challenges another for 'copying' his style the accusations are directed at designs centred in section 4 only. Because all other sections on the prow and splashboard are conceived according to standardised rules of design patterning and animal representation, these areas are not even brought into the argument as evidence for the theft of one's designs.

In section 4, the variation in 'animal' representation is considerable. Carvers tend to group forms schematically to represent animals they wish to carve. On the other hand, forms may be patterned to conform to a standardised marker of an individual carver and the way he was taught to organise design units. Nevertheless, there is generally some degree of variation between an apprentice's and master carver's patterns. Further, a carver may label the patterns he carves in section 4 differently on separate occasions. In other cases carvers cannot or do not want to label their designs at all. They simply refer to the pigment terms. Usually the animals chosen as labels are birds and fish, or other creatures associated with water such as frogs.

Another interesting variation from the other sections is that in section 4 alternative body parts are represented. Although heads, eyes and mouth continue to receive attention, the most significant body part of section 4 is the chest. Indeed, the area of the splashboard occupied by section 4 is commonly referred to as the 'chest of the splashboard'. The chest is a significant locus of emotion and the centre of consciousness. Within the 'chest' of the splashboard the chests of specified animals also occur.

Unlike other sections, the largest proportion of category C forms can be found in section 4. This is probably a factor relating to the greater freedom to utilise space in less restricted ways, placing category A forms into varying configurations and allowing category C forms to emerge. However, it is significant that category C forms occur more frequently in the 'chest' of the splashboard. Previously it was noted that large areas of black are 'good' to look at, offering a degree of balance to the predominance of white forms. Additionally, black is conceptually associated with men past their physical prime; those who have lost the youthful beauty but who are nevertheless strong, influential and in control of power through the magic they have acquired during their passage from physical beauty in youth to social maturity in age. Section 4 of the splashboard represents the *kabitam* carver who, past his youth, possesses the magic of carving and the knowledge associated with it.

In conclusion, section 4 has a major role to play on the kula carvings. Firstly, it is an important identifier of particular 'schools' of carving, as well as the individual creativity of specific carvers. Creativity, although conforming to acceptable parameters of design application, is a further mark of an individual carver's more potent internalised carving magic as it compares with that of other master carvers. Similar to the aesthetic value placed on dense black, here, too, the 'density' of internalised magic, signified by a carver's ability to balance creative innovation while at the same time retaining acceptable relationships between forms, is valued and respected.

Section 5 is not an essential part of the kula carving complex and is often excluded on Vakuta. The choice is entirely left to the carver. If he decides to incorporate it, however, there are two ways in which it should be oriented. One 'style' uses a relatively realistic representation of a snake either consuming a bird or, more simply, left on its own (Plate 13). On occasion, the snake was identified as a gecko or other type of lizard. This distinction, however, does little to alter the semantic intention. Most reptiles are conceptually classified as animals that inhabit domains under as well as on top of the ground (see also Malinowski 1927a: 110 regarding 'animals of the below'). This conceptualisation is related to the origin myths prevalent in the area, as well as to beliefs in ancestral spirits residing underground who periodically return to terrestrial haunts on certain occasions and for reincarnation. It is significant that reptiles, particularly snakes, periodically shed their skins. This act is thought to represent a snake's reincarnation. It is also of interest to note that the reptile in the carving is usually in the process of consuming a bird, a creature 'of the above'.

The second choice for section 5 is the 'little butterfly' (*beba nakekita*).[15] This is incorporated into form A1.2 and is a repetition of the outline of section 1 (Plates 10–12). The form of the 'little butterfly' is repeated in red, then black. The 'fern frond' (form A2.2) creates visual cohesion as the two meet in the centre, curving around, then under, and finally ending in the *doka* (form A3.4; see Plate 8). In this section several visually related volute forms are carved. Flight and speed, together with knowledge and creative thought, are the main themes of this section. Section 5 contains in microcosm the most important elements to successful kula.

The Meaning of the Kabitam Carvings

In Chapters 4, 5 and 6, form, representation and colour were isolated so as to aid in the presentation of the basic framework within which various meanings and relationships are encoded. In so doing, however, the continuity and integration of a wider range of meaning was compromised. In this chapter there has been an attempt to redress this by discussing the various elements in conjunction with their orientation within the carved and painted environments of each section. The intention was to draw together form, representation, body-part and colour associations to reveal the complexity of meaning operating within the carved surfaces of the boards. However, our focus must ultimately change yet again as we take an even wider angle and view the collective context where further layers allude to the goals of kula and the men who seek fame and wealth through it.

The repertoire is composed of a variety of visual components (form and colour) which are ordered variously according to structural principles of design organisation: dimension (deepest, middle, surface), section and repetition. The corpus of forms, too, is finite. The limitations are prescribed by Vakutan principles generating form and must ultimately comply with a Vakutan style and aesthetic value. The forms, however, are not merely decorative. Most of them have associations with the natural world. These are generally derived from the familiar animals and plants within the Vakutan environment. The possibilities for animal or plant representation, however, are virtually infinite. Thus we have a finite corpus of forms to which are attached labels derived from an almost infinite number of animals and plants. What, then, is the basis for choosing certain plants and animals over others?

There are three kinds of design units used in kula carvings (I refer here, and subsequently, to the combination of form, animal, colour and body part as a design unit). The distinction is based upon a differing complexity of meaning and partially corresponds to the three divisions of form outlined in Chapter 4 (i.e. versatile, restricted and fixed). The first type of design unit is based upon a highly motivated relationship between the form, its animal association, colour and body-part representation. These design units communicate multiple layers of information, triggering the complex cross-referencing mechanisms of the receivers who are socialised to interpret, or make meaningful, the encoded messages. The animals identified with these forms suggest particular kinds of information that in turn communicate further layers of meaningful associations. The relationship of an animal to its representational form is but one step towards discovering richer layers of symbolic reference. Examples of these kinds of design units are the *boi/doka*, *buribwari, kapaiyauwa, weku* and *tokwalu*. While the majority of forms associated with these representations are from category A (the versatile forms), two are not. *Kapaiyauwa* (C3) and *weku* (C1) are associated with forms from category C (the fixed forms).

Much has already been said about the multiple meanings encoded in these design units. In the succeeding chapters, too, further analysis will reveal deeper connections and suggest a Vakutan philosophical engagement with their world. In anticipation, a brief exposition of one of these design units will serve to illustrate the sense in which they are all pregnant with multiple layers of meaning.

The representation of a bat in section 3 of the prowboard triggers in a Vakutan mind (whether conscious or unconscious) the following basic characteristics: it possesses admirable flight capabilities, it is a creature of the night and it bears live young. But why should these be of value to the *kabitam* repertoire?

In the flying canoe myth of Kitava, first reported by Malinowski (1922: 311–321) and similar to two texts I recorded on Vakuta, men lose the ability to make their canoes fly by the inopportune slaying of the only man who knew the magic. It is obvious from the myth and from contemporary accounts, both in magic and in deed, that Vakutans consider a truly successful kula canoe to be one that is capable of flight. A canoe able to fly would avoid the inherent dangers of the sea and, more importantly, would arrive at its destination before other canoes. According to the myth, the slain man's sisters flew away in anger following the murder of their brother. There is clear inference here that the sisters, like their brother, possessed the knowledge of flight, taking that knowledge with them in their angry departure. Thus while men lost the ability to make their canoes fly women did not.

Belief in flying witches is still prevalent in the Massim area. Vakutans believe that they continue to plague the night skies both over land and sea. Although inherently malevolent, it is ironic that the flying witch provides a model for the kula outrigger canoes.[16] In magic, men call upon the canoes to 'bind their skirts and fly' (see also Malinowski 1922: 132, 138) – a clear association with flying witches. The canoes are also decorated with pandanus streamers in imitation of the paraphernalia said to be carried by the flying witch on her nightly escapades (Malinowski 1922: 215–217). The ambivalence is striking. While the flying witch is in possession of an attribute much desired by men for their canoes, an attribute that in myth was once almost theirs only to be lost by an untimely fratricide, she is also the agent of a much feared death.

This ambivalence is in part resolved by the representation of a bat on the kula prowboard. The bat demonstrates many of the powers of the flying witch, for they are symbolically related. One of the main characteristics favouring the bat over other nocturnal flying creatures is that it bears live young, as do human females. The attribute that separates ordinary women from witches is flight, and, in a kind of ironic reversal, the parturition of live young and the practice of suckling them distinguishes the bat from other flying creatures. Both witch and bat are associated with the colour black. The bat, then, represents a visual euphemism for the flying witch.

The schematisation of the bat (rather than a more iconic representation) leaves open the symbolic relationship between its representation on the prowboard and flying witches. To actually represent the flying witch and call the design unit *mulukwausa* would be a dangerously provocative act, so Vakutans have built into the carving system a means of bypassing potential danger by schematically signifying the bat.

Returning for the moment to the discussion of the three kinds of design units, the second type consists of forms that show an iconic relationship to their animal counterparts in that the form bears some physical resemblance to its namesake. This relationship, however, does not seem to go beyond that of a relatively simple iconic reference. For example, the repetition of form B2.1 is said to be the 'footprints' of the hermit crab. The form's motivation is aesthetically linked to this small crab's mark in the sand as it scuttles along. Although certain characteristics of these animals' behaviour may be relevant to a broader interpretation of the system, the relative depth of meaning is limited when compared to the first type of design unit described above. Other forms belonging to this type of design unit are detailed in Table 7.1.

With the exception of form A3.1, the others all belong to the restricted (B) group. It is significant that these design units not only occupy the space determined

Table 7.1 Design units with simple iconic relationships

Duduwa (garden snail)	○ ◎	B1.1
Ubwara (wild yam)	◎	B1.2 and B1.3
Dodoleta (leaf of a shrub)	⟨⟨⟨⟨⟨⟨	B2.2
Kaidada (wood)	⊐=⊏	B3.1
Boi, doka, weku (egret, mythological animal)		B3.2
Taregesi (shell fish)	▵▵▵▵▵▵	B4.1
Dodoleta (leaf of a shrub)	∿∿∿	A3.1

by white forms (A), but that the 'animal' representations also have limited symbolic depth.[17] In discussions concerning the significance of the animals and their 'work' (a value made by Vakutans), they were said to be insignificant in relation to the 'work' of other animals represented on the prow and splashboard. They are there merely to 'hold the lime' and thus their purpose is to emphasise the significance of the white forms, as well as the latter's relationship to the black and red forms. The choices made by master carvers, who favoured these animals over others, were based not on the actual 'work' of the animals (with respect to their 'wisdom') but on the physical forms or the marks they make. Their inclusion, then, is primarily based upon aesthetic considerations relevant to their form. In conclusion, these forms are generated by other design units that have a more direct role to play in the communication of multilayered meaning.

The third kind of design unit generally includes those forms that have no animal or body-part term of their own. On the few occasions when a carver would assign these forms an animal label, together with its relevant body part, the form would take on the associations of those design units within their immediate environment. When discussing the designs with carvers it was clear that nearly all of these design units were given secondary roles in the communication process. With the exception of forms C1–C3, their importance is derived from their close proximity to other design units that are more meaningful. A further, perhaps more telling, indication of their role in the system is that these forms, by and large, emerge from the execution of other design units. Further, these forms are generally referred to by their colour term. Examples of this kind of design unit are forms C4–C10. The importance of their role in the system is aesthetic. These design units provide a balance of form and colour, throwing more meaningful design units into relief.

The spatial organisation of design units on the prow and splashboard is ordered in such a way as to provide yet another means of interpreting the meaning of the boards. Attention has already been drawn to the inappropriate suggestion that any physical likeness between people exists. It is also unacceptable to indicate likenesses between boards. To make comparisons between boards not only implies that a master carver has 'copied' another's designs but, in competition with other boards on other canoes, also calls into question the 'power' of the board's 'animal' crew to attract kula shell valuables.

The fact that there are a wide variety of ways in which the design units, their sectional orientation and the boards themselves can be interpreted is itself significant. The multiplicity of encoded meanings and the different levels at which these emerge are facilitated by a relatively small number of elements. The range of meanings conveyed by the colour arrangement on the boards elicits certain kinds of interpretational responses different, yet ultimately related to the meanings inherent in the 'animal' representations. Further, in relation to the 'animal' repertoire, it is not necessarily the details of each animal that are significant, but rather specific characteristics such as flight, colour, form and inherent wisdom that attracts attention. The 'animals' are, more or less, tools that assist one to interpret meaning: the *kapaiyauwa* (bat) indirectly refers to the flying witch; the *kaidada* (wood) suggests man's immortality through renown and fame; the *doka* represents human thought; the *boi* (egret) encompasses the most significant form in the symbolic system, referring to a tree idiom; the *buribwari* (osprey) embodies male values while further evoking the tree idiom; the *karawa* (fern frond), though a minor design unit, is also related to the tree idiom; and the snake has reference to the subterranean abode of the ancestors from whence humanity initially came and is periodically regenerated. While the symbolic content of some design units is relatively straightforward, in that the iconic relationship between form, animal, colour and body part requires relatively little interrogation, other design units seem to be more dense. They contain multiple layers of meaning that, when situated within other contexts of Vakutan social and cultural life, suggest significant conceptual constructs. This will be the subject of the remaining chapters.

The design units on the kula prow and splashboards are fundamentally about the representation of desired characteristics seen in the natural world to be 'successful'. The 'animals' used for representation on the boards are enlisted for the success of a kula expedition. This is marked by the boat's ability to negotiate the dangerous open sea, as well as the board's ability to woo kula partners and bring home shell valuables. With the multiplicity of representations on the prow and splashboards, together with special beauty magic and the magic to protect the canoe from possible dangers encountered at sea, the kula expedition is guaranteed success in the minds of Vakutans; that is, as long as the magic is more powerful than anyone else's and is efficacious enough to distract or deter the dreaded 'women'.

Part III
Kula

–8–

The Rituals of Kula

> When, on a trading expedition or as a visiting party, a fleet of native canoes appears in
> the offing, with their triangular sails like butterfly wings scattered over the water with
> the harmonious calls of conch shells blown in unison, the effect is unforgettable. When
> the canoes then approach, and you see them rocking in the blue water in all the splendour
> of their fresh white, red, and black paint, with their finely designed prowboards, and
> clanking array of large, white cowry shells – you understand well the admiring love
> which results in all this care bestowed by the native on the decoration of his canoe.
> (Malinowski 1922: 108)

The preceding chapters have focused on the meanings inscribed on the kula boards
while the context for which they are created has remained in the background. The
time has come to assemble the boards on the outrigger canoe and prepare to launch
upon the well-chartered 'waters' of kula. In this chapter we will explore the rituals
of kula.

The Making of a *Masawa*

There are several activities men attend to following the selection of a tree for a
new kula outrigger canoe. Generally, these are concerned with making the tree and
emergent canoe light. Shortly after selection, men place a shell valuable at the base
of the tree. This valuable is called *ulaula* or *sosula* and is presented to the *tokwai*,
spirits thought to inhabit trees (cf. Malinowski 1922: 126–128). After a suitable
period has elapsed (several hours to one day) the valuable is reclaimed, the tree
cut and the bark removed. On the following day men go into the forest to cut
lengths from a particularly strong vine they call *duku*. Vakutans use this to pull
the log into the village. The creeper is tied to both ends of the log: the *uuna* and
dogina. When this has been accomplished the man at the *uuna* end shouts at the
tokwai:

> *Tokwai* you go to that tree over
> there and stay
> leave our tree, our canoe
> Wagela kasailova

– 153 –

Wagela kamnamwana
Wagela uvalaku.

He then strikes the end of the log to expel the *tokwai*. It is now the turn of the man
at the *dogina* end, who shouts:

Mulukwausi you go to Kadimwata
You disappear.
You throw away our canoe.
Wagela kula
Wagela kasailova
Wagela kamnamwana
Wagela uvalaku.

With these words he strikes the *dogina* end. This rite is performed to make the log
light so that its removal from the forest is made easier (cf. Malinowski 1922: 129–
130). It is also, however, the first opportunity to secure the canoe as an artefact of
men. They are claiming the log from its wild state with the intention of transforming it into a cultural object to be used by men in the pursuit of male wealth
and renown.

It is significant that *tokwai* are expelled from the *uuna*, or base of the tree, while
mulukwausi (witches) are told to vacate the *dogina*, or top of the tree. This concern
for excising entities from both ends of the tree reflects Vakutan issues associated
with land and sky. More specifically, witches are asked to go to Kadimwata, a place
in the southern D'Entrecasteaux archipelago thought to be a meeting place for all
flying witches. Vakutans say that the most evil witches come from this region. It
is from Kadimwata mountain that they call to their 'sisters' to join them. The
gathering of witches includes participating in particularly gruesome rituals where
communal feasting on decayed human corpses is enjoyed by all. It is from the tops
of trees that Vakutan witches scan the land and sea for potential victims and
communicate with other witches. From this vantage, it is thought that they can
either bend the tree towards their destination or simply take flight. *Tokwai*, on the
other hand, are strictly land-based tricksters, eager to cause trouble whenever
possible. Their presence on the canoe causes it to remain heavy.

The significance of invoking weightless characteristics onto the felled tree is
twofold. As a pragmatic strategy, it is thought necessary to lighten the log in order
to ease its transferal to the manufacturing site. Secondly, the conversion from
heavy to light has extensive symbolic significance. Men entreat heaviness to depart
the tree so that as a canoe it will be light and able to perform well on the open seas.
At a more general level, land is associated with weight, stability and anchoring
while sea is associated with qualities of lightness and mobility (see also Munn

1977: 41, 1986). This can be expressed as the following: land is to sea as heavy is to light as anchored is to mobile. Thus, at one level, endeavours to remove the heaviness of a tree, while at the same time removing it from the forest, represent a simultaneous detachment of the tree's previous association with land and preparation for its new association with the sea. Further, the ultimate desire, as we shall see, is to make the hollowed log so light that it becomes detached from land and able to 'fly'. Two spells recorded by Malinowski make reference to a lightening of the canoe to facilitate its capacity for flight. The first is used in order to lighten the tree and thus enable its easy removal from the forest to the village. The second is chanted while the creeper used to pull the log to the village is ritually cut. In both spells reference is made to the Kitavan myth of the flying canoe (1922: 311–321).[1] As noted in the previous chapter, much of the value accorded to certain animals is their ability to fly and to the imagery of easy and effective flight. Similarly, the rituals related to the construction of a kula outrigger canoe allude to the qualities of flight, hoping to imbue the new canoe with this characteristic.

The shaping of the tree into a canoe is of obvious functional value. However, its symbolic significance is less clear. The shaping of the tree represents a transformation from natural matter to cultural artefact, from an object fixed to the earth into a vehicle for travel on the sea. This transformation goes further than merely involving a shift from nature to cultural artefact, however. The transformation of a tree into an ocean-going canoe represents for men a conversion of the tree from an abode for uncontrollable, anti-social beings into a vehicle to accommodate men on their highly social pursuit of inter-island exchange.[2] The conversion is based upon transferring a weighted and anchored object into a light and mobile one. It also represents, at a more heightened symbolic level, men's reclamation of their own agency in the promotion of themselves beyond their mortal lives as well as their ability to transcend the anchoring forces of *dala*. We will return to this issue later.

At its simplest, an object is taken from its anchored state and transformed into something essentially mobile. The tree is severed from the land to become an object of the sea. In this domain men generate an imagined, third transformation, via magic, towards a symbolic replication of flight. But how does this happen? We know that canoes will not fly despite all the intentions mustered by men in their endeavours towards this end. To understand this, let's return to the transformation of the tree from anchored to mobile.

The log, while undergoing structural transformation, also undergoes a spatial shift from forest to village where it is shaped. It is here that the canoe's maker, sometimes with the assistance of other male kinsmen, but more often on his own, painstakingly shapes the hull with his single adze. Once the body of the dugout canoe has been formed in the village it is ready for further transformation into an ocean-going canoe *(masawa)* rather than a simple fishing outrigger canoe *(kewou)*.

This process takes place at the water's edge.³ For an ocean-going *masawa*, planks are attached to the sides of the dugout log. These are lashed together by use of an especially strong vine from the *weyugwa* creeper (Malinowski spells it *wayugo* [1922: 137]). Finally, the outrigger is shaped and attached to a platform lashed to the side of the canoe (see Figure 4.1).⁴

This movement through space echoes the concurrent change in status for the log. While it is anchored to the earth, the tree is considered to be in an uncontrolled, undomesticated state. Its orientation is vertical, anchored to the land but reaching to the sky. It is heavy from its association with land. This state is exacerbated by the presence of anti-social and uncontrollable beings. Magic is performed and words spoken to dispel these, while at the same time lightening the log. When it is moved to the village and reshaped, the log is being transformed into a controllable cultural artefact. In its transformed state the new canoe is washed in preparation for its emergence as a social entity. It is painted, decorated and has its name marked on its side plank. Its name associates the canoe with a particular *dala*. The canoe is now ready to be launched onto the open sea. It has been transformed from a vertical entity to a horizontal one designed to move horizontally in an uncontrolled domain, the sea. As a cultural artefact it is specifically designed to traverse this dangerous space. While mobility is considered a positive value for aspiring men, the sea represents excessive mobility with all manner of highly mobile elements lurking above and below the surface. Munn notes the significance of similar spatial and status transformations for Gawan canoes (1977, 1986).

The newly created canoe rests on the beach, a transitional space between land and sea. While land is predominately associated with women and their regenerative agency, the sea is associated with men. Like Vakutans, Gawans also associate land with feminine values of anchoring, weightedness and corporate identity whereas the sea represents that domain in which men achieve mobility and lightness. The beach, too, marks a point of transition between these two domains (Munn 1986). Vakutans consider the sea to be the enabling domain for their pursuit of wealth, an essential partner in the making of their social value and renown. On the other hand, Vakutans associate the land with feminine qualities. Both women and land are credited with fertility and regeneration. The beach represents the mediation between these two distinct domains. It is on the beach, or more precisely in the shallow waters rhythmically caressing the sands, that women conceive *dala* spirit children who have travelled across open sea from Tuma to make their way into the womb. The beach is also the place where men perform their beauty or love magic prior to a kula expedition and where, on the return home, they wash and arrange the shells they have seduced from their kula partners (Plate 18). Male and female influences meet on the transitional space of the beach. It was here, according to mythology, that love magic had its origins through the incestuous liaison of brother and sister (Malinowski 1932: 456–459). It is significant that a woman in her first pregnancy is ritually bathed in the shallow waters off the beach (Malinowski 1932: 185–186; see also Munn 1986: 97–101). Similarly, a newly constructed kula outrigger canoe is ritually bathed in the same shallow water (Malinowski 1922: 135). Both acts symbolically impart beauty and lightness to a woman and to a *masawa*.

An important ceremony during this stage of a kula canoe's transformation involves the ritual insertion of the four carved boards on both ends of the hull. Until the boards are inserted into the ends of the canoe, they remain with the master carver in the village. Prior to insertion, the *dogina tabuya* is taken to the ocean beach and ritually bathed by the master carver. While he washes the *tabuya*, gently rubbing it with charmed leaves, he recites a spell imparting to the board qualities of speed, lightness and, more importantly, the power of attraction. Thunder and lightning are said to accompany the spoken magic, thus informing villagers that the master carver is ritually bathing the *dogina tabuya*. Later all four boards are ceremonially carried to the beach and put into place on the prows of the *masawa*. The boards are carried in strict order on the shoulders of four men; the *dogina tabuya* leads, followed by the *dogina lagim*, the *uuna tabuya* and finally the *uuna lagim*. While being carried from the village to the beach the leader shouts, 'Tabuyoo', followed by the others answering, 'Oooooyo'. Arriving at the *masawa*, the procession, led by the *dogina tabuya*, encircles the *masawa* from the *uuna* end, passing to the right side of the canoe and progressing counter-clockwise around it. Then, standing on the left of the *dogina* prow (with the outrigger on the left), the *dogina tabuya* is knocked into place together with a charmed bundle of *sulumwoya* (mint bush) leaves. These are a necessary ingredient in all love and beauty magic. This is placed under the 'nose' of the *buribwari* design (see also Malinowski 1922: 134–135). The bundle contains *kaimwasila* magic and is meant to affect the minds of partners. Once the *dogina tabuya* is in place, the other boards are similarly knocked into position without, however, a magical bundle of leaves.

Although Malinowski discussed at length the magic system of *mwasila* employed exclusively in kula (1922: 102, 147, 334–349, and 1932) he made no mention of another form of kula magic called *kaimwasila*. Vakutans make a distinction between these. *Mwasila* refers to spoken incantations that impart powers of attraction and persuasion to objects associated with the body such as face paint, oil, body decorations, combs, and so on. *Mwasila* is thought to act upon the bodies of the practitioners, making them beautiful, glossy, healthy and irresistible. Mythical heroes with particularly potent *mwasila* were Kasibwaibwaireta (see also Malinowski 1922: 322–324; Young 1983a: 383–394) and Tokosikuna (Malinowski 1922: 307–311). *Mwasila* magic, then, is personal beauty magic used to attract lovers and exchange partners. I was told that another use of the word *mwasila* is to refer to someone who has a smiling, happy face.

Kaimwasila, on the other hand, is magic that is contained within specially selected and charmed vegetable matter.[5] The potency of this magic is said to affect the minds of partners, making them 'soft' and easily 'turned'. Most of the magic ascribed to the *mwasila* system of kula magic by Malinowski is, according to Vakutans, *kaimwasila* in that the desired effect is to change the minds of others rather than to alter one's own body. Malinowski wrote that *mwasila*: 'consists [of] numerous rites and spells, all of which act directly on the mind of one's partner, and make him soft, unsteady in mind, and eager to give kula gifts' (1920: 100).

Based on Vakutan distinctions between *kaimwasila* and *mwasila*, the only magic of the latter category described by Malinowski is the actual beauty magic performed by the crew on the beach of Sarubwoyna prior to landing on the Dobuan beaches: 'The main aim of these spells is to make the man beautiful, attractive, and irresistible to his kula partner' (1922: 335–336).

A third form of magic associated with kula and the attraction of women is *kaributu*. This is spoken magic and is said to intensify the speaker's beauty so acutely that anyone who sees him is compelled to shake with desire.[6] *Kaributu* also refers to the giving of a solicitory gift in the hope of acquiring an especially fine valuable (see also Malinowski 1922: 99, 354, 358). *Mwasila* and *kaimwasila* are symbolically represented by two of the *kabitam* animals carved on the prowboards – recall the osprey *(buribwari)*, which personifies *mwasila*, and the egret *(boi)*, which is thought to have access to particularly effective *kaimwasila*. Although Malinowski describes the magical rite associated with the placement of the *tabuya* on the prow as *mwasila*, Vakutans say that it is *kaimwasila* because the magic is contained within charmed leaves and its desired outcome is to soften the minds of the hosts. By 'blinding' them with the beauty of their *masawa* (the effects of the *mwasila* of the *buribwari*), the crew's intention is to draw their hosts' attention to themselves (the effects of the *kaimwasila* bundle under the nose of the *buribwari*) and thereby eclipse the others in their fleet. A veritable double whammy of magical power!

Finally, it is significant that the *dogina tabuya* is singled out for special treatment. As has already been argued, the *dogina tabuya* is considered the most important of the four prowboards, particularly the presence of the *buribwari* symbolising the power of men to attract an adoring audience, be they kula partners or women. In the context of kula, the *buribwari* represents the desire to be unfailing in procuring 'prey'. The egret *(boi/doka)*, however, alludes to human frailty by comparison to the powers of the *buribwari*. Its beauty does fail, necessitating access to the specific magic of attraction embodied in *kaimwasila*. Only men know and use *mwasila* and *kaimwasila* magic.[7] If a woman wants to attract a particular man she must ask a mother's father or a father's father to perform personal magic on her behalf. This ability gives men a special power over women who, although credited with considerable say over which of their suitors they choose as sexual partners, are otherwise helpless in countering the effects of love magic. It is not surprising then that the ultimate symbol of this male ideal, the *buribwari*, receives ritual attention in the placement of the boards on the kula outrigger canoe.

Before the newly transformed canoe can make a public debut it must be painted and have shells attached to its *lagim*, prow and outrigger platform (Figure 4.1, Plates 1 and 15). Both ends of the hull are carved and painted. Forms utilised on both ends are the same and include forms A2.3, A3.4, B1.1, B2.1–3 and B3.1. Vakutans did not give these forms names, preferring to refer to them by their colour terms. The *dogina* end of the hull is called *pusa* Dobu while the *uuna* end is called *pusa* Gawa. Form C2 is carved along the upper rim of the hull and painted alternately red and black on a strip of white background (Plate 1). This form is called *papa*, or 'wall'. It is the 'wall' of the hollowed log to which the vertical planks are attached. The actual hull is painted black except for both prow ends which are painted white. The side planks are painted red (Plates 1, 2a and 2b). The aesthetics of colour is extremely important to Vakutans. They wince at the wrong combinations of the three colours as if the visual affront were a physical blow. The colour associations of Vakutan *masawa* are fixed. White on the prow seems inoffensive, the red of the planks evokes beauty and attraction, clearly visible as the *masawa* comes to shore, while black is confined to a less dominant place on the hull, barely seen by their hosts as the fleet sails towards them (Plate 14).

While men attend to the task of painting, others attach the *buna* (*ovula ovum*) shells. These are sometimes secured along section 1 of the *lagim* in a double or triple row (Plate 15). The preference for shells attached to the *lagim* is more common among Kitavans than Vakutans, but Vakutans do sometimes follow suit. *Buna* shells are always, however, attached to the prow of the canoe (Figure 4.1, Plates 1, 2, 15, 18). The shells are attached in such a way as to resemble a mouth; a double row meets in the middle forcing the free ends to splay outwards (Plate 1). Vakutans call the placement of these shells the 'mouth of the canoe' and to make it more authentic they paint the convergence of the shells in the middle red, saying, 'it chews betelnut'. This creates a striking contrast between the colours white and red, and is evocative of the social practice of chewing betelnut in company. Love and beauty magic are often spoken into betelnut, a practice not lost in the symbolism of painting the shell 'mouths' red. The significance of the 'reddened mouth' of the canoe is further related to its role in the process of attracting and seducing kula partners. The mouth and teeth are used metaphorically to imply success; the mouth speaks eloquently as well as making magical utterances into betelnut, while teeth 'bite' or secure the shell valuables.

Soon the completed canoe is ready for its maiden kula voyage. Prior to this, however, the new *masawa* must have its public debut. When the construction and decoration have been completed the crew 'break' the wall previously hiding the *masawa* from public gaze. Once it comes into the public eye it must demonstrate its speed and strength against other *masawa*. A race (*tasasoria*) is called. One wise man, famed for his knowledge of 'tradition', exclaimed, 'We will see its strength, we will see its penis' ('*Batagisesa la peuri, batagisesa wila*'; Ruguna, Kuweiwa hamlet, Vakuta village).

The race is conducted by means of paddling rather than sailing (cf. Malinowski 1922: 148, where he describes the race). Malinowski claimed that the *tasasoria* was not a competitive race on Kiriwina Island, arguing that the chief's canoe would always be allowed to win. For Vakutans, however, it is a competitive race. Each crew is eager to demonstrate the superior quality of their *masawa* and, by implication, of their own strength and efficiency at manoeuvring the canoe through water. Winning the race, however, is a mixed blessing. Following their success in the water, the winners receive an unwelcome visit in the night. Villagers go to the successful crew's houses and take away anything that is removable (*bikwaiyasi*; Chapter 1).

Departure of a Kula Expedition

Prior to the departure of a fleet, each owner (*toliwaga*) of a *masawa* makes an offering (*kalavausi*) to male ancestors (*baloma*) of the *dala*. This offering consists of betelnut, bananas, and coconut. The aim is to entreat the *baloma* to remain at home rather than accompany the crew on the expedition. The presence of *baloma* on the *masawa* is thought to adversely affect the canoe's ability to manoeuvre rough open seas. *Baloma* reside underground while waiting to be reborn. Their subterranean abode connects them to the heaviness of land where they are immobile, in stasis between death and rebirth. It is interesting that root crops are not part of the offerings made to *baloma* on this occasion, only the produce that ripens above the ground, in the tops of trees, is considered appropriate. A pattern of oppositions is beginning to emerge, highlighting key relationships in a Vakutan universe:

female	male
earth	sky
root crop	tree crop
anchoring	mobile
heavy	light
corporate	individual
regeneration (*baloma*)	immortality (kula)

While many of these oppositions have already been suggested in various contexts, their significance in relation to providing some framework with which to make sense of the designs carved on kula canoes needs further exploration. To accomplish this we must return to the fleet as it sets sail in the direction of its kula partners.

For kula voyagers the sea poses many threats to the success of a kula expedition. Of particular note are the moving stones – *vineylida* in the language of the Trobriand Islands and *nuakekepaki* for those in the southern D'Entrecasteaux archipelago (Malinowski 1922: 235; Roheim 1948: 286). Sharks, together with other malevolent creatures of the sea, are also considered potentially threatening to the crew (Malinowski 1922: 244–245; Roheim 1948: 287). Sources of fear from above are primarily formulated in the agency of flying witches, but a black cloud, *sine matanoginogi*, also heralds certain disaster (Malinowski 1922: 235; Roheim 1948: 286). Flying witches, however, are the most dangerous because, once aroused, they influence all the other dangers of the sea, enlisting their evil to thwart the intentions of the crew.

Sine matanoginogi, according to Roheim (1948: 286), is the patron of all witches in Normanby belief. Indeed, the noun *sine* refers to a woman from a specific place (*sine* Dobu, *sine* Duau, etc.). In many of the D'Entrecasteaux languages *sine* also occurs as part of the adjectives denoting feminine beauty or otherwise (*sinebwoina*, for example, means a beautiful woman, while *sinegeyogeyoi* refers to an ugly one in Dobuan). The moving stones are likewise associated with females and feminine qualities of weight and anchoring. Malinowski notes the connection of *vineylida* with women through an analysis of the word: '*vine* – female, *lida* – coral stone' (1922: 235). But the very mobility of these stones, like that of flying witches, represents danger to men.

Women on Vakuta have symbolic association with stones.[8] Stones symbolise fertility and the perpetual reproduction of the sub-clan. The prime repository for this association is the hearthstone. This is a woman's most important possession, given to a woman by her husband's mother a year or so after marriage (see also Weiner 1977: 184). It symbolises the nurturing role of a woman and, according to Vakutans, serves to anchor her in marriage. The giving of a hearthstone to a woman by her husband's mother signifies a transfer of the latter's role as nurturer of her son (a member of her *dala*) to another woman (son's wife). Following marriage, a woman leaves behind the relative mobility of a single woman and begins to reproduce and nurture new members to her sub-clan. This again is symbolised by the hearthstone, suggesting a woman's anchoring in marriage; a condition necessary to the viability of conception and pregnancy. Another example of stones used as anchoring devices are *binabina*. These are basaltic stones imported from the D'Entrecasteaux. They are used in yam houses and in gardens to 'anchor' or weigh down the yam crops. In this sense the stones are thought to hold down and make 'heavy' fertility. If fertility were to lighten and become buoyant, Vakutans fear that it would dissipate.[9]

The *vineylida* stones are not feared by Vakutans so much for their habit of jumping out of the sea and holding fast to a canoe, although this poses an obvious threat on the open seas. This characteristic, however, is merely a manifestation of a greater fear. The anxiety caused by these 'moving stones' stems from their very mobility. Unlike normal stones, mobile ones demonstrate unexpected and unpredictable behaviour. Similarly, women who habitually take to the night skies and fly are feared because they are detached from land. They 'shed' their weight as they do their social obligations and civilised behaviour, becoming light and able to fly. It is not just the threat these women pose to men's participation in kula and their potential loss of life, although these, too, are of major concern, but more the unpredictable and out-of-control nature of this reversal that is disturbing and the basis of fear. Both *vineylida* and flying witches represent a collapse of the established order. Stones that are characterised by their weight and ability to anchor become dangerous when weightless and mobile. Some say that *vineylida* are thought to be inhabited by flying witches (cf. Malinowski 1922: 235; Roheim 1948: 287). The ideal characterisation of women can be contrasted to its antithesis, as represented by flying witches, in the following set of oppositions:

women	*mulukwausi*
hearthstones	*vineylida*
anchored	mobile
predictable	unpredictable
giver of life	destroyer of life

Apart from the external dangers that lurk on the open seas, men also carry with them the seeds of their own destruction. These malignant forces are harboured by various parts of the canoe and the 'animals' carved on the prow and splashboards. Recall from Chapters 5 and 7 that certain 'animals' are magically restrained from feasting upon the human crew. Should the human crew endanger the canoe the restraint on the *tokwalu* and *boildoka* lifts and they order the rest of the 'animals' to turn on the human crew and feast. Hence, the threat of being eaten comes not only from flying witches and jumping stones, but also from the very vehicle upon which they sail.

In the face of these inherent dangers, however, men continue their quest for shell valuables, embarking upon their voyages armed with magic to help them along their course. Shortly after launching, the winds are called to fill the sails and thus speed the fleet towards its destination. It is desirable for the canoe to take on the characteristic of the butterfly, effortlessly speeding ahead over the tops of waves. There are many magical spells documented by Malinowski (1922) that engender the canoe with qualities of lightness and flight epitomised by the butterfly. Examples of these are found in the '*kaygagabile* spell', where the incantation runs:

I lash you, O tree; the tree flies; the tree becomes like a breath of wind; the tree becomes like a butterfly. (1922: 130)

And in the '*ligogu* spell':

I shall make thee fly, O canoe. I shall make thee jump! We shall fly like butterflies, like wind; we shall disappear in mist, we shall vanish. (1922: 132)

Finally, the dangers of the open sea are left behind as the fleet prepares to land the canoes upon the beach of their hosts. Conch shells are blown announcing the imminent arrival of the Vakutan kula fleet. Before landing, however, each *masawa* is turned so that the *dogina buribwari* 'sees' land first and is 'seen' first by the hosts. The *dogina* end of the *masawa* is the first to 'pierce' the land as it is thrust onto the beach of the host community. Thus the Vakutans arrive.

The landing of the *dogina* end is significant. The *dogina* symbolises aspects of masculine ideology. It represents a behavioural ideal that Vakutan men seek to emulate. Conversely, the *uuna* end of the *masawa* represents feminine characteristics. The *uuna* never forgets its roots, its origins. Upon landing on a foreign beach, it gazes back to its land of origin where it was once anchored. However, the *dogina* is anxiously looking ahead in search of adventure and fame. From the time the tree is cut and removed from the forest the *dogina* receives primary attention, with a focus on behavioural attributes concerning mobility. The *uuna* end is of secondary importance. It represents immobility, retaining associations with women and thus conceptualised as anchored. In turning the canoe so that the *dogina* end beaches first (if the *uuna* end was forced, by the direction of the wind, to lead the way), the hosts are presented with symbols representing Vakutan men's assured powers of mobility, seduction and success. It is with these qualities that they 'strike' the land of their hosts.

Munn describes a somewhat different gender scheme for Gawan kula canoes. Initially, while still anchored to the ground and undergoing transformation, a Gawan canoe carries female associations. A canoe's feminine attributes are gradually shed as it moves from 'static' to 'mobile', or from female associations to male associations in its transformation into a mobile, detachable Gawan construction (1977, 1986; see also Damon 1998). Vakutan canoes, on the other hand, continuously embody both male and female associations. Indeed, Vakutan's conceptualisation of a tree incorporates both genders. Although a tree, as an anchored natural object, can be transformed into a canoe, a mobile cultural artefact, it cannot be disassociated from its past. The relationship between the two ends, however, is changed in the transformation. While the tree is anchored to land it is the *uuna*, or female part that is the most important. It is the *uuna* that not only nurtures the tree as a whole, but also anchors it to its place. It is the determining condition of the tree. When the tree has been cut down and transformed into a canoe the *dogina* becomes the more important part. It receives ritual and symbolic attention and is charged with ensuring the success of the canoe in its role as a vehicle to transport men across dangerous spaces. It is also partly responsible for the success of men in attracting the kula shells.

The association of the *dogina* end of the *masawa* with the prominent *buribwari*, and the magical bundle of *kaimwasila* under its 'nose', is also worth remembering. The *buribwari* represents basic male ideals, reinforcing male associations with the *dogina*. *Buribwari* are seen to sit at the tops of trees (*dogina*) watching for their prey, and from there they strike. This same image bears a direct relationship to the goal of doing kula. A man who possesses very strong *kaimwasila* magic is able to attract and acquire all the highly ranked shell valuables in the same way that the *buribwari* 'attracts' (through embodied *mwasila* magic) and catches his prey.

Before the crew move into their hosts' villages and commence the business of kula, preparations of beautification are undertaken on the beach (see also Malinowski 1922: 334–349). Betelnut, tobacco and other small gifts are charmed to influence the minds of the partners. The hosts' wives must likewise be influenced so that they do not place adverse pressure on their husbands to give the shells to their own kinsmen in a network of affinal exchange obligations. The preparations taking place on the beach prior to entering the villages closely resemble the preparations made by men for festive occasions when their full beauty is 'worn on the skin' so as to attract the available women. The magic of beautification for kula (*mwasila*) is the same used in love magic.[10] In the preparations on the beach, each individual is trying to make himself more beautiful and attractive than his companions. He wants to be the chosen partner who attracts all the shells. As backup, an individual might use *kaimwasila* magic on specific objects intended as gifts to potential partners, or on articles of personal adornment to be worn so as to 'turn' the mind of the hosts. When each man has made himself beautiful and ready to seduce his partners the party heads for the villages where their 'prey' awaits them.

In the event of a maiden voyage for one of the *masawa*, its crew make a ceremonial advance into the villages.[11] The advance is overtly aggressive and features as its principal symbol the pole used to punt the *masawa* in shallow water. A pandanus streamer (*bisila*) is attached to the end. The name of the pole in this context is *kaibisila*, and the advance itself is referred to as *bibisilasi* ('they will engage in *bisila* display').[12] The advance is distinctive as members of the crew aggressively run at partners' houses shouting: 'Get ready your pigs, kill them and we will eat. Get ready your yams and long yams, throw them to us. Get ready your armshells and give them to us. This is your *bisila*.' A 'spear' is thrust into the sides of a house with the pandanus leaves (*bisila*) left to flutter outside. This marks the house and reminds its occupants of their obligation to the new canoe and its crew.[13]

The *bisila* symbolises speed and mobility. A charmed *bisila* is tied to the top of the mast while others are attached along the boom of the *masawa*. Malinowski records a spell chanted over *bisila* invoking qualities of speed, the strength to break through physical obstacles and flight. By way of comment he writes:

> There is a definite association in the minds of the natives between the pandanus streamers and the speed of the canoe. The decorative effect of the floating strips of pale, glittering, yellow is indeed wonderful, when the speed of the canoe makes them flutter in the wind. Like small banners of some stiff, golden fabric they envelope the sail and rigging with light, colour and movement.
>
> The pandanus streamer, and especially their trembling, are a definite characteristic of Trobriand culture. In some of their dances, the natives use long, bleached ribbons of pandanus while they dance. To do this well is one of the main achievements of a brilliant artist. On many festive occasions the *bisila* are tied to houses on poles for decoration. They are thrust into armlets and belts as personal ornaments. The *vaygu'a* (valuables) when prepared for the kula, are decorated with strips of *bisila*. In the kula a chief will send to some distant partner a *bisila* streamer over which a special spell has been recited, and this will make the partner eager to bestow valuables on the sender. (1922: 216–217)

The *bisila* also recalls the flying canoe of the Kudayuri myth in the Wayugo spell (Malinowski 1922: 137–138) and refers to flying witches: 'The flying witches are supposed to use pandanus streamers in order to acquire speed and levitation in their nightly flights through the air' (Malinowski 1922: 217).

The *bisila* ceremony on a kula expedition further reinforces the image of male aggression against other communities, asserting the superiority of one group over another. Both Vakutans and Kitavans told me that *bisila* recalls the threat of war that existed between communities in the past and the role that kula played in smoothing over latent hostility. Far from being ignorant of the functional implications of kula, Vakutan men themselves brought this aspect of kula to my attention (cf. Malinowski 1922: 83; see also Brookfield and Hart 1971; Egloff 1978; Irwin 1983; Macintyre 1983c; Uberoi 1962). The spears thrust through the walls of partners' houses and the war chants of the crew, as they move from village to village, evoke the memory of a time when war was a real threat.

Finally, the *bisila* ceremony represents male sexual vigour. Men leave their own homes, detaching themselves from the heaviness that would anchor them to their land, and sail across the open sea acquiring qualities of mobility and lightness. Arriving on the island threshold of their kula partners, they 'pierce' the beaches with the *dogina tabuya*, laden with its male symbolism and the magical powers of attraction and seduction. Their partners, meanwhile, remain attached to the land with their womenfolk, helpless to withstand the alluring powers of their visitors. It is indicative that these men do not go to the beaches to welcome their overseas visitors. Instead they remain in the villages and gardens, sending young men and women to take food and refreshment to the voyagers. Significantly, before going to the villages to seek out their partners, the kula crew make themselves beautiful and anoint their skins with oils and perfumes charmed to seduce those who await them in the villages. Accordingly, the male hosts are sitting by the hearths with their wives while the visitors embody ideal qualities of mobility and sexual persuasiveness. The goal of the crew is to enter the villages so as to attract and seduce partners. Gifts are charmed and given to partners in the same way that men charm and present women with gifts in attempts to solicit a night of sexual dalliance. A woman, although empowered with a good deal of choice over which admirer to favour, is nevertheless thought to be a passive recipient of solicitations emboldened by the use of magic. Similarly, the hosts, for their part, have to be wooed and cajoled into giving up the valuables in their possession. It is perhaps not surprising that during kula, unmarried women of the hosts' villages enter into sexual relationships with the visitors. Malinowski writes: 'It was considered right, and sanctioned by custom, that the local girls should sleep with the visitors' (1932: 220).

Viewed from a host's perspective, when a man receives his partner from overseas he is usually entrenched within his house alongside his wife. Together they entertain their overseas visitors. As she is engaged in preparing food, her husband enters into small talk with his partner. In the context of kula, this juxtaposition suggests that the role of the host is that of a 'female' who, while granted the final decision, waits to be solicited and finally seduced into giving up the shell valuables. This same representation of visitor as 'male' and host as 'female' is the subject of a much-loved legend, Imdeduya. The hero, Yolina, travels from the Dobuan area by canoe in search of a beautiful girl, Imdeduya, whose fame has spread throughout the islands. He makes stops at each island and village en route. In each one he is invited to come ashore to enjoy the sexual favours of an important man's daughter. He always refuses, however, instead giving gifts and then sailing on singing a chorus:

> Imdeduyo, Imdeduyo
> Imdeduyo, Imdeduye make a place for me,
> I will lie down.
> I am Yolino
> Tossed by the waves.
> My body is tired, but
> I will go every day
> I will go every night
> Imdeduyo, Imdeduye.[14]

Yolina finally arrives at his destination, Muyuw, where Imdeduya, who has dreamt of him, waits. They marry and he sets up house in his wife's father's village.

Yolina is given gardens so that he can provide for Imdeduya and their son. One day, while Yolina is out fishing, Imdeduya makes her way to the garden and there commits adultery with a former lover. Her son witnesses the incident and tells his father who packs his belongings and, together with his son, pushes the canoe out to sea. Imdeduya entreats them to return but Yolina is so resentful he refuses to do so. To show his anger and disappointment he breaks their son's neck on the side of the canoe and tosses the body into the sea. Yolina sails back home to the D'Entrecasteaux.

In this legend the symbolic relationship between visitor and visited is clearly set out. Yolina, a male imbued with the power of mobility, sets sail across the seas in response to the fame of a beautiful woman. He detaches himself from his land and journeys until he reaches the land of Imdeduya. The strength of Yolina's *kaimwasila* magic, apparent by Imdeduya's knowledge of his imminent arrival, 'turns' Imdeduya's mind towards him and secures her for himself. Upon landing, Yolina gives her parents all of the valuables in his canoe. Thus wooed, Imdeduya is his. But, as she is so beautiful and desired by others, she succumbs either to their love magic or her own, inherently fickle nature, in the same way that kula partners are apt to turn their favours to others. She momentarily surrenders to another partner's solicitation. Yolina's reaction is to break all ties with her, tossing the broken progeny of their relationship into the sea.

Although the plot is simply that of a love story and the journey to find a beautiful woman, the parallel between success in attracting women and success in kula is potent. This theme is further exemplified by another myth about a man named Tokosikuna who was so ugly that he was unable to marry because of his inability to attract women. Tokosikuna, however, journeys far away in search of a flute. Finding the flute, he returns with it and a particularly potent magic that enables him to change his appearance *(mwasila)* so that he becomes a beautiful young man when he so desires. With these advantages he succeeded in attracting all the women and kula shell valuables to himself, raising the rancour of his fellow travellers.[15] Again, there is an obvious correlation between success with women, kula partners and kula shell valuables. In the jealous attempts of Tokosikuna's comrades to rid themselves of this enviable male, the men of his village organised a kula expedition, giving Tokosikuna a boat with a hole in it. However, not only did Tokosikuna succeed in sailing from island to island in a defective canoe, he also managed to get to their destinations first and thus acquire all the kula shell valuables!

Further indicators suggesting the association of male hosts with feminine characteristics are found in several Kitavan spells which, according to Scoditti, belong to fragments of a *mwasila* magic associated with Monikiniki. Of particular note is a translation of the fragment given to Scoditti by Togenuwa of Okabulula village in 1974:

O men who are desired with corollas of flowers gently recumbent!
O men who are desired, with corollas of flowers recumbent!
With your faces painted black with black faces
With the pretty basket of woven leaves I shall tremble in excitement
I shall stimulate myself, the two of us will stimulate each other and,
entwined, will be a single body
I don't hear the man with the turgid red lips
I don't hear the men who are desired!
I hear monikiniki
the sweet memory of the mountain
the mountain of fire
my mountain
the mountain that trembles
the mountain that flies! (1980: 100–101)

In Scoditti's rather free translation of a Kitavan spell there are obvious references to sexual embraces between the kula partners. The speaker describes how he is blinded by his partner's beauty and unable to 'see' the faces of other potential partners (owing to their *kaributu* and *mwasila* magic).

In the entire process of preparing oneself, charming solicitory gifts, going to the villages where partners await and then, in the verbal discourse peculiar to kula, seducing one's partners into giving up their possessions, there are parallels of men's behaviour when wooing and seducing women. In kula, however, the actors are all male. Their roles alternate according to which group of men, at any given time, are in possession of the shell valuables and which group sets sail for the purpose of attracting and seducing them.

The activities leading up to the transference of shell valuables are not the only ones laden with meaning. The transactions themselves are also symbolic. Until the point when the visitors seek out their partners, the kula men revel in their personal beauty as well as powers of attraction and seduction. Masculine splendour is reinforced and activities demonstrating the ideology of male behaviour are the prime focus. When finally in face-to-face dialogue with their partners, however, Vakutans are forced to recognise their vulnerability. The seduction of kula partners, and women for that matter, is not so easily achieved as the ideal suggests. It takes more than external splendour *(mwasila)* and internal powers *(kaimwasila)* to persuade a partner to hand over that which is desired. If a man's initial impact upon his partner does not succeed in securing what the spells claim, the visitor must fall back upon his oratorical abilities in an effort to bring about the desired outcome.

The verbal exchange between partners can go through several stages before a valuable is transferred, each stage becoming less amiable and more insistent. The first stage begins with the initial encounter between partners. The visitor may merely walk by his partner's house when the latter throws the valuable at his feet. Although an expected reaction to his personal beauty, according to myth and the content of the spells, this immediate and public transferral of a valuable precludes much of the challenge and intrigue normally provided by kula solicitations. Intrigue is much preferred by an experienced kula man as it allows him the challenge of 'hard' kula. A non-compliant host provides the opportunity to demonstrate a kula man's skills in the art of persuasive argument peculiar to kula, as well as furnishes evidence of the ultimate power of his magic. In the event that there is an immediate transference of a kula shell valuable, the recipient has only the effectiveness of his beauty magic to brag about around the evening fire with his companions. Far better for a man's social and political reputation are elaborate stories about the hardness of a partner who finally succumbs, being unable to resist his persuasive skills of argument and *kaimwasila* magic. 'Hard' kula requires far more skills than the ability to enhance one's physical beauty.

The verbal discourse between partners may consist only of the pleasantries shared between two friends meeting after a time of separation. Following the convivial consumption of betelnut and tobacco, the shells are unceremoniously shown and handed over. However, on other occasions this small talk may not 'soften' a partner, who might even deny that he has any 'kula' for his guest. At this stage the visitor might accuse his partner of evasion and demand to see the valuables. The host may only have been prevaricating and may now bring the shells out for his guest to admire. Discussion of past and future routes (*keda*, see Campbell 1983a) is an important part of the transaction. If a transaction does not occur at this stage, however, the guest is in for hard bargaining. The host may begin delaying tactics by commencing a meal with his guest, which the latter declines to eat. The host may go to cut down some young coconuts for his guest to drink. This too is refused. He may go to get some betelnut, or to borrow tobacco, all of which are refused as a method of eliciting sympathy from the host and his family in an effort to encourage the eventual surrender of the valuables. A verbal strategy used by the guest when negotiations become difficult is to boast of planned routes for the shells and the successful acquisition of other desired shells. In this way a man can excite the desire of his 'hard' partner by reciting the names of various famous shells that are in the hands of partners on the other side. This may or may not be the truth, and one's partner will be aware of possible deceit. Nevertheless, this method does sometimes prove successful in loosening a 'tight' hold over desirable shells.

After some time, and even days of this kind of behaviour, a man may resort to verbal abuse as a further strategy to acquire the shell. At the commencement of this stage the guest accuses his host partner of lying, stealing and upsetting everyone's kula. Finally, a threat is made implying that if the host does not give up the shell on this occasion, he will end up attending exclusively to his garden because no one will engage in kula with an unfair and 'hard' partner. The guest threatens to make his host's 'hardness' known to others.

The ultimate defeat occurs when on another morning of negotiations the host does not even show up to receive his guest, preferring instead to remain in his gardens or to take up temporary residence elsewhere while his guest returns day after day to meet with him. This represents an insult for which there is no immediate redress. The guest in this case never gets a chance to perform his skills at 'seducing' a partner and thus is not even able to boast of his efforts. The partnership inevitably is terminated, the host changing the route of the shell while the guest seeks revenge by accomplishing the acquisition of a shell intended for the former partner's kula, or by sorcery to bring about the man's death.

The strategies involved in the acquisition of shell valuables resemble more closely the day-to-day struggle of men to achieve success in attaining political, economic, social and sexual status than the latent ideology represented in the symbols, rituals and mythology of kula would suggest. In order to achieve these in his lifetime, a man must know how to manipulate situations to his advantage as they arise and be able to maintain a degree of control so as to remain influential during the perpetual shuffling of personalities in and out of the social limelight. The work involved in the transactions of kula force men to face the real difficulties involved in achieving and maintaining social status and, by extension, their renown. The contrast between the ideology, as it is encoded in the symbolism of kula, and the actual behaviour of the hosts is profound.

When the seduction of a man has been accomplished and the two men enter into an exchange relationship through which shell valuables are passed, Vakutans say that a 'marriage' has been contracted.[16] Although modelled upon a male/female relationship, a kula partnership represents a union between men. Kula facilitates the detachment of men from their roles as sons, sisters' sons, brothers, mothers' brothers and husbands; in other words, relationships that bind men to women. Thus it allows men to form unions directly with other men that are not mediated by women. Further, the inheritance of kula partners is more usually bestowed on a man through the male line rather than through a woman. In demonstrating why he conducted kula with a particular person from Dobu, one kula man told me:

> Anton and I kula together because our fathers kula together. Fathers give all their knowledge of kula to their sons and very little to their sister's sons. It is better for sons of men who were good kula partners to kula together because their knowledge is already worked out between them. (Kunabu, Kuweiwa hamlet, Vakuta)

The aim of a kula 'marriage' is not only to initiate relationships between men where women have no part, but also to reproduce male wealth. Further, the wealth that cements a kula 'marriage' is notionally the means by which men achieve immortality for their names. Thus, through the combined efforts of men, their personal status and immortality can be accomplished.

The analogy of marriage used to illustrate the kind of relationship entered into by kula men is also extended to the shell valuables. When a 'marriage' between two men has been accomplished a shell is transferred and sent through a set of partners to 'attract' and 'seduce' another shell. If the initial shell is famous, a specific companion shell is identified and all efforts are made to secure it. If the initial shell is not so famous it is simply released to attract any unnamed shell of equal or better quality. When the two 'meet' – that is, when one is successfully 'seduced' and becomes part of the *keda* (route) – a 'marriage' is said to be made (see also Malinowski 1922: 356–357). During the 'marriage' between shells, other shells are attracted to the partnership, thus increasing the flow of shells handled by the men who constitute the *keda*. Shells attracted to the *keda* are sometimes referred to as 'children' produced by the 'marriage' between the 'parent' shells. When a *keda* ends, a 'divorce' is said to have occurred. Thus, the relationship between shells is not only conceptualised as constituting 'marriages', in much the same way as a man and a woman are married, it is also generative in that it reproduces through their 'marriage' other shells which are considered offspring.[17] Whereas women reproduce people who are born into social categories differentiated by women, shells 'reproduce' shells that remain separate, or outside those categories. Indeed, shells are 'born' into categories generated and controlled by men. When temporarily detaching themselves from land and relationships with women, men embark on kula expeditions to seduce other men, forming partnerships with them so as to facilitate a flow of shell valuables that will generate male wealth and ultimately an individual man's renown. At the end of an expedition, however, men must load their canoes, turn sail, and head for home.

The Return Journey

While the final transactions are being brokered the boats are loaded, promises secured, goodbyes made and sails hoisted. Vakutans set sail and begin their journey home, returning to their roles as male actors within a matrilineally defined world. However, the return journey involves the crossing of physically dangerous seas, full of those same malevolent agents that threatened their outward expedition. When safely close to home the men stop on a beach to wash, admire, count and display the valuables acquired during their kula transactions (Plate 2). They catch fish, and a small, exclusive feast is consumed while men laugh and joke about the encounters made when engaged in kula. In this way men enjoy the remaining moments of their heightened identity, symbolised by the *buribwari*. They are men who have swooped and made their 'kill', accomplishing the seduction of their partners and the safe return home with their prizes.

The Art of Kula

Before returning the voyagers to their womenfolk, however, a digression to a tale recounting a return voyage that ended in a shipwreck highlights the relief men experience as they share their last meal and exchange kula stories with their comrades. The text was recorded by Malinowski:

The canoe sails fast; the wind rises; big waves come; the wind booms, du-du-du-du . . . The sails flutter; the *lamina* (outrigger) rises high! All the *usagelu* [crew] crouch on the *lamina*. I speak magic to calm the wind. The big spell of the Sim-sim. They know all about *yavata* (North-Westerley [*sic*] Monsoon wind). They live in the eye of the *yavata*. The wind abates not, not a little bit. It booms, it gains strength, it booms loud du-du-du-du-du. All the *usagelu* are afraid. The *mulukwausi* scream, u-u, u-u, u-u, u; their voices are heard in the wind. With the wind they scream and come flying. The *veva* (sheet rope) is torn from the hands of the *tokabinaveva*. The sail flutters freely in the wind; it is torn away. It flies far into the sea; it falls on the waters. The waves break over the canoe. I stand up. I take the *binabina* stones; I recite the *kayga'u* over them, the *giyotanawa*, the spell of the Underneath. The short spell, the very strong spell. I throw the stones into the deep. They weigh down the sharks, the *vineylida*; they close the Gaping Depth. The fish cannot see us. I stand up, I take my lime pot; I break it. The lime I throw into the wind. It wraps us up in mist. Such a mist that no one can see us. The *mulukwausi* lose sight of us. We hear them shout near by. They shout u-u, u-u, u-u, u. The sharks, the *bonubonu*, the *soka* do not see us; the water is turbid. The canoe is swamped, the water is in it. It drifts heavily, the waves break over us. We break the *vatotuwa* (the sticks joining the float to the platform). The *lamina* (outrigger float) is severed; we jump from the *waga* [canoe]; we catch hold of the *lamina*. On the *lamina* we drift. I utter the great *Faytaria* spell; the big fish *iraviyaka* comes. It lifts us. It takes the *lamina* on its back, and carries us. We drift, we drift, we drift.

We approach a shore; the *iraviyaka* brings us there, the *iraviyaka* puts us on the shallows. I take a stout pole, I lift it off; I speak a spell. The *iraviyaka* turns back to the deep sea.

We are all on the *dayagu* (fringing reef). We stand in water. The water is cold, we all shiver with cold. We do not go ashore. We are afraid of the *mulukwausi*. They follow us ashore. They wait for us ashore. I take a *dakuna* (piece of coral stone), I say a spell over it. I throw the stone on the beach; it makes a big thud; good; the *mulukwausi* are not there. We go ashore. Another time, I throw a stone, we hear nothing: *mulukwausi* are on the beach; they catch it; we hear nothing. We remain on the *dayaga*. I take some (ginger) I spit it at the beach. I throw another stone. The *mulukwausi* do not see it. It falls down; we hear it. We go ashore; we sit on the sand in a row. We sit in one row, one man near another, as on the *lamina* (in the same order as they drifted on the *lamina*). I make a charm over the comb; all the *usagelu* comb their hair; they tease their hair a long time. They are very cold; we do not make the fire. First, I put order on the beach; I take the piece of *leyya*, I spit it over the beach. One time, when the *leyya* is finished, I take some *kasita* leaves (the beach is always full of these) I put them on the shore, I put a stone on them, uttering a spell – afterwards, we make fire.

At day time, we don't go to the village; the *mulukwausi* would follow us. After dark, we go. Like on the *lamina*, we march in the same order, over a *libu* plant. I efface our traces. I put the *libu* on our track; I put the weeds together. I make the path confused. I say a charm to the spider, that he might make a cobweb. I say a charm to the bushhen, that she might turn up the soil.

We go to the village. We enter the village, we pass the main place. No one sees us; we are in mist, we are invisible. We enter the house of my *veyola* (maternal kinsman), he medicates some *leyya*; he spits (magically) on all of us. The *mulukwausi* smell us; they smell the salt water on our skins. They come to the house, the house trembles. A big wind shakes the house, we hear big thuds against the house. The owner of the house medicates the *leyya* and spits over us; they cannot see us. A big fire is made in the house; plenty of smoke fills the house. The *leyya* and the smoke blind their eyes. Five days we sit in smoke, our skin smells of smoke; our hair smells of smoke; the *mulukwausi* cannot smell us. Then I medicate some water and coconut, the *usagelu* wash and anoint themselves. They leave the house, they sit on the *kaukweda* (spot before the house). The owner of the house chases them away. 'Go, go to your wife;' we all go, we return to our houses. (1922: 256–258)

In this tale it is evident that men, faced with the possibility of a shipwreck, do not fear the prospect of drowning as much as death by some other malevolent means. This is in the form of attacks from fish, the 'animals' of the prowboard carvings and flying witches, who follow the 'smell' of sea water on men. Likewise, it is apparent that those individual women who habitually use their powers of flight and take to the night sky are feared not only on the open sea – even on land they are a continuing source of fear. However, there is another, implicit agent of fear. In retelling the story, the commentator describes how the men, having survived the dangers of the sea, have still to hide from the witches who are thought to have followed them onto the beach. We are told that the shipwrecked men cannot go to the village because the witches might follow them there. They wait until the next night to steal their way into the village, preferring to go to a house of a maternal uncle of the *toliwaga* rather than their own house where their wives and mothers wait. It is not until the smell of salt water on their skins has been replaced by the smell of smoke, followed by the smell of ginger and coconut oil, that the men are able to return to their wives. It might seem odd that the men do not go to the safety of their own homes and wives before the smell of the sea is removed from their bodies. In explanation, I suggest that this purposeful delay in returning to their womenfolk is related to a fear that all women are potential witches and therefore collectively dangerous to men. This is especially so when the latter, having been shipwrecked and bathed in the waters representing their mobility and detachment from the anchored soil of their matrilineages, smell of the sea.

I put the possibility that all women are potential witches, if not actual *mulukwausi* to a number of men. Many denied the suggestion outright. A few, however, hesitated before quashing the suggestion. They acknowledged the possibility that all women, if they wanted to, could become flying witches at night, leaving their bodies asleep on the mats next to their husbands. These same men, however, denied that their own wives, sisters, mothers and daughters fell into this category, pointing to 'other' village women who were known to be so inclined, or exhibited characteristics akin to those attributed to flying witches.

Seligman suggested that all women have the potential for becoming malevolent spirits in his description of witches from Bartle Bay on the mainland: 'At Gelaria the "sending" was called *labuni*. *Labuni* exist within women and can be commanded by any woman who has had children' (1910: 640). Closer to the Trobriands, Roheim discusses the witchcraft beliefs of Normanby Islanders: 'The people of Normanby Island say that the sorcerers' way is the fathers' and the witches' way is that of the mothers. It is therefore correct to say in a sense that potentially every man is a [sorcerer] and every woman a [witch]' (1948: 279). Because few women professed to be witches, however, Roheim decided that there were more male sorcerers than there were female witches.

Vakutan men believe that the biggest threat to their success in negotiating the *masawa* across open seas is in the form of flying witches. Not only are these women able to detach themselves from land, thereby defying the anchoring necessary for the perpetuation of the matrilineage, soil fertility and regeneration, but they can also fly. This enables the witch to enter the highly mobile, seductive sphere that men claim as their domain and through which they traverse aboard their specially constructed *masawa*. If all women have the potential to become mobile through flight, they represent a collective threat to the endeavours of men who claim this domain as their pathway to personal fame and immortality. Thus, women as flying witches represent a restraint on men's desires to achieve renown.

The Meaning of Kula

For Vakutans, kula is the arena within which men express their powers of attraction and seduction. While men engage in kula activities primarily for political and economic expediency there is also an emotive undercurrent playing out each individual's dreams of possessing irresistible charms and powers. Kula presents opportunities for men to achieve influence within Vakutan society by encouraging them to acquire shell valuables. Their economic responsibilities towards their female relatives necessitate some level of participation in kula (Campbell 1989). In order to acquire these items men must demonstrate personal abilities that accord with the ideal qualities of male behavioural standards as these are symbolised by the *buribwari* and *boildoka*.

Kula plays a significant role in balancing two perspectives within a Vakutan conceptual framework. It provides a means for conceptually differentiating a man's individual identity, constructed by his own endeavours, from his corporate identity, sociologically defined by women. Whereas individual women, through their reproductive power, are guaranteed immortality for their names by the very principle that accords their gender the fertility needed to reproduce each generation of *dala* blood, men are given no such place in the cosmic order. Instead, men must rely upon their powers of attraction and seduction to achieve personal renown and the immortality of their own names, as these are attached to the 'marriage' of famous shells and their trajectory through time and space. Kula provides the opportunity for each man to establish and build upon his own individual identity separate from the corporate group identity defined by *dala* blood. Thus in kula, men free themselves to compete as individuals in the political and economic spheres of social interaction (see also Uberoi 1962: 146–147, 159; Weiner 1977: 232). The competition is not only between men of different clans, but also between individuals of a single clan and sub-clan. In other words, kula allows individual men to compete with each other regardless of the constraints binding them into social groupings defined by woman.

Through the successful operation of kula relationships each man has the opportunity to achieve immortality through the renown of his name. In this endeavour, however, men often experience failure. This receives symbolic expression in the form of flying witches, in the same way that flying witches in myth took with them the power of flight when they flew from their slain brother on Kitava. Although Vakutan women also believe in and fear the *mulukwausi*, these flying women represent no real threat to the ambitions of women. Indeed, during my fieldwork there were women who used men's fear and anxiety of flying witches as a means of political and economic leverage. Those women who behaved in a dominant and self-assured way inevitably received respect from men in their day-to-day relations. Suspected *mulukwausi* were given a greater degree of attention in issues concerning village matters. Rarely were they refused any of their demands. When I enquired why some men would marry such dangerous women I was told that as long as a *mulukwausi*'s husband behaved according to his wife's wishes, she would offer him protection from other witches. In effect, men would say, 'husbands of *mulukwausi* take the coward's way out by marrying such women'.

Once a man succeeds in seducing a male partner and a formal 'marriage' is contracted between shells, men use a model of reproduction and regeneration to validate their kula partnerships. Men beget 'offspring' in the form of male wealth. This in turn establishes social relationships ('marriages') outside the Vakutan community. One of the purposes of these 'marriages' is to establish the immortality of a man's name. The shell 'offspring' of these 'marriages' is one means by which this is achieved. The model is based upon the ideology of matriliny as it is understood within Vakuta. Through marriage, women's fertility is anchored, thereby enabling women to reproduce offspring who are the regeneration of *dala* blood. A woman's own children immortalise her name as a symbol of *dala* identity. Thus women, through their own reproductive power, are able to achieve immortality for their names and the perpetual reconstitution of *dala*. Men establish an alternative means of immortalising their names by being successful operators of kula shells contracted in 'marriage'. The 'offspring' that these 'marriages' beget circulate throughout the kula communities to immortalise the names of men.

In kula, men are able to accumulate fame through the circulation of their wealth along individually created paths (Campbell 1983a). One of the main forces motivating men to enter the competition is the acquisition of fame and renown abroad, as well as the enhancement that this brings to their position at home (see also Munn 1977: 50, 1983; Damon 1980; Weiner 1983). Even after a man's death, his fame ideally continues to circulate through kula, thus extending his name beyond the duration of his lifetime. Uberoi correctly emphasised in his analysis of the kula that the shell valuables exchanged through kula always passed between different *dala* rather than within them in internal relations. Kula shell valuables are items of male wealth and as such are identified with individual men. They are not used 'as the emblems of a corporate solidarity' (Uberoi 1962: 135; see also Weiner 1983). Whereas land, trees, canoes and other wealth items are passed to brothers or to sister's sons at a man's death, kula shell valuables are usually given to a man's own sons.[18] Kula shell valuables are identified with a man's personal achievements during his lifetime and symbolise these after his death. Finally, the circulation of male wealth establishes social relationships between different communities whereas women are restricted to maintaining the social continuity of Vakutan society. While women actually regenerate society, men act out their own regeneration by invoking their powers of attraction and seduction in the pursuit of kula and the renown it affords.

–9–

Women of the Land, Men of the Sea

The *dogina* end of the *masawa* is also called *buribwari* because this bird is very sharp [*sena kakata*]. It does not fool around and so always gets its fish, never missing. That is why the *buribwari* always lands first in kula, because it will always get all the *vaiguwa* and *mwari*. The Kitavans and Dobuans will see the *buribwari* and throw away their shell valuables, they want the *masawa* to win by getting the most valuables.

Men are *buribwari*, they are like the *dogina* [top] of the tree. Women are like the *uuna* [base] of the tree. If a man wants a woman he walks around because he is like the *dogina*. A woman is like the *uuna*, she sits on the ground and peels yams and cooks. A man will see which woman he wants while walking around and he will catch her, like the *buribwari* catches his fish.

The *buribwari* sits at the top of the tree and then falls. He plunges into the water and when he re-emerges he has his fish.[1] He never simply strikes here and there. He always catches his fish and so a man is like the *buribwari* and when he catches the woman he wants, he will hold her.

A woman is *uuna*, like the roots of a tree. She stays in one place and gives birth. While the tree is growing she gives the rules. Once the tree has grown, her sons then rule her, they are *dogina* and she just sits and gives birth and peels and cooks food. The *uuna* of the *masawa* is woman and the *dogina* is man. That is the way [*keda*]. (Youwa, Wakwega hamlet, Vakuta village)

The imagery used by Youwa in this statement succinctly captures some of the dominant themes that are the focus of Vakutan symbolism as it relates to kula. Particularly the recurring theme around the status of the *buribwari* as a dominant male symbol, the relationship between the tree metaphor and the *masawa*, together with the images of success, as these are embodied in the *buribwari* perched on the *dogina* end of the *masawa*. Youwa takes the imagery further, however, and offers insight into the relationship between men and women, as well as how this is reflected in the structure of a tree, transforming in time and space. While it should be noted that these characterisations were given by only one Vakutan man, many of his insights were shared as separate reflections by other Vakutan men, though they were less able to draw the analogy so clearly. Throughout the course of fieldwork many of these relationships were apparent, but it wasn't until Youwa shared this imagery in a conversation we were having that they began to make sense in a holistic way. As I became more versed in the rituals and magic of kula, this metaphor became noticeably prominent when male and female spheres of agency were being referred to, either directly or obliquely. Youwa simply put this into a single, concise statement setting out the 'way things are'. The perspective of men, however, is not necessarily an accurate reflection of how things are in reality. Indeed, real experiences are forever contradicting this ideology. In particular, the experience of difficult kula transactions is not uncommon. Nevertheless, it is worth pursuing the ideological perspective that men harbour because the analogies help to clarify what kula is for Vakutan men and illuminate the symbolic content of the designs carved into the kula boards. In following Youwa's lead then, we will take a closer look at other aspects of Vakutan life in this chapter and explore the wider implications of the tree metaphor.[2] Not only is it a vehicle for the expression of dominant messages related to kula symbolism, it is also a means by which the relationships between men and women find symbolic expression.

The tree/canoe is a composite symbol encoding on the vertical (tree) and horizontal (canoe) planes characteristics differentiating male and female spheres of influence. While anchored to the ground, a tree represents on a vertical plane the spatial distinction between earth and sky. When detached and made into a canoe it represents on a horizontal plane the distinction between land and sea. In the process of making a *masawa*, the tree is transformed from an object of the land to one of the sea. Encoded within these distinctions is a differentiation between men and women.

Women of the Earth, Men of the Sky

In comparing women to the base or foundation of a tree, I suggest that Youwa was giving expression to a collective preference for women to be essentially immobile and anchored, making their sexuality and fertility less threatening and more predictable for men. A prime example of women whose sexuality is aggressively perpetrated against men is found in the image of the *kaytalugi* women (Malinowski 1932: 356–358). These women are said to live on an island not far from the Trobriands. If an unfavourable wind fills the sails of a *masawa*, blowing the helpless crew to the shores of this island, men know their fate is sure death from these sexually insatiable women. Another example of women, free from the social conventions restricting the expression of their sexual appetite, is female *baloma*. These ancestors, while enjoying the period between death and rebirth, sexually assault men when they posthumously arrive in Tuma (Malinowski 1948a: 159). Flying witches, however, pose the greatest threat. They are not restricted to one island nor are they encountered only at death. They are living women from the numerous islands around the Massim. They are men's sisters, mothers, daughters and wives. As well as representing the agency of death, witches are a threat to men in their endeavours to acquire economic and political standing within their island communities. Flying witches thwart men's attempts to achieve inter-island fame in their pursuit of kula. These women defy all attempts to anchor and control their behaviour. In likening women to the *uuna* of a tree, Youwa expressed the need to counter a perceived tendency for women to be mobile, and thus dangerous to men. Like other uncontrolled women, flying witches have an insatiable sexual hunger which extends to the desire to consume human flesh. By invoking an ideal image of the relationship between men and women, there is the hope that women's uncontrolled tendencies can be restrained.

Men characterise themselves as analogous to the tops of trees. These 'touch' or 'hold onto' the sky. Birds, particularly the *buribwari* representing all the attributes dearly desired by men, live in the tops of trees where they achieve ultimate mobility through flight. Essentially, men see themselves as mobile. They are the one's who make solicitous advances to would-be lovers and leave their island home to traverse seas in search of male wealth in the form of shell valuables. They seduce their male partners to acquire these objects of male desire, bring them home as emblems of their persuasive and seductive prowess and, with these, achieve status within their own community. The ability to continue to demonstrate one's success is rewarded by the immortality of their names throughout the kula exchange community. However, in realising these goals men must somehow anchor women to the earth so that they are not a threat to men's mobility.

In myth there are several symbolic associations equating earth and women. In the creation myths typical of the area, brothers and sisters popped out of holes in the ground, the siblings emerging from a single 'hole'. These sites of origin become the property of their descendants. By implication, the 'hole' in the earth is equated to a mother and the place of emergence her birth canal, since siblings, by definition, are born from the same mother. The emergence of a brother/sister sibling set supports the dogma of matriliny and safeguards *dala* claims to land. It is the brother in Vakutan myth who ventures away from the place of origin to make gardens and bring food to his sister while she remains near the emergence site tending to the hearth and preparing food for consumption. The avoidance of all things sexual pertaining to brothers and their sisters has forced the detachment of women from *dala* land. It is the brother who, being mobile, has to go out and seduce another woman, while his anchored sister waits to be seduced by another man. In reality though, men are the ones who are anchored to *dala* land, bringing their wives to live with them. A man's sister becomes detached from *dala* land and goes to live with her husband, her sexuality separated from her brother. The reality is at odds with the ideology.

The birth of Tudava, a Trobriand culture hero, also suggests a symbolic equation between women and earth. In the myth, Tudava's mother, Bolutukwa (also named Mitigis according to Malinowski 1927c, 1932: 155) lay sleeping in a grotto.

Dripping water from a stalactite (*kaibua*) 'pierces her hymen, penetrates the vagina and thus "opens her"' (Malinowski 1932: 359). Tudava emerges from the hole thus 'opened'. It is significant that Bolutukwa was 'lying' on the ground. The water dripping from above eventually pierces Bolutukwa/earth, making a 'hole' from which Tudava was born. In this myth the agency responsible for enabling Tudava's birth comes from above Bolutukwa as she reclines on the earth.

In the origin myth of Vakuta, Togamolu's sister was able to return to her underground domain through the hole from which she and her brother had emerged. Togamolu, on the other hand, once he had emerged, was unable to do this. In this myth brother and sister maintain different connections to the earth; the sister retains her connection while her brother is irrevocably severed from it. It is significant that the means by which Togamolu finally secured his sister above ground was by fishing. He catches his sister and pulls her above ground in much the same way as a *buribwari* snatches his fish from the surface of the water.

In Youwa's statement he likens women to the *uuna* of a tree; 'they sit on the ground'. This is, indeed, what women do. According to Vakutan etiquette, women regularly sit with their buttocks on the ground. It is considered inappropriate for men to sit on the ground. Instead, men have a preference for squatting without touching the soil, or they find some object to sit on. Again, women make physical contact with the earth while men avoid doing so (see also Malinowski 1935 Vol. 1: 101).[3]

Associations symbolising the relationship of women to land and men to sky are likewise found in the context of the garden. Here too, there are several explicit references to women and their fertility. Although gardeners in the latter half of the twentieth century rely more on prayer and solicitous gifts to the Christian God, by way of substantial offerings placed around the church, many were trying to reclaim their past usage of magic as part of an effort to sustain their heritage.[4] In many of the spells uttered by garden magicians there were references to securing the 'fertility' of the soil. Images of female fertility were also used in the text of spells. For example, the garden magician asked the 'belly' of the garden to 'swell as with child' in his spells. The association of the garden with the female body, and, in particular, its nurturing quality, is suggested in the naming of the corners of the garden plots *nunula*: 'its breast' or 'its breast milk' (Malinowski 1935 Vol. 1: 100, Vol. 2: 140). In the collective activity of planting yams, men give expression to their communal labour by engaging in chants (*vinavina*). One of those recorded by Malinowski contains obvious references to female sexuality: 'Boginai . . . is recently deflowered . . . But your vulva, Bomigawaga . . . over there at the corner of the fence, has for long time had a considerable circumference' (1935 Vol. 1: 135–136). While these allusions to the circumference of female genitalia may be no more than what is common ribaldry amongst groups of men in many cultural settings around the world, there is a more serious purpose to these. By way of comment, Malinowski adds: 'The obscene allusions in this spell are connected with the planting; the deeper the soil is broken up at the planting-spot, and the more thoroughly it is worked, the better will grow the [yam]' (1935 Vol. 1: 136). In this sense, men are drawing upon their agency in the preparation of the soil's fertility in the same way they facilitate the fertility of their wives.

Garden soil requires its fertility to be renewed annually so that men can plant their seed yams in the 'belly of the garden' where they will regenerate. Only men plant yams.[5] For this purpose men gather in consecutive gardens to plant the yams as a collective activity. Using long, stout digging sticks men break up the soil, forming small mounds by thrusting their poles deeply into the ground and, in a circular motion, breaking up the clods while thrusting deeper into the mound. The soil is loosened into a fine loam. It is perhaps not surprising that it is during this activity that chants similar to the one recalling Bomigawaga's large orifice are recited. After the soil has been prepared to the right consistency, it is mounded and a seed yam is inserted into the side of the mound.[6]

When the yams have been planted men later gather in the gardens to collectively 'plant' large poles *(kavatam)* for the vines to cling to when growing. With this accomplished, the gardens are festooned with erect poles struck deep into the earth (Plate 16). The community now awaits the rains that 'feed' and nurture the soil as well as the growing yams. Rain, an element from the sky, represents male sexuality and its penetrative role in preparing the fertility of the garden.[7] Men control rain magic. Raindrops strike the earth to penetrate deep into the soil and mould the growing yams in the 'womb' of the garden. Raindrops represent the combined energies of men who labour collectively in the garden and facilitate magic to ensure the growth of the yams. The erect poles can be likened to a corporate penis facilitating the piercing effect of the rain as it penetrates the earth, moulding the growing yams that, when harvested, will nurture the entire community as distributions binding people together, and as cooked food feeding the population.

The connection between rain, 'opening up' a woman and facilitating the necessary conditions for pregnancy is further illustrated by a Trobriand myth describing how 'an ancestress of one of the sub-clans exposed her body to falling rain, and thus mechanically lost her virginity' (Malinowski 1927c: 50–51; see also Barton 1917). Recall, too, the means by which Tudava was conceived; his mother, Bolutukwa, lying on the grotto floor receiving dripping fluid from a stalactite above her. This myth suggests an above/below spatial orientation similar to that of rain and earth. The continuous dripping from above, although not a generative substance, facilitates the conception and birth of the culture hero.

The imagery of 'opening' the soil with a stout digging stick, making the hole large and soft thereby preparing the necessary conditions for soil fertility, the poles permanently thrust into the garden soil, together with the hitting and penetrating fluid of raindrops accords well with Trobriand beliefs concerning the role of the male in preparing the fertility of women. Prior to this, however, men must anchor women's fertility. This they do through marriage.

Unmarried women enjoy considerable freedom in their social lives. Barring intimate relations with male kin, they sleep with many different unmarried men. Generally their lives remain free of the responsibilities that weigh down their married sisters. Unmarried women do not worry unduly about conception despite their freedom to explore many and varied sexual encounters. It is thought that a woman cannot conceive as long as she sleeps with different men. People say that a woman is only in danger of becoming pregnant when she repeatedly sleeps with one man. It is not that people today are ignorant of the fertilising consequences of mixing male and female fluids. It is simply that repeated intercourse with one person tends to result in a pregnancy.[8] When a woman begins to prefer one boy over others and has repeated nights with him, an attachment begins to form tantamount to marriage. This endangers her carefree lifestyle. Once married, a woman is said to become 'heavy'. Marriage anchors her to the responsibilities of an adult woman, including being anchored to one man who prepares her for conception. Thus marriage marks the onset of a woman's fecundity. Hearthstones given at marriage represent the anchoring of a woman's sexuality, together with her responsibilities as an adult.

The Trobriands have become famous in the anthropological literature for a number of cultural attributes. Significant among these is the absence of the male role in fathering offspring. Debates have raged on the extent of Trobriand beliefs regarding 'virgin birth' and the denial of male procreative powers (Austen 1934–35; Leach 1967a, 1967b; Malinowski 1932; Powell 1968; Rentoul 1931, 1932; Scheffler 1973; Spiro 1968, 1972).[9] Instead, a man's role is to 'open up' a woman through repeated intercourse, thereby making it possible for a spirit child to enter and be nourished in her womb (Austen 1934–35: 105; Malinowski 1927c: 31–44, 1932: 154). Once 'opened up', regular intercourse is thought to check a woman's menstrual flow, causing the necessary condition preliminary to pregnancy (Austen 1934–35: 103–105; Powell 1969b: 603). The father's role, following conception, is to nurture the growth of the foetus by continued sexual intercourse. It is this action, together with the accumulation of seminal fluid, that is considered necessary for the growth and formation of the foetus (Austen 1934–35: 112; Malinowski 1932: 176–177; Montague 1971, 1989; Munn 1986; Weiner 1977: 122–123; see also Leach 1967a, 1967b; Rentoul 1931, 1932). While a woman may conceive without the generative aid of a husband, the latter is essential in the process of preparing the passage and forming the foetus.

Moving for the moment away from phenomena located 'above' and their penetration of the earth below, we return to the explicit reference made by Youwa equating the *buribwari* with men. Recall the image of the *buribwari*, sitting high in a tree, suddenly swooping down to make a spectacular dive before sailing high above the surface of the water, a fish firmly secured in his talons. While much has already been said about the relationship between men and *buribwari*, the implicit association between women and fish has yet to be explored.

Fish are symbolically connected to women and used in many contexts to represent women's sexuality and fertility. Fish are not so much symbols of women as they are symbols of the agents of female fertility. One of the preparatory activities described by Malinowski for the imbuing of fertility into the soils of new gardens requires men ritually to offer fish to the garden magician (1935 Vol. 1: 93–96). The magician makes a selection of the offering and places this on the hearthstones in his house. In catching fish and offering these to the garden magician, men are collectively engaged in the weighing down, or anchoring of the garden's fertility in the same way they weigh down and anchor their wives in marriage. The garden magician places a selection of fish on hearthstones prior to entering the gardens and performing magic to weigh down the soil's fertility. The combination of hearthstone and fish in these inaugural rites links the weighing of women's fertility with that of the garden.

Fish are used in other contexts too, particularly when the community needs to re-establish order. Immediately following a death, men who are not among the deceased's clansmen go fishing. The catch is taken to the senior man of the deceased's *dala* who distributes the fish amongst his clansmen. The objective is to free the entire village from restrictions placed on normal village activities incurred immediately after a death (Campbell 1989). Symbolically, the harvested fish can be seen as representing an assurance to the deceased's clan of its continued fertility. This assurance comes from the labour of those very men responsible for preparing the deceased's clanswomen's fertility.

The myth describing the origins of love magic, recorded by Malinowski, also draws an association between human fertility and fish (1932: 454–474). In this myth a brother and sister succumb to incest and then death having been enchanted by the power of love magic.[10] A man from Iwa Island dreams of the incident and travels to Kitava to find the magic. He returns to Iwa and bestows the magic to the youth of Iwa with the following words:

> The water of this magic is Bokaraywata . . . the youth of our village only should come and bathe in it. But a fish caught in these waters is taboo to them . . . When such a fish is caught in the nets, they should cut off its tail, then the old people might eat it . . .
>
> When they come and bathe in the Bokaraywata and then return to the beach, they make a hole in the sand and say some magic. Later on in their sleep they dream of the fish. They dream that the fish spring (out of the sea) and come into that pool. Nose to nose the fish swim. If there is only one fish they would throw it out into the sea. When there are two, one female, one male, the youth would wash in this water. Going to the village, he would get hold of a woman and sleep with her. He would go on sleeping with her and make arrangements with her family so that they might marry . . . (1932: 458)

Although most of this text is self-explanatory, of particular interest are the two separate directives with respect to the handling of any fish found in the pool. The prohibition on eating fish found in the pool safeguards young people's sexual freedom from being anchored too soon. The myth clearly makes an association between physical contact with fish and marriage. It is suggested that bathing in the water when two fish swim 'nose to nose' has the effect of anointing one's skin with their sexuality. This is thought to empower a man with the magic of attraction so that he cannot fail to seduce a woman, 'capture' her and make her his wife, thereby anchoring her sexuality and preparing her for reproduction.

Perhaps the most direct association between fish and fertility is found in conception beliefs. According to the Trobriand doctrine concerning conception, it is said that fertilisation usually takes place in the shallow waters of the surrounding reefs:

> To receive the *waiwaia* [spirit child] whilst in the water seems to be the most usual way of becoming pregnant. Often whilst bathing a woman will feel that something has touched her, or even hurt her. She will say, 'A fish has bitten me.' In fact, it was the *waiwaia* entering or being inserted into her. (Malinowski 1948a: 218)

It is not that fish are the agents by which women are impregnated; indeed, this is decidedly not the case. Rather, fish represent fertility and are used metaphorically to refer to it. Thus, when a woman exclaims that 'a fish has bitten her' she is alluding to the triggering of her fertility; she has conceived and the reincarnating *baloma*, in its foetal phase, is being nurtured internally.

It makes good sense that in a matrilineal society symbols associating women with forces restricting mobility also reflect the desire to control them. In a society where young women are free to explore their sexuality, and move with few restrictions between sexual partners, it is important at a certain point to rein in and curtail them so as to enable *dala* reproduction. While 'mobile', women's fertility is unanchored; women cannot become pregnant, *baloma* cannot be reincarnated and *dala* cannot be regenerated. Marriage is the key anchoring force that tames a woman's sexuality and anchors her fertility. This finds symbolic representation in various contexts associating women with the earth, weight, heaviness, immobility and anchoring. These conditions are carried over to a third domain where women's access should be restricted.

Women of the Land, Men of the Sea

In the foregoing, several examples have illustrated the extent to which men's ideological characterisation of their relationship to women has found symbolic representation in diverse contexts. This is most explicitly developed in the imagery contrasting immobility with mobility. Returning to the analogy of the tree, this contrast is played out in the transformation of the tree into a canoe. The canoe remains conceptually identified with the tree that it once was by retaining terms recalling its vertical axis and the perception that the *uuna* end looks home while the *dogina* looks away. The *uuna* end retains its association with the Vakutan earth and women, while the *dogina* end represents the ability of Vakutan men to become detached from Vakutan earth/women and achieve mobility. Youwa explicitly characterises the *dogina*'s association with the *buribwari* and man. While perched on the *dogina* of a tree, this master of embodied knowledge and magic attracts and then acquires its prey, symbolising men's desire to capture all the kula shell valuables.

The prerogative of men to embark on overseas voyages and visit distant islands in search of shell valuables is the ultimate symbolic representation of their ability to detach themselves from their own island. This detachment from Vakuta is not only a physical one but also represents a symbolic detachment from the group identity that retains their membership within a *dala*. In Trobriand social organisation women are the focal points of diverse social units constituting *dala* and clan identity. In this context, women are paramount, despite men's role in women's fertility. Clearly this model reflects a symbolic as well as practical complementarity between men and women, highlighting the essential connection between them as generators of society. However, the names of women are structurally immortalised in time while men's are not. In the context of beliefs relating to the continuing cycle of life, women are essential to the reincarnation of ancestors. As Weiner has powerfully argued:

> Trobriand women control immortality through the recapitulation of *dala* identity. Thus women's power over cosmic (ahistorical) time is singularly within their own domain. Men cannot enter into the ahistorical domain of women, in which the continuity of *dala* identity is recapitulated through unmarked time; nor can men reclaim *dala* names lent to others; nor can men alone secure the indigenous reconstitution of *dala* hamlet and garden lands. From this view, Trobriand women participate on both the social and cosmic planes, but men are limited to the social. Even on the social plane, women are an integral part of control and power. Men can only control objects and persons which remain totally within a generational perspective of social time and space. Men, therefore, remain destined to seek their measure of immortality through perpetuating individual (as opposed to *dala*) identity. (1977: 231–232)

While the emphasis on women's power is perhaps to forcefully put by Weiner, she makes the important observation that within the ideological context sustaining matriliny at least, men have a limited role in maintaining it. There is no organisational means by which a man's claim to immortality is guaranteed within the structural framework supporting matriliny. The memory of a man's name is not essential to future generations. Men are simply reincarnated. In contrast, women's names are remembered, their immortality ensured because it is through them that *dala* continuity is achieved.[11] This lack of significance, at the level of ideology, receives support in the symbolism of kula.

At birth children are given at least two names: one by the mother, the other by the father. The name given to a child by its father is not necessarily a name from the father's *dala*, while the name given by a mother is always a name that belongs to the child's *dala* (see also Weiner 1977: 126). On Vakuta, the father's name is used more regularly than the mother's. The name given by the mother, however, is inalienable and considered the formal name of a *dala* member. The different-iation of the two names and their application in different social contexts supports the contrast between women's perpetuation of group continuity and men's devel-opment of an individual identity. A woman regenerates individuals into a corporate identity by recycling the dala's ancestors and their names. A father, on the other hand, does not confer to his children a group identity. He is responsible for moulding the reincarnating *baloma*'s features into a distinct individual while the mother is responsible for transferring group identity through blood. The different names represent the complementary contributions made by a child's mother and father to its physical and social identity. The often preferred use of the name given by a father throughout one's life is indicative of an individual's attempt to build upon individual identity and personal renown. This is true of both girls and boys. However, the life path for a girl is to consolidate her individual identity with that of her identity as a *dala* woman whereas a boy's destiny is less secure and certainly not confined to his identity within his *dala*. It is important for men in Vakutan society to have mobility and the means to detach themselves from a context in which women are the most valued members of society according to the principles of Trobriand matriliny. It is the role of women as generators of *dala* identity and the vehicles through which men, in the end, rely for their physical reincarnation that gives women heightened status within a Vakutan ideology. In this context, there is no avenue for realising a man's renown beyond his own lifetime. By transforming a tree into a canoe, however, men are creating a vehicle through which they achieve mobility and upon which they search for those items that enable them to create a different kind of immortality.[12] In kula, men capitalise on their powers of beauty, attraction, persuasiveness and magic to build upon their own name and thus, if successful, achieve fame and renown.

The *dogina* of the tree and canoe represents the mobility of men, their ability to detach themselves from women and thus free themselves from *dala* corporate identity. As mobile agents they are free to build upon personal renown. This achievement is represented by the *buribwari*: '*Manana buribwari naveka, yagala bogwa orakaiwa. Titolela lakarewaga.*' (The *buribwari* is a very big 'animal'. Already its name is above. By itself it makes the rules. (Ruguna, Kuweiwa hamlet, Vakuta village).

The representation of the egret on the other hand, symbolises the continual efforts of men to detach themselves from the land to achieve a measure of detachment and immortality. Recall that the egret, standing in the shallows, is sometimes unsuccessful in catching fish. Periodically he must renew his magic of attraction by returning to the woods (land). Like men, the egret never fully succeeds in absolute detachment from land. Men always have to return home and sublimate their mobile quest for personal renown. It is true that at one level men return home from kula parading their success so as to enhance their status within the community. This is an important function of kula for Vakutans. But status is only temporarily enjoyed and does not circumscribe their immutable identity and obligations to *dala* membership, either as kinsmen or affines. The fact that men never achieve total detachment from group identity is explained by beliefs in extenuating influences that further impede men's achievement of personal renown. These beliefs see women transformed into the highly dangerous witches who have achieved the very powers that men perpetually strive for.

Flying witches are enabled by their means of locomotion to invade the spheres ideally controlled by men. They detach themselves from land and invade the sky over the sea. Access to the skies through flight was lost by men and achieved (or retained) by women in the myth of the flying canoe. As witches, moreover, women are anti-social because they defy the anchoring necessary to perpetuate the principle of matrilineal descent. They represent the ultimate detachment and mobile state desired by men – the antithesis of the ideal condition for women. If women were to become uncontrollable and detached, there would be no regeneration of society, no vehicle through which *baloma* are reincarnated. Accordingly, women's reproductive powers are highly dangerous if not anchored; in the form of flying witches, women's reproductive powers are uncontrolled, their sexuality unfettered to such an extent that they engage in the consumption of human flesh. Flying witches also represent the greatest danger to men because they can, by invading the spheres of men, destroy the process by which men seek their personal immortality and nullify their only avenue for personal renown. It is because of this potential for unanchored and mobile women to threaten men's endeavour that men represent the anchoring of females in the tree metaphor and activate their control of female fertility through marriage.

Setting sail on a kula expedition effectively marks a symbolic detachment of the individual from his social persona, normally embedded in the identity of *dala* membership, clan membership and marital affiliations. When on kula business, a man is symbolically and effectively released from this identity. In kula a man acts as an individual in pursuit of his own personal ambitions. These remain, of course, grounded to the aims and goals valued by the community to which he must, in the end, return. But in kula, he breaks free from the obligations and duties owed by him to his group. For instance, in attempts to attract particular valuables brothers compete with brothers, sister's sons with mother's brothers and fathers with sons; their individual beauty is personified and enhanced. It is personal magic that is jealously guarded *(mwasila* and *kaimwasila).* Uberoi also recognised this tendency from his reading of Malinowski's argonauts:

> An examination of the social situations at these rituals reveals that the rites which punctuate the progress of an overseas expedition serve to mark out the social categories operative at home, within one district, and progressively loosen up their internal solidarity, so that canoe competes with canoe within the same fleet, and one man against another within the same canoe . . . For the *kula* has two prongs: . . . [and it suspends] the political identity between two *fellow* tribesmen. (1962: 146–147)

The pursuit of kula is indeed an occasion on which men are able to detach themselves from the identity given them through their association with women. Kula is a vehicle for the realisation of men's mobility (at sea) in contrast to the immobility of Vakutan women (on land).

The foregoing argument has outlined the boundaries between male and female symbolic spheres and can be illustrated diagrammatically. Figure 9.1 maps out the spatial orientation of men and women according to a male ideology as it is variously represented in the rituals of kula and the representations encoded on the kula carvings. By comparing certain characterisations, we can further contrast these spheres in order to reveal the symbolic associations of male and female realms respectively:

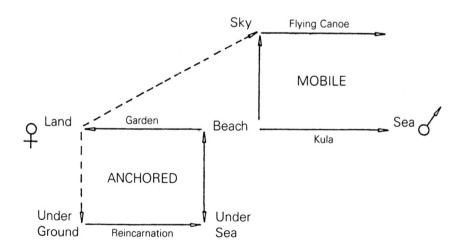

Figure 9.1 Spatial orientation of male and female spheres

Male	Female
Top of tree	Base of tree
Sky	Earth
Sea	Land
Above	Below
Mobile	Anchored
Individual identity	Corporate identity
Infertile	Fertile

Whereas in the domestic sphere a man's identity is rigidly bound to a specific corporate group and is controlled by the regenerative power of women, in kula a man becomes detached from the time he sets sail on a canoe to cross the open seas. In kula a man works for himself, drawing upon all his available resources in an attempt to build upon his own name. A man's individual renown, however, is extremely fragile. Ultimately a man's name is sustained through his manipulation and control of other men, many of whom he has no face-to-face contact with and who are, at the same time, pursuing their own goals and ambitions. The shells that carry a man's name must, if they are to generate his immortality, pass through the hands of other men. At every stage in the circulation of shells the fragility of a man's name is highlighted with the loss of shells that carry it.

In attempting to extricate their personal names from a corporate identity defined by women, men enlist symbols of male success. These symbols, in their various contexts, represent goals men try to achieve so as to succeed in the acquisition of status and renown. Although the symbolism associated with the ritual activities of kula conveys messages concerning these values, it is the canoe, together with its elaborately carved and painted boards, that silently transmits the force of these symbols. The designation of one end as *uuna* and the other as *dogina*, together with several of the design units on the boards *(ginareu, ubwara, kiadada, weku,* for example), recalls the boundaries marking spatial transformations between spheres of female influence to spheres of personal male power. Vakutan concepts of cyclicity and the movement in time from birth to death and thence to rebirth, are incorporated into colour symbolism and the imagery of particular body parts. Further, concepts of success, beauty, flight and knowledge are incorporated into the *kabitam* repertoire to give symbolic emphasis to men's personal endeavours to satisfy individual ambitions. Finally, kula is concerned with the achievement of mobility and the search for personal renown.

Matrilineal values require that women should be heavy and motionless. Male ideology requires that women's fertility is anchored by men. Men, however, are not bound in their regenerative role to stay put; they are merely members of the particular groups defined by women and only responsible for preparing women's fertility. Men symbolise an urge to escape any subversion of their personally created renown via kula. The canoe represents this endeavour on the horizontal plane and is symbolically as well as quite literally the vehicle by which men experience their mobility. Accordingly, while the tree is anchored, matrilineal values prevail. Women 'give the rules'. As the tree grows, men gradually take control and transform the tree into a canoe. This affords men the detachment they require so as to facilitate their mobility. On the sea and in kula the 'rules' of men prevail. Men define their own course, charting the waters towards their own renown. In this realm, corporate group identity is thrown overboard while men pursue the emblems that will carry their personal renown. Corporate group identity, however, in the form of flying witches, pursues and threatens to reclaim the personal renown men attempt to build when detached from Vakuta Island.

In its former state, the canoe represents the mediation between earth and sky. When transformed it represents the mediation between land and sea. The *uuna* end of the tree and canoe represents the essence of women's fertility and matrilineal values linking people into corporate groups, defined by women through a regeneration of time. These represent the anchoring forces of Vakutan society. It is to the land of their birth that men must return from the pursuit of kula. Their corporate group identities, alas, can never be lost or wholly discarded. In kula, however, men search for and augment personal renown. By enlisting symbols that embody powers of attraction, magic and persuasion men seek to enhance their own individual immortality.

Conclusion: A Composite System of Communication

In the preceding discussion, I have tried to establish what meanings are encoded in the graphic designs carved on kula prow and splashboards. However, a grander plan has been to situate this analysis within a wider social and cultural context. The boards are created for a purpose. Structurally they pierce the water, making way for the canoe, and block the end of the hull to prevent water from filling the boat. They decorate the canoe to enhance its beauty. While these are passive benefits, there is agency in their purpose. Prior to embarking on a kula expedition, Vakutan men take great care in applying a fresh coat of paint to the canoe and its boards. Likewise, shell decorations are cleaned, polished and finally attached to the top of the *lagim* and to the prow of the canoe. Only after the boards have been placed into position do the encoded meanings become fused with the dynamics of kula. Once these essential preparations have been accomplished, the fleet is ready to set sail. The prow and splashboards become intrinsic participants in the pursuit of kula, their powers enlisted to assist the human crew to acquire kula shell valuables and achieve fame.

As an opening premise I argued that Vakutan artists do not randomly carve forms onto the surface of the boards. Instead, lines are carved into the wood in precise patterns executed by the skilled hand of a *tokabitam* artist. The predictable nature of these patterns enables us to identify a Vakutan style, which is a variant of a Trobriand and, ultimately, a Massim style. The forms and the representations they delineate have a purpose. They are expected to influence the minds of other kula men, turning them into adoring givers of shell valuables. The meanings, however, have a further value. They reflect upon Vakutan men and women as well as to the conflicting values men entertain; values that reinforce their role as partners in the procreation of other people's *dala* while at the same time acknowledging the desire to become detached from this role and achieve personally constructed value enhancement for themselves (Munn's 'qualisign', 1986).

The nature of the system of meaning worked into the carved boards is multi-dimensional; meaning is encoded on the boards in different ways. Attached to form is a labelling system through which people identify key themes relevant to Vakutan cosmological constructions. The system of representation can be interrogated by way of body parts, 'animals', and colour. Each enables one to follow a separate pathway leading to a variety of connected meanings. While these are unique within their own 'spheres', they ultimately reflect on coherent views about the nature of the world, as understood and constructed by Vakutans. The islanders have devised a complex system communicating particular ideas, at one level, and central themes at another. By employing the word 'level' to describe the system I do not wish to imply a relationship of hierarchy. Indeed, the system is not characterised by the dominance of one mode of encoding meaning over others. Each level, or layer, is distinct, encoding meaning independently.

Throughout much of this analysis my objective has been to introduce these levels and to demonstrate the kinds of information conveyed by each. Graphic forms are combined in meaningful ways to convey certain kinds of information. For example, the relationship of continuous curvilinear forms to those which are essentially self-contained, and the relationship between curvilinear forms to angular forms, may suggest an understanding of Vakutan aesthetics. The formal properties of a graphic system reflect the way in which people 'see' aspects of the world around them. Again, the predominance of volute and scroll patterns over more angular configurations indicates particular aesthetic preferences in Vakutan visual codes of representation. The volute delineating sections 2 and 3 on the *lagim* recalls the tree; the base is anchored to the canoe prow while the top is curved to represent mobility and the desire to become detached. The use of form also enables space to be broken up in a meaningful way. Body-part terminology, on the other hand, encodes different kinds of information. Vakutans use body-part terminology as a referential means by which they attach meaning to form and the spaces broken up by form. Value is attributed to certain body parts and transferred to the boards. Another way in which meaning is encoded is through the representation of the natural world. By labelling a form *buribwari*, for example, certain outstanding characteristics attributed to this bird are encoded and drawn together in the form. In the representational system forms are labelled according to an iconic or schematic relationship between them and the desired meaning. Colour symbolism, on the other hand, evokes further interpretations that focus attention on central issues concerned with Vakutan experiences, and encode beliefs about transformations that take place in the human life cycle. In combining the different meanings conveyed by these distinct modes of encoding information, broader conceptual issues emerge and compel further investigation.

The graphic system employed by Vakutans on the canoe prow and splashboards is a cultural construct. Forms do not necessarily look like, nor are they necessarily intended to resemble, the natural species with which they are associated. The 'work' attributed to the 'animals' of the *kabitam* repertoire is not necessarily a realistic characterisation of these animals' natural behaviour. Rather, the behaviours of the *kabitam* 'animals' are themselves elaborate conceptualisations reflecting the ambitions of Vakutan men and the means by which they set out to achieve these. The representational system merely offers one line of interrogating the forms.

Conclusion

From there, cultural characterisations can be explored and a new kind of 'animal' emerges. The relationship is not merely one between natural phenomena and their representation, be it iconic or schematic. In the case of the Vakutan graphic system the meaning attached to form elicits the 'work' of particular 'animals', encoding specific ideologies associated with the natural environment that, together, encode the presumptive success of kula and the significance this has to Vakutan men. In understanding the various conceptualised representations, one is able to build upon levels of interpretation so that the encoded meaning is revealed.

The graphic system does not exist in isolation, however. Unlike Western concepts of art which often view it as something that can exist for its own sake, and be placed in institutions devoted to its display, in most other societies art is created for specific contexts and fulfils particular functions. It is a part of everyday experience. Taken out of its context, much of the value is lost, the 'stories' they have to tell remaining untold. The *kabitam* repertoire, in its entirety, has a job to do, and it is for this purpose that the designs are carved into the boards. They are to assist men in the acquisition of shell valuables and thereby achieve success in the pursuit of status and renown. It is in this context that the graphic system becomes a part of the process of kula, agents in the pursuits of ambitious men. An examination of the meanings emerging from the various rituals associated with kula, including the preparation of the canoe, the voyage to distant islands, the transactions between partners and the rituals related to the return voyage, enriches the value of the encoded meanings on the prow and splashboards.

The art of kula is a dynamic medium of communication in which the associated systems of meaning are integrated with others to reflect Vakutan spheres of social experience. Rituals connected to the garden, those employed in fishing, in marriage, conception and childbirth encode information that formulates a Vakutan world-view. In this way themes that are concerned with basic Vakutan ideologies receive endless elaboration and permutation. In seeking to understand the meanings operating within different contexts of communication we begin to understand the complexity with which ideologies are constructed and reinforced. We cannot hope to understand what the graphic forms used to embellish canoe prow and splashboards mean without also seeking to understand the art of doing kula. Likewise, the rituals of kula, the transactions and the tensions associated with it, can only be fully understood when the meanings encoded within the carvings have also been investigated. The relationship these have in a wider social context must also be explored before we can begin to appreciate the significance of the *buribwari* and *boi*, the *uuna* and *dogina* to Vakutans. The art of kula cannot merely be reduced to the relationships that exist between individual representations and the forms they take, nor to ideal and experienced aspects of behaviour between kula partners. The art of kula is about Vakutan social experience as a whole, reflecting in particular the ideological relationships between men and women on Vakuta Island.

Notes

Introduction

1. The term was first used by Italian Marists who set up a mission in 1847 on Muyuw (Woodlark) Island (Affleck 1983). See also Young (1983c), who provides a historical sketch of the Massim.
2. Seligman wrote a few brief articles examining the meanings carved into canoe ornaments (1909, and with Dickson 1946) and encouraged Malinowski to pay attention to it. However, Haddon wrote two books dedicated to the subject of art (1894, 1895).
3. I am grateful to Dr Michael Young for bringing both Haddon's and Malinowski's letters to my attention. Malinowski's reply, dated 26/6/1918, is in the Haddon Collection in University Library, Cambridge, and Haddon's letter, dated 4/10/ 1916, is in the Malinowski archive in the London School of Economics Archives.
4. From the correspondence attached to these, Halls was seeking to undertake study at the London School of Economics with the support of the Department of External Territories, Canberra. Professor Firth intervened on his behalf, but it seems that nothing came of his application. The materials were deposited with Professor Firth who later passed the manuscript on to Professor Anthony Forge. It has now come into my care.
5. There are other significant analyses that have been developed to ask similar kinds of questions. For example, Ben-Amos (1980) and Biebuyck (1973) have extensively investigated the meaning and value of Benin and Lega art, respectively. In choosing Munn, Forge and Morphy, I am reflecting the importance these analyses have had on my own attempts to make sense of Vakutan carvings.

Chapter 1

1. In telling me the Vakutan origin myth, Ruguna instils contemporary significance by including the name of Lepani Watson, a prominent political figure both locally and nationally. He was a member of the Kiriwinan local government prior to becoming chairman of the Tonenei Kamokwita movement in opposition to the Kabisawali organisation in 1973. He was a member of the Papua New

Guinea House of Assembly from 1964–1972 and premier of the Milne Bay provincial government in 1983

2. There is a seventh inhabited island, Muwa, in the lagoon south-west of Sinaketa village. I do not include it here because it has only been inhabited by an Australian family operating a coconut plantation. Generally, the plantation used labour from the D'Entrecasteaux archipelago. As far as is known this island was never inhabited by Trobriand islanders. However, it is now owned by the Trobriand entrepreneur, John Kasaipwalova, who is hoping to develop it further.

3. See Leach (1983) for a discussion of the confusing array of names applied to these islands.

4. I do not intend to enter into the debate about the constitution of *dala* in the Trobriand Islands. For those interested in pursuing this, one might start with Malinowski (1932), Powell (1969a) and Weiner (1977). For my purposes, the conventional use of sub-clan is retained here. People who claim to be related according to real or presumed links connecting people by blood to a founding ancestress are said to belong to the same *dala*. Accordingly, a clan is made up of several such *dala* claiming descent from a fictive ancestress who emerged from the ground at the beginning of time.

5. Gawa has a similar origin history recognising only one *dala* as the auto-chthonous residents of the island. All other *dala* ancestors immigrated to Gawa from other islands (Munn 1986: 27).

6. Although there is no resemblance between Trobriand clans and those found on Dobu, it is common practice to accommodate any newcomer into the Vakutan clan structure. A stranger is asked for his or her totemic animals so as to determine which of the four clans and sub-clans he or she belongs to. If clan and sub-clan identity cannot be determined in this manner the palm of the stranger's hand is examined and the clan identity thereby discovered. In 1976 a Dobuan residing in Vakuta village was associated with the Lukwaisisiga clan. If Rurupa's family was indeed originally from Dobu, and this is quite possible given the frequent communication between these two islands, it is likely that this process of identity construction took place.

7. The institution of chiefly rank on Vakuta is not as strong as that reported for northern Kiriwina (Hutchins 1980; Leach 1983; Malinowski 1922; Powell 1960, 1969a, 1969b; Weiner 1980). From what Vakutans said, particular men are acknowledged as having superior qualities and are accordingly given the status of *guyau*, or 'chief' (as this has been translated in much of the literature). This status recognition is similar to other parts of the Massim where people accumulate characteristics that afford them status and influence (Battaglia 1990; Damon 1990; Lepowsky 1993; Liep 1991; Macintyre 1994; Munn 1986; Young 1971). I prefer to see these 'wars' as indicative of status rivalry between men and the groups they represent.

8. Details of Fellows's experiences in the Trobriand Islands are recounted in his diaries. The entry of 28 August 1894 describes his arrival in the lagoon. The Fellows diary is currently held by the National Gallery of Australia, Canberra, together with a large portion of his collection of artefacts. Recently, the diary was transcribed by Kim Akerman, but remains unpublished.

9. Malinowski's last entry in his letter to Elsie Masson, later his wife, was on 23 April while still on Vakuta. He describes his rage at the Vakutans who, although paid handsomely by his estimation, refused to take him back to Sinaketa. His next addition to the correspondence was on 2 May from Sinaketa (Wayne 1995: 136).

10. In a later report MacGregor says the two coastal villages on Vakuta are 'Sikwea' and 'Wokinai' (1892–93: 9). The village name 'Toula' dropped from use entirely after the 1891–92 report. I assume that 'Wokinai' is a respelling of 'Bokinai' found in the 1891–92 report and is today called Okinai (see Figure 1.2).

11. This must be a gross overestimate as it would give the village a population of 600–900 people, using a calculation of three people per house. Austen likewise questions MacGregor's population figures, suggesting they were greatly inflated (1945–46: 16–17).

12. In his letter to Elsie Masson, dated 'Sunday 21 April 1918', Malinowski describes Vakuta village in terms remarkably consistent to the village in 1976:

> It is a complex of villages, 13 in number, each rounded up well. Many such sub-villages are extinct and there are big empty spaces among the settlements. The terrain is not even and some 'suburbs' are higher on dry, stony grounds whilst others are on the black mud (Wayne 1995: 132).

13. Malinowski spells it *sayda* and describes the nut as, 'a spirally coiled up nut, longish and pointed in shape, with somewhat the taste of the hazel-nut' (1935 Vol. 1: 311). See also Fortune (1932: 90), who refers to these nuts in the Dobuan language as *saido*. To me, the term 'native almond' captures more accurately the taste and look of the kernel once it is removed from its rather heavy outer casing.

14. By using the term 'mythological charters' here to refer to the basis upon which people lay claims to parcels of land, I do not wish to imply the absence of any historical basis underlying the myth.

15. While Malinowski and Powell focused upon the village as a political unit, identifying the man in authority for each village as either a chief or headman depending upon relative status, Weiner identified the hamlet as the socially significant unit. She argued that the organisation of each hamlet centres around a 'hamlet manager' (1977: 42–43). While in agreement with Weiner's argument positioning the hamlet as the principal organisational unit, I prefer

not to use the term 'hamlet manager' because within Vakutan hamlets the equivalent person in no way displays the managerial role outlined by Weiner for northern Kiriwina. These men do not behave as 'headmen' or 'chiefs'. They behave instead as senior male representatives of their respective *dala* (see also Hutchins 1980).

16. *Pokala* refers to a range of wealth items given repeatedly to someone who possesses a particularly desirable item: for example, magic, land and kula routes. *Pokala* represents a solicitation of the thing desired and can go on for years (Campbell 1978, 1983a; Leach and Leach 1983; Munn 1986).

17. Some men plant a fourth garden, the *kuvi*, or long yam garden. *Kuvi* (*Dioscorea alata*) are grown exclusively for display and exchange. Vakutans claimed they only eat *kuvi* when given to them by Kitavans on kula voyages.

18. See Weiner (1977, 1978) for her complementary interpretation of the significance of men's yams. See also Forge (1972) for his discussion of male and female yam classifications.

19. More recently, Liep has argued that historical processes have resulted in the devolution of hierarchical systems throughout the Massim, and now retained only in northern Kiriwina (1991). In particular, the work of the colonial government and missionaries instigated complex transformations in social and economic systems, bringing about the varied forms of competitive and non-competitive social relations found throughout the Massim. For Liep, there is no easy trajectory from hierarchical to egalitarian structures now common in the Massim. The apparently anomalous existence of hierarchy in northern Kiriwina continues to draw comment. See Macintyre (1994) and Mosko (1995) for equally compelling discussions of this phenomenon.

20. Compare with Macintyre (1983a, 1983b) where she describes Tubetube exchange networks that have no internal or external boundaries. Weiner, too, notes the distinction made between these two spheres in northern Kiriwina (1983).

21. These are not *urigubu* payments as Malinowski so meticulously outlined (1922, 1932, 1935). See also Weiner (1977: 140) for a reanalysis of *urigubu*.

22. Refer to the following for a selection of publications discussing the exchange networks between affines: Campbell (1989), Hutchins (1980), Leach (1983), Malinowski (1922, 1932, 1935), Montague (1989) and Weiner (1977, 1978, 1980, 1988).

23. See also Malinowski (1922: 69, 1932: 231, 1948c: 121–122) for further discussion on the hostilities existing between Vakuta and its neighbours. Uberoi (1962: 121) makes similar points based upon his analysis of the data provided by Malinowski (1922), Fortune (1932), and others.

24. On many occasions during my fieldwork, public meetings were called but the 'chief' did not attend.

25. It was fortunate for me that he did not go on this particular expedition because his absence gave me the opportunity to accompany the fleet. Indeed, he gave me his kula business and, in so doing, the privilege of participating in 'hard' kula. His kula routes were not uncontested and his Kitavan partner was unhappy with the 'chief's' past kula transactions.

26. The status of a wealth item as *kitoum* has been the subject of considerable attention. A *kitoum* on Vakuta is a shell valuable that comes to a man with no path of transactors attached to it (Campbell 1983a). By initiating a path using a *kitoum*, a Vakutan potentially launches his own fame beyond his own community and into other kula communities handling his *kitoum*. See also Damon (1983, 1990), Macintyre (1983a), Munn (1983, 1986) and Weiner (1983).

27. The Vakutan word for moon is *tubukona* and is used to correspond to our concept of month. All 'months' are calculated from the full moon.

28. Although some confusion has existed about the importance of the lunar phases in Trobriand temporal calculations (cf. Malinowski 1927b: 209 and Austen 1939) there can no longer be much doubt of its significance. In Malinowski's later publication focusing on gardening (1935) it is clear, even if implicit, that the phases of the moon are important markers to the passage of time and particularly to the associated activities in the gardens (see also Damon 1982; Leach 1950).

Chapter 2

1. Austen spells it *tokatalaki* (1945: 194). The distinction Austen makes, however, is between an 'engraver' (*tokabitam*) and a 'handicraftsman' (*tokataraki*) (1945: 195). I think that Austen has misunderstood the difference between the two. Those Vakutans and Kiriwinans I have spoken to on this matter say that the difference is dependent upon whether the carver has taken magic or not. The drinking of magic is unequivocally a precursor to becoming a *tokabitam*.

2. I prefer to use the more recent spelling of this village: Boitalu.

3. Conversely, no one in the Kuboma district had master carver status.

4. These tourist carvings are not to scale. The pig is located at the Institute of Anatomy, Canberra (M-AF7); the seated figure is in the Malinowski collection held at the National Museum of Victoria, Melbourne (75462); the lime spatula is part of the MacGregor collection held by the Queensland Museum, Brisbane (Mac. 1061); and the bowl is held by the Institute of Anatomy, Canberra (M-DCW 30).

5. *Tokwalu* is a general term used by Kiriwinans to refer to carved figures. On Vakuta it has a more specific usage in relation to the graphic forms carved on a canoe splashboard. In the latter context, *tokwalu* identifies the human figure(s)

at the top of the splashboard. This will be discussed in greater detail later (see pp. 106–107, 141).

6. In the early 1980s, Weiner conducted a survey of cash obtained from carvings for a village in northern Kiriwina. She estimated an average income from carving to be A$62 per week (1982: 66).

7. In the 1960s through to the 1970s the Local Government Council discussed plans to initiate a system of certification in which carvings could be officially classified as 'good' (Weiner 1982: 67), but this never eventuated.

8. Weiner argued that the distinction between artists and craftsmen was maintained: 'Trobrianders . . . never lost sight of what constituted a fine carving. Distinctions were always made between the "real" carvers, ie. those who had knowledge and magic passed down through generations, and those who "carved for the money"' (1982: 67).

In relation to people's aesthetic assessment of carvings, I am in agreement with Weiner. Trobrianders continue to be articulate about the aesthetics of good carving and are quick to dismiss sloppy and uninspired work. Where I depart from Weiner's perspective, however, is in the distinction between *kabitam* artists and other carvers. This distinction did become blurred, particularly as it was obvious that *tokataraki* artists produced equally fine carvings for sale to tourists. The fact that there were, to my knowledge, two carvers from Boitalu village in the 1970s who were commissioned to carve canoe prow and splashboards, formally the exclusive repertoire of *kabitam* artists, also suggests a blurring of the distinctions on Kiriwina Island.

Chapter 3

1. Some of the material in this chapter appeared in *Canberra Anthropology* (1978: 1–11).

2. *To-* is the male noun classifier. Women have access to highly valued knowledge in the form of skirt-making magic. A woman possessing this level of knowledge is referred to as *nakabitam*, the female classifier *na-* replacing the male classifier.

3. I refer here to public garden magic. Private garden magic is owned individually. Most individuals have some personal corpus of magic (see also Malinowski 1935 Vol. 1: 78, 152–157).

4. Today public garden magic emanates from the church. To all intents and purposes, Yaubada (God) is the community's garden magician par excellence.

5. Weiner was the first to call attention to the importance of women's wealth in mortuary distributions on Kiriwina Island (1977). In contrast to Kiriwina, however, Vakutan women do not make banana-leaf bundles. Only fully

constructed skirts are used as women's wealth in mortuary distributions (Campbell 1989).

6. To my knowledge there is no specific, single word in the Vakutan dialect referring to the 'ownership' of knowledge. Other words implying 'ownership' are *toli-* and *kitoum*. It is not linguistically appropriate, however, to say *tolikabitam. Tolikabitam*, or owner of *kabitam*, is redundant because *kabitam* already implies ownership. *Toliginigini*, while linguistically acceptable, has a different meaning to that conveyed here. It means 'the owner of a carving' and would be used to refer to the person who had commissioned a *tokabitam ginigini* to create a carving. *Kitoum*, likewise, denotes that an object is owned. This particularly refers to kula valuables that have become detached from kula routes. *Kitoum* distinguishes those valuables that are owned by a man from those committed to routes and thus to other men. A man can do as he likes with a *kitoum*, but he should not change the route of other shell valuables (Campbell 1983a).

7. Occasionally a master carver will transgress this rule and give his knowledge to more than one apprentice. This is against *kabitam* conventions and inevitably causes conflict, as will be described below.

8. The *-la* suffix is used here to indicate that the magic (school) belongs to these areas; for example, 'Sopila Gawa' means literally the 'magic of Gawa'. The use of *sopi* without the suffix is also used and carries the same meaning: *Sopi Gawa*, etc. My thanks to Ralph Lawton for pointing this out to me, amongst other linguistic conventions peculiar to the Kirwinan language.

9. *Mina-* is the classifier which is used to refer to people in general; *minakabitam* for example, means the 'people of the *kabitam* profession'; *minavakuta*, the 'people of Vakuta', and so on.

10. Spells are spoken over the substance intended to carry the magic to the recipient. When this is done the person speaking does so with his or her mouth close to the substance so that the words are not only said, but breathed into the magical concoction.

11. The forehead and chest represent separate storage areas for knowledge that are qualitatively different. This is further explored in Chapter 7.

12. The 'ocean side' of the island (*olumata*) is distinguished by Vakutans from its opposite, the 'lagoon side' (*wa pasa*). This distinction has symbolic significance and is discussed in Chapters 8 and 9.

Chapter 4

1. See Morphy (1977b) for a fascinating examination of Aboriginal *toas*, or 'message sticks'. He demonstrates how these seemingly idiosyncratic forms encode culturally specific knowledge about the landscape.

2. Style can also be identified by differing conventions for breaking up space, colour patterning and so on. See the volume edited by Ucko in which various authors investigate form (1977). More recently, Gell examined the issues in determining style (1998).

3. This is not an uncommon phenomenon. There are a number of art systems where an apparent economy of form prevails, underpinning complex systems of meaning. Sometimes these are hierarchically arranged into levels of meaning that are progressively revealed in successive stages of initiation (Morphy 1977a), while in other artistic traditions these systems are contextual; the meanings applied to form changing according to the context. Munn's contrast between women's sand drawings and men's *guruwari* designs is a good example (1973a).

4. See Beran (1996) for a contemporary analysis of Massim style.

5. Although reasoned differently, Munn makes a similar observation for Gawan distinctions in the relative 'hardness' of kula towards the west as opposed to the east (1986). Gawans consider the pursuit of necklaces, obtained from their west, to be far more precarious than the acquisition of armshells from their Muyuw partners.

6. *Nugwenigwe* is also a noun used to differentiate weeds from cultigens. *Pitupitu* refers to something that is chipped or full of holes or lesions. The use of the word *pitupitu* to describe a carving too heavily worked refers to the condition of a pockmarked surface or face.

7. Plate 12 is a splashboard carved by Gigimwa of Kaulaka village. He also carves with *Sopila* Kitava magic. His designs, however, are quite different to Youwa's. Youwa carves in the 'traditional' Kitavan school. Gigimwa was once accused of 'stealing' Youwa's designs and his boards were broken. He told me that he had stopped carving until one night he dreamt of new 'animals'. He recommenced carving with his totally innovative designs and is now considered to be one of the best carvers. Although he was formally given magic for the Kitavan school, he has created a new design complex that may become incorporated into a new school if he decides to pass it on formally. He was, at the time of my fieldwork, preparing his son for the receipt of magic and *tokabitam ginigini* knowledge.

8. The formal analysis of Massim artefacts held in Australian museums prior to fieldwork reveals results corresponding closely to what I observed in the field and to the further analysis of the kula boards (1982, and n.d.[a]).

Chapter 5

1. Ralph Lawton has argued extensively that the -*na*- classifier signifying female humans and the -*na*- classifier signifying all non-humans are of differing

semantic domains and that these do not overlap (1980). Lawton argues that the -*na*- classification used to refer to *kabitam* forms and colours belongs to the animal and not the human female semantic domain. However, even if it is the case that the -*na*- classifier formally refers to different semantic domains, in actual speech the sounds do not differentiate. It could be argued that there is some basis for collapsing the domains so that some relationship, even if it is only homophonous, exists. For example, when identifying gender in animals, females are implicit within the -*na*- classification; *manana bunukwa* means implicitly 'that female pig', unless the context demands a differentiation between genders. If this is required, a male is simply identified as 'its husband' (*la mwala*). Hence, in speech it might be said: 'this pig came with that pig, its husband' ('*manana bunukwa lema toya manawena bunukwa, la mwala*'). Occasionally, when it is necessary to emphasise the gender of animals the female can be stressed by use of the noun *vivila*, which means woman (or women). The male, however, remains classified as a 'husband' in this context and is not given the noun *tau* used to designate a human male. Moreover, when the -*na*- classifier is applied to animals in its generic sense, it refers to all animals regardless of gender. When referring to a specific animal, however, its unmarked meaning remains female, hence the need to specify maleness by using an additional noun: 'its husband'. Although Lawton's insistence that -*na*- animal and -*na*- human female belong to different semantic domains may be well founded, I suggest that these need not be unrelated.

2. Yet another noun used to refer to flying witches is *nayoyouwa* (or *nayouwa*); *na*- is the female classifier specifying the root -*youyouwa*, meaning 'to fly'. Thus, a literal translation is 'female fliers'.

3. Linguists refer to this language as 'Kilivila'. It is one of the many belonging to the Austronesian family of languages. The accent falls on the penultimate syllable, enhancing the flow of the words when spoken in conversation.

4. Further south, Normanby Islanders believe that a young girl is initiated into witchcraft by her mother, or grandmother, who swallows the child and emits her again through the vagina (Roheim 1948: 280–281).

5. Another 'animal' that may function to organise space is known as *tubuniwola*. The term refers to the rounded 'head' of the prowboard:

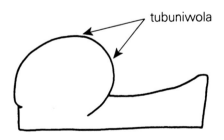

tubuniwola

A morphological breakdown of this word may translate as 'body of the moon'. *Tubukona* is the noun used to refer to the moon. *Wowola* means (its) body with the first possessive form suffix *-la* attached. *Woula* is a generic noun referring to the body. Thus, a translation of *tubuniwola* could be 'the body of the moon'. As this is more speculative than other aspects of the *kabitam* repertoire, I prefer to only mention it in a footnote rather than treat it more formally in the analysis. The form of the moon has aesthetic value that focuses upon its smooth roundness when in full display. Further, the moon is an important navigational instrument to a kula expedition. It is also important for its role in the temporal organisation of the garden cycle.

6. Malinowski has translated *buribwari* as 'fish-hawk', another word for osprey. I prefer to use the term 'osprey' as it is the more common name for this bird amongst ornithologists (Rand and Gilliard 1967).

7. An accomplished carver from northern Kiriwina, Nalubutau, calls the snails represented on northern Kiriwinan boards *susawiwi* (1975). The forms Nalubutau associates with *susawiwi*, however, correspond to the forms Vakutans call *ubwara*, which is the name given to a wild yam.

8. As with all other aspects of human society, art systems are always, if imperceptibly, changing. New ideas, ways of seeing and representing the world will continue to bring about an ever-developing form of expression. There should be no illusion that the system of carving I have attempted to understand in the latter part of the twentieth century is, and has been, timeless.

9. The Vakutan dialect has a set of prefixes denoting the direction of people relative to Vakutans. Using Vakuta as the central point, a Vakutan speaker can refer to other people by including in his grammatical construction information identifying the relevant direction in which 'those' people reside:

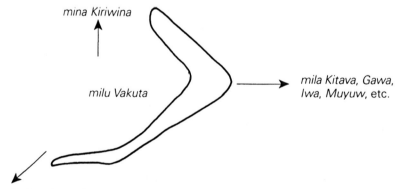

It is interesting to note that Vakutans make a change in the prefix according to the direction of kula partners. In the case of Kiriwina, it shares the same term that is used for Dobu and adjacent communities because Vakutans have no kula relationships with Kiriwinans and therefore no need to differentiate them. Concerning the word *minutoula*, I suggest that *minu-* is connected to *milu* (people of Vakuta) because in choosing an *a* or *u* ending people are creating a semantic change in the word, while the change from *-l-* to *-n-* in the penultimate sound of the prefix is a usual dialectic shift in the Trobriands. Kiriwinans commonly use *-l-*, where Sinaketans use *-n-* and Vakutans use *-r-*. In other words, if *minutoula* were *minatoula* the word is more likely to be connected to the Dobuan directional prefix, not because they share the same structural form but because of their hypothetically shared ending, *-a*. The ending, however, is *-u*. Sometimes in Vakutan speech an *-l-* is used instead of an *-n-*, or vice versa, so that the word is more euphonious within its linguistic environment. Therefore, *milu-* is changed to *minu-* in the word *minutoula* because it sounds better than stumbling over two *-l*'s and conforms to conventions in Vakutan speech. *-Toula* means 'to go first' (*kutoula* – you go first, before me). Therefore, the noun *minutoula* could mean 'the people of Vakuta who go first'.

10. The Vakutan term for snake is *kaiuna*. The *kabitam* snake, however, receives its name from the Dobuan generic term for snake, *mwata*. I could not discover why this was the case.

11. The *sawila* can just be seen emerging over the top of the shells attached along the top of the *lagim*.

12. Scoditti refers variously to *susawila* as sea eagle or frigate bird (1980).

13. A picture of this shellfish is published in *Sago bei den Sawos* by Schindlbeck (1980).

14. People sometimes harvest these wild yams in times of hunger when cultivated produce is not available. Vakutans say they only look for *ubwara* if the yam harvest was a poor one due to drought.

Chapter 6

1. In a brief article, Nalubutau discussed the qualities of carvings held in the Papua New Guinea National Museum collection. He described one splashboard as being carved by a man who 'broke all the rules'. In particular, the 'paths' were not carved properly and, 'if an attempt were made to apply paint to this carving it would soon be discovered that it could not work. The artist has failed to create the proper paths that keep the white, red, and black paint apart' (1975: 4).

2. Munn also argues for the specific primacy of colour patterning on Gawan canoe prows (1977: 48–49). Indeed, there is a good deal of convergence between Gawan and Vakutan symbolic, conceptual and aesthetic ideology (1986).

3. See Jones and Meehan (1978), Strathern and Strathern (1971) and O'Hanlon (1989) for detailed analyses of colour terminologies that include hue, density, gloss and flakiness, to name a few very different ways of identifying colour. In these systems of colour recognition the significance of colour symbolism is more than a means of differentiating a number of visually distinct hues. For further analyses of colour see Bulmer (1968), Conklin (1955), Coote (1992), Forge (1970), Gell (1975), Morphy (1992), Segall *et al.* (1966).

4. In many languages the term for blood can often be associated with the term denoting red. In Kilivilan the word for blood is *buyai-* and does not appear to have any closer morphological relationship to *bweyani*. Indeed, when asked, people declined to make any association between blood and the colour red. Instead, white and black were the colours more usually chosen as representing the colour of blood.

5. In fact, initially a corpse is stiff and rigid before decomposing but Vakutans, when evoking the condition *mwenogu*, are referring to the loss of muscle tone in the body and the absence of healthy vigour otherwise present in living bodies.

6. Mature betelnut is predominantly a very strong yellow to gold in colour. But its association on these kinds of public displays with sexuality is common. This is possibly due to its narcotic strength, but also because betelnut is the most prevalent gift given to a girl when her sexual favours are desired by a boy. After marriage, men should continue to provide their wives with betelnut to secure their affections and sexual exclusivity.

7. According to Malinowski the *mwari* was female and the *vaiguwa* its male partner. The shape of the shell valuables seemed to reinforce this supposition. However, it is interesting to note that information from Vakuta and the lagoon area of Kiriwina suggests quite the opposite. The reasons people gave for this were that the *mwari* is generally worn by men while the *vaiguwa* is worn by women. Further, the relative ease of handling *mwari* in comparison with *vaiguwa* reflects everyday relationships between men and women. For example, obtaining a *mwari* was likened to the day-to-day distribution of betelnut between men, whereas obtaining the *vaiguwa* was likened to the more tricky process of soliciting sex from women. It was easier to obtain *mwari* from Kitava than *vaiguwa* from Dobu. On Tubetube the male–female association of the shells corresponds to Malinowski's assertion (Macintyre 1983a, 1983b), while on Gawa and Muyuw the association is the same as Vakutan classification (Damon 1978: 85, 1990: 96; Munn 1983: 290–291, 306).

8. John Liep (1983) has argued conclusively that the necklaces were not made exclusively from *spondylus* shell. Indeed, the ones collected by Malinowski

now in the British Museum are made from *chama* shell. It is likely that the necklaces were made of a variety of species.

9. This characterisation was made independently by Youwa of Wakwega hamlet, Ruguna and Kunabu of Kuweiwa hamlet, Vakuta village. Youwa and Ruguna are both master carvers. Kunabu, while not a master carver, is a respected and knowledgeable man.

Chapter 7

1. Bomatu is the name for the south-east winds and may have inspired the name of the beach, Kadabomato, upon which these winds blow.
2. People living in Kaulaka village keep some of their boats on an ocean beach close to the village. But they also maintain boats on the same tidal creek as people of Vakuta village. Kaulakans choose to fish the lagoon rather than launch fishing boats into the ocean past the fringing reef. Fishing does occur beyond the reef, but far less regularly than in the lagoon.
3. It is the black areas of this section that Vakutans always point out and discuss spontaneously. From their discussions it is clear that the main impact of this section is the black area, even though red and white also feature here.
4. I do not wish to imply here that anyone other than Vakutans can 'read' the messages encoded on the prowboards in the same way as Vakutans. Although there is some evidence that similar kinds of symbolic associations occur between Massim societies, there are also obvious divergences (cf. Munn 1977, 1983, 1986; Scoditti 1975, 1977, 1980, 1990; Seligman and Dickson 1946). From the perspective of Vakuta, it is enough that Vakutans think their messages are so powerful as to affect their partners' behaviour, even though the latter may not be able to interpret them in the same way as Vakutans. Gell made much of this in 'The Technology of Enchantment and the Enchantment of Technology' (1992: 40–63).
5. In the past, the fibrous husk of the coconut was burnt and added to the flesh of young coconuts and coconut oil. These were mixed together to make a pigment painted on a baby's fontanelle to protect it from dampness *(numila)* and wind *(yagila)*, thought to be potentially dangerous to a baby's head. An affected baby would become crazy or 'soft-headed' if exposed.
6. In the analysis of each section of the splashboard the *dogina lagim* is the point of reference. The *uuna lagim* is the equivalent except that sections 2 and 3 are reversed. Their content, however, remains the same as the corresponding sections on the *dogina lagim*.
7. An alternative colour scheme is to interchange the outer ring red–black–red–black. It is said, however, that the outer-ring scheme should all be in red, its complement being the 'black' (perforations) of the inner ring.

8. *Kaimwasila* utilises vegetable matter as the main agent in this system of magic. Substances are combined, spoken over and swallowed.

9. Sometimes there are two *tokwalu* figures, often represented as male and female. However, there does not seem to be any significance attached to the use of two figures instead of one. It is simply a choice made by the carver, depending largely upon the space he has to fill. There are never more than two figures, though. If there is only one figure, its gender is usually specified. Scoditti argued that, relative to more contemporary carvings, older splash-boards display *tokwalu* with more emphasis on genital representation (1990). However, I do not think that his sample was big enough to place any great significance on this observation. Nor am I satisfied that the selection of boards chosen for his analysis, based on museum collections, escaped the bias of collectors. Regardless of whether any sex is attached to the figure(s), it is always referred to by use of the female/animal classifier *-na-*.

10. G. Roheim and F. E. Williams independently interpreted the human figure on the top of splashboard from the D'Entrecasteaux Islands as a representation of a 'baby' *(wame'a* on Fergusson Island), or a 'newly-born child' *(guama* on Normanby Island). These interpretations were subsequently compared and analysed by Seligman and Dickson (1946).

11. One carver labelled the spatially central bird design *miludoga*, a mythical 'animal'. It should be noted that this design unit is the same as that of section 1 on the *tabuya* featuring the *buribwari*. This same carver also calls the bird in section 1 on the prowboard *miludoga*. I was told that some carvers call the *buribwari* design on the prowboard *miludoga* or *muluveka* (sea eagle) but that it really is *buribwari*. Judging from the range of information given to me by people I do not think that any significance should be attached to this altern-ative label. The symbolic representation is motivated by the same image: that of a bird of prey. It need only be noted that there is some variation in label and form attachment. What is important, however, is the predominance of the *boi/doka* association to these design areas by most people. Nalubutau refers to form A3.3 as '*minodoga*' in his commentary on the splashboards held by the National Museum of Papua New Guinea (1975). Vakutans call this form *sawila*.

12. In 1977 Taduwasi of Kaulaka village was an old man. He was also an old man renowned for his knowledge of magic. One of his major concerns was that when he died people should remember to gag his mouth tightly and lay his corpse face down so that none of his magic would escape him and thereby endanger the survivors (cf. Weiner 1977: 69).

13. Scoditti also notes the significance of the head for Kitavans (1975, 1977, 1980, 1990).

14. Malinowski found that Trobrianders refused to recognise physical likenesses between matrilineal kinsmen, while they commented openly upon such

similarities between a man and his children. This particularly perplexed Malinowski because of their denial of physiological paternity. Vakutans told me, however, that one should not point out the physical likeness of a child to either of its parents. Although it is considered intolerable to point out physical similarities between matrilineal kin it is also impolite to point out likenesses between children and their fathers. Vakutans stressed that people were born different and that they were given different 'names' upon which to build personal reputations. They considered this to be very important and quite unacceptable to be physically identified with someone else. It should be remembered that for a time in one's life it is thought that one's physical appearance is potentially a source of power and can be advantageous in accruing useful alliances, not to mention wealth and sexual activity. The difference between Kiriwinans' willingness to accept some degree of individual likeness to others and Vakutans' aversion to accepting any at all may again demonstrate the degree to which Vakutans value a more egalitarian milieu than their northern neighbours, or the many years between my time on the islands and Malinowski's.

15. Note the use of the classifier *na-*, in this case invoking a connection to animal or female classification rather than to wooden objects (which would be the implication if the *kai*-classifier were used). *Kai-* is used, however, when reference is being made to the butterfly structure of sections 2 and 3, the connection being to the physiological structure of a butterfly and the form utilised to delineate these two sections.

16. Tambiah similarly argued that flying witches and the flying canoe myth are symbolically connected (1983). However, Tambiah's efforts to link this relationship to Trobriand cosmology, though similar to my own aim, suggest quite different conclusions concerning male and female roles within a 'cosmological' order. These will be discussed at length in the following chapter.

17. Form B3.2 is said to represent the *boi, doka* and *weku* depending upon which white form it is incorporated within. The *boi, doka* and *weku* are given prominence in the process of encoding meaning. Form B3.2 does not receive such status, however. Its role in the system is to emphasise the main design unit within which it occurs. In this way, form B3.2 takes on different names according to the white form it is incorporated within. It is for this reason that form B3.2 is included in category B.

Chapter 8

1. Others have noted the significance of this myth in Trobriand rituals associated with kula (Scoditti 1980: 97, 1990; Uberoi 1962: 77–79; Tambiah 1983).

2. Munn has written extensively about the transformation of Gawan outrigger canoes as vehicles whereby Gawan men transport their fame and build upon their social value (1977, 1983, 1986).

3. The 'water's edge' can be conceptualised as the 'beach' and thus a transitional stage between land and sea. However, the 'water's edge' for the four villages of Vakuta are different (see Figure 1.2 and Plate 3). Giribwa village is surrounded by water on all but one side, as the site of the village is the beach on the south-ernmost tip of Kiriwina Island. Okinai village is situated on the lagoon beach where people construct their kula canoes both in the 'village' and on the 'beach'. Kaulaka village is close to the ocean side of the island. Villagers sometimes construct their *masawa* on the ocean beach or they join Vakuta villagers who have access to the lagoon via a tidal creek. They construct their kula outrigger canoes at the point where the tidal creek widens very near to the south-western part of the village.

4. Damon has written an intriguing paper on the use of wood on Muyuw, explor-ing the qualities of different species valued for canoe construction among other things (1998).

5. An etymological breakdown of the word explicitly conveys the content of this magic. Recall that *kai-* is a classifier used to specify nouns referring to a tree-like substance or structure. In the context of *kaimwasila*, reference is made to the vegetable matter used in this form of magic.

6. This word can be broken into two components, *kari-* and *-butu*. *Kari-* is a deriv-ative of the second form possessive, *kala-* (third person singular), specifying articles of body adornment that are semi-alienable. *-Butu* is a component of words referring to sound, noise and to fame or renown: i.e. *butula* – its/his/her fame, *mwaributu* – a class of armshell second in the hierarchy and specifically referring to the acquisition of fame and renown (Campbell 1983b).

7. Contrary to this, Malinowski writes that both men and women perform 'love magic' (1932). It is not, however, made clear whether both sexes have direct access to it. Malinowski is even more obscure when he writes; 'Although girls are said to practise [love] magic, it is more usual for the men to take the init-iative' (1932: 307). Vakutans assured me that only men can perform this magic, reminding me that this is an important magic also used in kula to attract partners and shell valuables. Women, it was argued, do not need this magic.

8. Other examples of women's association with immobility, weight and anchoring from the Massim come from Dobu (Fortune 1932), Goodenough Island (Young 1983a), Sabarl Island (Battaglia 1990) and Muyuw (Damon 1990, 1998). The association of stones with *dala* is also a characteristic of Gawan construction of their world order. Munn demonstrates extensively the way in which stones represent *dala* (1986: 76, 80–89).

9. Malinowski also refers to the stability induced by weight (1935 Vol. 1: 221–222, 476). Munn argues that similar ideas are held by Gawans linking fertility

and weight in their relationship to the soil (1977, 1986). Likewise, Young presents an anchored versus mobile dichotomy in Goodenough belief (1971, 1983a: 388–390). See also Damon (1990) and Hutchins (1980).

10. Vanoi, the late paramount chief of northern Kiriwina, was quoted as saying, 'Remember, a kula shell is like a young girl; she looks over every man until she decides which one she likes best. One man is chosen and the others are sent away' (Weiner 1977: 218).

11. On those occasions when there are no new canoes, each man goes on his own to visit his kula partners or to the house where a particularly fine shell valuable is known to be held. In the case of a new canoe, the crew, representing the *masawa*, travel as a single body through all the villages.

12. Gilmour refers to this activity without naming it (1904–5: 72).

13. Young describes a similar activity carried out by Kalauna villagers of Goodenough Island who make expeditions to neighbouring villages to 'ask for food'. The manner in which they do this, however, has aggressive overtones, akin to those displayed by Vakutans on *bisila* advances: 'The "aggressors" simulate a war-party in dress, paint and demeanour when they visit another village to ask for food' (1983b: 408).

14. A version of this legend was recorded by Leach (1981). The text closely resembles that which I recorded.

15. See also Malinowski's version (1922: 307–311) and Fortune's account of this myth (1932)

16. As the majority of transactions are between men already contracted to each other in a 'marriage', not every transaction of shells results in the inception of a 'marriage'. A new 'marriage' occurs when a new partnership is cemented by the transfer of shells and a new *keda* commences (see Campbell 1983a, 1983b; Damon 1983; Macintyre 1983b; Munn 1983).

17. See also Leach and Leach (1983) for a variety of complementary and contrasting views of how kula operates around the 'ring'. Vakutans perceive that the rules of kula are the same amongst all participating communities but are vaguely aware that others think about the process differently.

18. The pattern of inheritance discussed here can be compared to other parts of the Massim where kula is prominent. Seligman noted for Tubetube that:

> A man's landed property, that is to say his share in the clan garden land and any land in the bush that he might have cleared and planted during his lifetime, would be equally divided among his sisters' children . . .
>
> A dead man's house, if he were living in his own hamlet at the time of his death, would pass to one of his brothers or sisters or sisters' children . . .
>
> As regards inheritance two categories of personal property must be recognized. A man's drums, lime pots, lime spatulae and canoe or canoes would always pass to his sisters' children [or] his maternal uncle would take his canoe and other

property and only after the death of the maternal uncle would the property revert to the dead man's own brothers and sisters. The second class includes such valuable property as armshells and *sapisapi* necklaces which would in part go to a man's own children. (1910: 522–523)

See also Macintyre (1983b).

Chapter 9

1. At this point in the narrative one might question Youwa's knowledge of the behaviour of fish-eating raptors, for it is surely unusual for such birds to actually dive into the water and risk getting their plumage wet and waterlogged. Most sea-based hunters grab fish in their talons without getting wet. However, some European studies refer to the spectacular 'plunge' that the osprey makes as it goes for its prey: 'Best identified by hunting habits: systematically quarters water at heights from 15–50 m; hovers, plunges, entering feet first with spectacular splash' (Pizzey 1981: 76).
2. Malinowski also draws attention to the use of the tree as metaphor in several of his published material. On each occasion the analogy is made with different phenomena (1922: 433, 1935 Vol. 2: 92). Elsewhere he wrote:

> In many subjects they distinguish these three elements: the *u'ula* [*uuna*] the *tapwana*, and the *matala*. The image is derived from a tree or a pillar or a spear: *u'ula* – in its literal sense the foot of the tree, the base, the foundation – has come, by extension, to mean cause, origin, source of strength; *tapwana*, the middle part of the trunk, also means the trunk itself, the main body of any elongated object, the length of a road; *matala* – originally eye, or point (as in a spear) and sometimes replaced by the word *dogina* or *dabwana*, the tip of a tree or the top of any high object – stands for the highest part, or, in more abstract metaphor, the final word, the highest expression. (1932: 143)

There are two points concerning the words *u'ula* and *dogina* that need mention here. Firstly, Malinowski's use of *u'ula* is a dialectic preference. In the Vakutan dialect the -*l*- is often dropped and replaced by a -*n*-, making *uuna*. There are no glottal stops in Vakutan speech. Secondly, Malinowski is not consistent in his usage of *dogina*, *matala* or *dabwana*. In 1922 (p. 433) he used *dogina* as the common reference to the tip of a tree, commenting that *dabwana* ('top' or 'head') is sometimes used instead. *Matala* is not mentioned here. Later, in 1935 (Vol. 2: 92) he wrote that *dabwana* refers to the 'head' while *dogina* refers to the 'tip'. Again *matala* is not referred to at all. According to my observations, Vakutans rarely use *dabwana* and *matala*, although they are sometimes substituted. *Dogina* was by far the more common term in use while I was there. Others have noted the significance of trees to Massim people, particularly their use as metaphor (Damon 1990, 1998; Fortune 1932; Munn 1977, 1986).

3. There are, of course, occasions when sitting directly on the ground is unavoidable. However, even on these occasions men prefer to fashion some barriers, a fallen palm leaf often being a simple way to separate them from direct contact with the earth.

4. In the past these offerings were given to the garden magician (Malinowski 1935). Interestingly, Malinowski's books were being used to reclaim magical formulae. The activities of missionaries persuaded people to cease their belief in magic, teaching that these traditions are the work of the devil. There are a growing number of people, however, who are not so committed to this idea and who are keen to return to their use of magic.

5. This is not entirely true. Women also plant yams, but these are considered the lesser varieties (see Chapter 1). There is, however, a prevailing perception that only men cultivate yams. I was not aware of women's yams, and their cultivation of these, until late in my fieldwork – despite working alongside women in the gardens throughout my stay!

6. *Karisalem* refers to the action of planting the seed yam in the side of the mound (*pulu*).

7. See also Barton (1917: 109) who confirms what Bellamy said (1908) were the symbolic associations of rain.

8. Vakutan women use a wide variety of potions and technical aids to avoid conception or achieve an early termination of unwanted pregnancies. Some infertile women claimed that their inability to conceive was the result of especially powerful magical potions given to them by their mothers and grandmothers when they were young.

9. Vakutans acknowledge what was taught to them by missionaries, government personnel and doctors concerning the fertilising agency of seminal fluid. At a certain level, however, their indigenous belief is sustained to justify the principle of matriliny and the regeneration of *baloma* into *dala*. To them the coexistence of what might appear to be substantially different beliefs is not a problem as long as they remain separate.

10. A sister becomes crazy with desire for her brother when she accidentally knocks a container hanging above her, releasing magically impregnated oil imbued with her brother's love magic. This spills onto her head causing the calamitous events that follow.

11. What is being expressed here is the ideology of *dala* immortality. I do not wish to imply that in reality all *dala* achieve immortality in the sense that they are able perpetually to reproduce themselves. It is not out of the question that

existing *dala* may cease to exist should there be no women to reproduce them. People recognise the tenuous future of a *dala* with very few women, saying: '*Bogwa bikariga matausina dala*' ('Already it will die, those people's *dala*'). However, it is significant that *dala* with no living members may continue to be remembered, together with the names of those women who were respons-ible for its reproduction. Further, it would be misleading to suggest that men's names are entirely neglected. However, these are not the names used to identify rights over land and other important resources. Their names are recalled as individuals who received notoriety during their lifetime.

12. Women who are unable to reproduce face the same fate as men, but with the added disadvantage of being unable to participate in kula. Becoming a famous witch may be their only means of achieving renown for their names.

Glossary

baloma	spirits of the dead
beba	butterfly; the name given to part of the *lagim*
bisila	pandanus streamers attached to the sail and boom of canoes; the name of a ceremonial advance on kula partners when a new canoe has made its maiden voyage (*bibisilasi* – they will engage in *bisila* display)
boi	egret; the name given to one of the forms in the *kabitam* repertoire
budakola	a mixture of charred coconut flesh and coconut oil used as black pigment
bulebula	without colour
bulubwalata	the magic of sorcery; magic enlisted for evil
buribwari	osprey; the name given to a form in the *kabitam* repertoire
bwabwau	black
bwagau	sorcerer
bwau	rain clouds
bweyani	red
dabila	head
dala	sub-clan
debumwoya	banana leaf skirt
digadegila	sulphur crest of the cockatoo; sometimes used to refer to green, brown or yellow colours
dodoleta	forms on canoe boards carved to hold the white pigment; a particular shrub
dogina	the top of a tree; refers also to the 'male' end of a canoe
doka	mythical animal, related to thought (*-doki* is the verb stem meaning 'to think'; a name given to a form in the *kabitam* repertoire
dudubila	dark or dull
duduwa	small, light green garden snail; name given to a form in the *kabitam* repertoire
duku	a strong creeper used to pull heavy loads
geguda	unripe
genata	raw
ginareu	hermit crab; name given to a form in the *kabitam* repertoire
gogosu	antennae of insects
gwadi	child

igavau	first pregnancy
kabisivisi	giving seed yams to a man's sister(s)
kabitam	a high order of knowledge achieved through magic and training
kabitam ginigini	the knowledge of carving
kabulu	beak
-kai-	noun classifier for tree, or wood-like objects
kaibua	stalactite
kaidada	a horizontal piece of wood, referring particularly to the front boards of a yam house platform
kaigilagela	wooden paddle or hammer used to drive the *kaiwawaiya* through wood to create incisions
kaimalaka	pigment produced by red ochre or the dye extracted from *Bixa orellana*
kaimata	new garden cleared and planted with seed yams following harvest festivities
kaimwasila	magic involving the use of particular plants or trees that, when mixed together, become powerful and are believed to act on the minds of others
kaisipu	a particular snake residing in mangrove and swampland; a magical component of *kabitam*
kaiwawaiya	sharp tools, these days nails, used to carve lines into the surface of wood
kaiyau	throat
kaiyaula	an exchange relationship between a man and his wife's brother involving the building of a kula canoe for the former
kamgwa	a small, second garden cultivated as a back-up source of food when the *origabu* becomes depleted and the new garden is not yet ready for harvest
kamkokola	the upright supports of a yam house roof that are removed upon the death of the yam house owner and kept as symbols of the deceased
kapaiyauwa	bat; name given to a form in the *kabitam* repertoire
karawa	fern frond; name given to a form in the *kabitam* repertoire
karibudaboda	payment of yams at harvest for the building of a kula canoe
karisalem	action of planting a seed yam in the side of a prepared mound
-kateta	to be sharp, as a knife; carvings may also be called 'sharp' if they have been finely carved; sharp of thought
kavasaku	the carving of an initiate's first boards inside his house
kavatam	poles inserted into the earth as supports for the yam vines
kaytalugi	a community of women believed to inhabit a distant island and thought to have insatiable sexual appetites

keda	route, path
kema	axe
kewou	fishing canoe
kipoum	small hand knife used to dig out carved lines
kitoum	a term which distinguishes the personal ownership of valuables from non-ownership; used particularly in relation to kula shell valuables
kosobu	holes carved through the bottom of the *lagim*'s loops through which ropes are passed so as to secure the *lagim* to the prow of the canoe
kovesa	yam harvest festival
kudila	teeth
kudu-	possessive form for teeth; the closing transaction to a kula path
kuvi	long yams (*Dioscorea alata*)
-kwai-	noun classifier distinguishing all round or amorphous objects
kwaikwaiya	an institution whereby people raid the household of someone who 'comes first' in kula, yam competitions, boat races
kwila	penis
kwita	octopus
lagim	splashboard on the kula outrigger canoe
lilau	white clay taken from the foot of the reefs to use as white pigment
masawa	kula outrigger canoe
matila	eyes
matua	ripe
menu	cooked
migila	face
miludoga	name given to specific designs carved on the *lagim*, *tabuya*, and steering paddle
minakabitam	people who possess valuable knowledge of the *kabitam* order
minutoula	name given to a specific form utilised in the *kabitam* repertoire and associated by Vakutans with a mythical 'animal'
mulukwausi	flying witches
muluveka	sea eagle
mwari	kula armshell
mwarikau	highest ranking classification for armshells
mwata	Dobuan generic term for snake
mwenogu	mature
-na-	noun classifier referring to women, all non-humans, and heavenly bodies
nagega	style of kula outrigger canoe used by people of Iwa, Gawa and Muruwa

nakubukwabuya	female youth
nanoula	'mind', located in the chest/stomach
nugwenigwe	grass, weeds; used as an aesthetic term to describe something too confused and cluttered with too many lines
-nukwari	to know
numila	dew
nunula	breast or breast milk
Olumata	the name given to the ocean side of the island
orakaiwa	above
origabu	the old garden, declared after yams have been harvested from it and while it continues to yield other foodstuffs in the second year of its cultivation
otenauwa	below
papa	wall; name of an 'animal' in the *kabitam* repertoire
pepeni	a gift of raw yams given by a bride's kin to the bridegroom's kin immediately following marriage
pinipanela	wings
pitupitu	a description of something that is chipped and full of dents or lesions
pokala	a noun describing a gift of wealth items given in solicitation of magic, land, kula routes, etc.
pokiyou	ashes
pulu	mound in which a seed yam is inserted
pupwakau	white
pwaka	lime baked from coral
pwanana	hole
pwanasi	mixture of water or oil with charred coconut husk and ashes used for black pigment; used particularly for putting on a baby's fontanelle and for face paint
rigogo	adze
sagali	ceremonial distribution
sawila	sandpiper; a name given to a form in the *kabitam* repertoire
sigala	brightness
soba	face paint
sopi	water, or liquid; the term applied to magical concoctions
sopila	school of carving
sosula	gift of a shell valuable offered to *tokwai* to appease them
sulumwoya	scented leaves from the mint bush used as body decoration and in magical concoctions
tabuya	prowboard on the kula outrigger canoe
takola	a marriage gift of male valuables given by the bridegroom's kin in payment for the raw yams given by the bride's kin

taregesi	a kind of shellfish that attaches itself to sago palms; a name given to a form in the *kabitam* repertoire
tasasoria	ceremonial race of kula canoes
tau	man
-to-	noun classifier specifying all human males; used to specify all humans in a context which compares humans with non-humans
tokabitam	a man who has received the magic and technical instruction to make him wise and in possession of a specific 'knowledge'
tokataraki	an uninitiated carver who has no specific carving knowledge
tokwai	a sprite believed to inhabit trees, stumps and boulders; thought to occasionally cause harm to human beings in the form of bites, swellings, etc.
tokwalu	the name given to the figure(s) at the top, centre of the *lagim*; the figure(s) is said to represent humanity; also used in contexts where an image of something is being referred to
toliwaga	owner of a canoe
toulatile	male youth
tubukona	moon, the Vakutan 'month'
tubuniwola	boy of the moon
tumila	foundations, hamlet land
ubwara	wild yam; the name of a form in the *kabitam* repertoire
ulaula	gift of a shell valuable offered to *tokwai* to appease them
ureri	striations that occur on *conus* shells once the epidermis has been removed
urigubu	gift of fruits of a tree or produce from a garden given by a man to any one of his female relatives
uuna	base or bole of a tree; also 'female' end of a canoe
vaga	opening transaction to a kula path
vaiguwa	kula shell necklace
vakapula	payment in the form of cooked and uncooked food, tobacco and betel nut for work rendered
vau	squid; ink from the squid is used as black pigment
vaula kaukweda	gift of uncooked pig flesh to a man's son(s)
vilakuri	return payment of *takola* in the form of raw yams given by the bride's kin at the harvest following the marriage
vivila	women
wadila	mouth
waiwaia	reincarnated spirit child
Wa pasa	name given to the lagoon side of the island
weku	a mythical 'animal' carved in the *kabitam* repertoire
weyugwa	a creeper used to lash gunwale planks to the hull
yagila	wind

yamila	arms
yeluyelu	the white, frothy water that follows the rise and retreat of a wave on the beach

Bibliography

Affleck, D. (1983), 'Manuscript XVIII – Information on Customs and Practices of the People of Woodlark Island, by Carlo Salerio', *The Journal of Pacific History*, 18 (1): 57–72.

—— (n.d.), 'Catalogue of the Civic Museum Collection, Milan, Italy: A Translation', Paper presented to the 2nd Kula Conference, Charlottsville, Virginia, 1981.

Allied Geographical Section, Southwest Pacific Area (1942), *Terrain Study No. 23, D'Entrecasteaux and Trobriand Islands*, October: 33–49 (plus maps).

Arnheim, R. (1974), *Art and Visual Perception: A Psychology of the Creative Eye*, Berkeley: University of California Press.

Austen, L. (1934–35), 'Procreation Among the Trobriand Islanders', *Oceania*, 5: 102–113.

—— (1936), 'The Trobriand Islands of Papua', *The Australian Geographer*, 111 (No. 2): 10–22.

—— (1939), 'The Seasonal Gardening Calendar of Kiriwina, Trobriand Islands', *Oceania*, 9 (3): 237–253.

—— (1945), 'Native Handicrafts in the Trobriand Islands', *Mankind*, 3 (7): 193–198.

—— (1945–46), 'Cultural Changes in Kiriwina', in *Oceania*, 16: 15–60.

Barnes, R. (1992), 'Textile Design in Southern Lembata: Tradition and Change', in J. Coote and A. Shelton, *Anthropology, Art and Aesthetics*, Oxford: Clarendon Press.

Barthes, R. (1967), *Elements of Semiology*, London: Jonathan Cape.

Barton, R. P. (1917), 'The Spirits of the Dead in the Trobriand Islands', *Man*, 17–18: 109–110.

Battaglia, D. (1990), *On the Bones of the Serpent: Person, Memory, and Mortality in Sabarl Island Society*, Chicago: University of Chicago Press.

Beier, U. (1974), 'Aesthetic Concepts in the Trobriand Islands', *Gigibori: A Magazine of Papua New Guinea Cultures*, 1 (1): 36–39.

—— (1978), 'The *Mwali* Shell as Art Object and Status Symbol', in *Oral History*, 6 (3): 78–86.

Bellamy, R. L. (1908), 'Notes on the Customs of the Trobriand Islander', *Annual Report on British New Guinea for the Year Ending 30th June, 1907*, Brisbane: Government Printer.

Ben-Amos, P. (1980), *The Art of Benin*, London: Thames & Hudson.

Beran, H. (1980), *Massim Tribal Art*, Wollongong: Wollongong City Gallery.

—— (1988), *Betel-chewing Equipment of East New Guinea*, Aylesbury, Bucks: Shire Publications.

—— (1996), *Mutuaga: A Nineteenth-Century New Guinea Master Carver*, Wollongong: University of Wollongong Press.

Berlin, B. and Kay, P. (1969), *Basic Color Terms: Their Universality and Evolution*, Berkeley: University of California Press.

Berlo, J. C. (1999), 'Drawing (upon) the Past: Negotiating Identities in Inuit Graphic Arts Production', in R. B. Phillips and C. B. Steiner (eds), *Unpacking Culture: Art and Commodity in Colonial and Postcolonial Worlds*, Berkeley: University of California Press.

Berndt, R. N. (1958), 'A Comment on Dr. Leach's Trobriand Medussa', *Man*, 64–65: 65–66.

Biebuyck, D. (1973), *The Lega: Art, Initiation and Moral Philosophy*, Berkeley: University of California Press.

Black, R. H. (1957), 'Dr. Bellamy of Papua', *Medical Journal of Australia*, 11, Aug. 10th 1957, 17th 1957 and 24th 1957.

Boas, F. (1927), *Primitive Art*, New York: Dover.

Brookfield, H. C. and Hart, D. (1971), *Melanesia: A Geographical Interpretation of an Island World*, London: Methuen.

Brunton, R. (1975), 'Why do the Trobriands Have Chiefs?', *Man*, 10 (4): 544–558.

Bulmer, R. (1968), 'Keram Colour Categories', *Kivung; Journal of the Linguistic Society of the University of Papua New Guinea*, 1 (3): 120–133.

Campbell, S. (1978), 'Restricted Access to Knowledge in Vakuta', *Canberra Anthropology*, 1 (3): 1–11.

—— (1982), 'An Analysis of Massim Material Culture from Collections in Australian Museums', *COMA: Bulletin of the Conference of Museum Anthropologists*, 10: 23–28.

—— (1983a), 'Kula in Vakuta: The Mechanics of *Keda*', in J. W. Leach and E. Leach (eds), *The Kula: New Perspectives on Massim Exchange*, Cambridge: Cambridge University Press.

—— (1983b), 'Attaining Rank: A Classification of Kula Shell Valuables', in J. W. Leach and E. Leach (eds), *The Kula: New Perspectives on Massim Exchange*, Cambridge: Cambridge University Press.

—— (1989), 'A Vakutan Mortuary Cycle', in F. H. Damon and R. Wagner (eds), *Death Rituals and Life in the Societies of the Kula*, DeKalb: Northern Illinois University Press.

—— (2001), 'The Captivating Agency of Art: Many Ways of Seeing', in N. Thomas and C. Pinney (eds), *Beyond Aesthetics: Art and the Technologies of Enchantment*, Oxford: Berg Publishers.

—— (2002), 'What's in a Name? The Search for Meaning', in A. Hearle, N. Stanley, K. Stevenson and R. L. Welsch (eds), *Pacific Art: Persistence, Change and Meaning*, Hindmarsh, South Australia: Crawford House Publishing.

—— (n.d.[a]), 'Massim Carved Art: A Formal Analysis of the Structural Elements within the Art System', MAq thesis, Australian National University.

—— (n.d.[b]), 'The High Status of Trobriand Women: Fact or Fantasy', Paper presented to the 'Highland and Seaboard Melanesia: Continuity or Contrast?' Conference held at La Trobe University, Melbourne, 1986.

—— (n.d.[c]), 'The Agency of Tokwalu: A Figurative Representation of Vakutan Humanity', Paper presented to the 2000 American Anthropological Association Meetings, San Francisco.

Caruana, W. (1993), *Aboriginal Art*, London: Thames & Hudson.

Chomsky, N. (1957), *Syntactic Structures*, The Hague: Mouten.

—— (1966), *Topics in the Theory of Generative Grammar*, The Hague: Mouten.

Cohodas, M. (1999), 'Elizabeth Hickox and Karuk Basketry: A Case Study in Debates on Innovation and Paradigms of Authenticity', in R. B. Phillips and C. B. Steiner (eds), *Unpacking Culture: Art and Commodity in Colonial and Postcolonial Worlds*, Berkeley: University of California Press.

Conklin, H. C. (1955), 'Hanunoo Color Categories', *Southwestern Journal of Anthropology*, 11: 339–344.

Coote, J. (1992), ' "Marvels of Everyday Vision": The Anthropology of Aesthetics and the Cattle-Keeping Nilotes', in J. Coote and A. Shelton (eds), *Anthropology, Art and Aesthetics*, Oxford: Clarendon Press.

—— and Shelton, A. (1992), *Anthropology, Art and Aesthetics*, Oxford: Clarendon Press.

Damon, F. H. (1978), 'Modes of Production and the Circulation of Value on the Other Side of the Kula Ring: Woodlark Island, Muyuw', Unpublished Ph.D. thesis, Princeton University.

—— (1980), 'The Problem of the Kula on Woodlark Island: Expansion, Accumulation, and Overproduction', *Ethnos*, 45: 176–201.

—— (1982), 'Calendars and Calendrical Rites on the Northern Side of the Kula Ring', *Oceania*, 52 (3): 221–239.

—— (1983), 'What Moves the Kula: Opening and Closing Gifts on Woodlark Island', in J. W. Leach and E. Leach (eds), *The Kula: New Perspectives on Massim Exchange*, Cambridge: Cambridge University Press.

—— (1990), *From Muyuw to the Trobriands: Transformations Along the Northern Side of the Kula Ring*, Tucson: University of Arizona Press.

—— (1998), 'Selective Anthropomorphization: Trees in the Northeast Kula Ring', in *Social Analysis*, 42 (3): 67–99.

Dickson, T. E. and Whitehouse, E. (1942), 'An Unusual Ceremonial Lime Spatula from British New Guinea', *Man*, 62 (29): 49–51.

Edge-Partington, J. (1969), *An Album of the Weaponry, Tools, Ornaments, Articles of Dress, etc., of the Natives of the Pacific Islands*, Part II, London: Holland Press.

Egloff, B. J. (1978), 'The Kula Before Malinowski: A Changing Configuration', *Mankind*, 11: 429–45.

Faris, J. C. (1972), *Nuba Personal Art*, London: Duckworth.

Fellows, S. B. (1891–1900), 'The Diaries of S. B. Fellows', held in the National Gallery of Australia, Canberra.

—— (1898a), 'Notes of Special Industries of Various Villages of Kiriwina', *Votes and Proceedings of the Legislative Assembly during the Session of 1898: Being the Third Session of the 12th Parliament*, Brisbane: Government Printer (4 vols) 2, App. ix GG: 147–148.

—— (1898b), 'Kiriwina Emblazoned Shield', *Votes and Proceedings of the Legislative Assembly During the Session of 1898: Being the 3rd Session of the 12th Parliament*, Brisbane: Government Printer, 2: App. JJ.

Finsch, O. (1888), *Samoafahrten*, Leipzig: F. Hirt & Sohn.

Firth, R. (1936), *Art and Life in New Guinea*, London: The Studio.

Forge, A. (1966), 'Art and Environment in the Sepik', *Proceedings of the Royal Anthropological Institute for 1965*: 23–31.

—— (1970), 'Learning to See in New Guinea', in P. Mayer (ed.), *Socialization: The Approach from Social Anthropology*, London: Tavistock Publications.

—— (1972), 'The Golden Fleece', *Man*, 7 (4): 527–540.

—— (ed.) (1973), *Primitive Art and Society*, London: Oxford University Press.

—— (1977), 'Schematisation and Meaning', in P. J. Ucko (ed.), *Form in Indigenous Art: Schematisation in the Art of Aboriginal Australia and Prehistoric Europe*, London: Gerald Duckworth & Co. Ltd.

—— (1979), 'The Problem of Meaning in Art', in S. M. Mead (ed.), *Exploring the Visual Art of Oceania*, Honolulu: University of Hawaii Press.

Fortune, R. F. (1932), *Sorcerers of Dobu*, New York: Dutton Press.

Gardner, H. (2000), 'Gathering for God: George Brown and the Christian Economy in the Collection of Artefacts', in M. O'Hanlon and R. L. Welsch (eds), *Hunting the Gatherers: Ethnographic Collectors, Agents and Agency in Melanesia, 1870s–1930s*, New York: Berghahn Books.

Gell, A. (1975), *Metamorphosis of the Cassowaries: Umeda Society, Language and Ritual*, New Jersey: The Athlone Press.

—— (1992), 'The Technology of Enchantment and the Enchantment of Technology', in J. Coote and A. Shelton (eds), *Anthropology, Art and Aesthetics*, Oxford: Clarendon Press.

—— (1998), *Art and Agency: An Anthropological Theory*, Oxford: Clarendon Press.

Gilmour, M. K. (1904–05), 'A Few Notes on the Kiriwina Trading Expeditions', *Annual Report of British New Guinea for 1904-05:71-72*, Brisbane: Government Printer.

Glass, P. (1978), 'The Trobriand Code: An Interpretation of Trobriand War Shield Designs with Implications for the Culture and Traditional Society', Unpublished M.Sc. thesis, Salford University.

Graburn, N. H. H. (1976), *Ethnic and Tourist Arts: Cultural Expressions from the Fourth World*, Berkeley: University of California Press.

Greenberg, L. J. (1975), 'Art as a Structural System: A Study of Hopi Pottery Designs', *Studies in the Anthropology of Visual Communication*, 2 (1): 33–50.

Guiart, J. (1963) *The Arts of the South Pacific*, London: Thames & Hudson.

Haddon, A. C. (1893), 'Wood-Carving in the Trobriands', *Illustrated Archaeologist*, 1: 107–112.

—— (1894), *The Decorative Art of British New Guinea*, Dublin: Academy House.

—— (1895), *Evolution in Art*, London: W. Scott.

—— (n.d.), Letter to Malinowski, 4/10/1916, held in the Malinowski Archives in the London School of Economics Archives.

—— and Hornell, J. (1938), *Canoes of Oceania*, London: Bishop Museum Special Publication 27, 28 and 29.

Halls, A. J. (n.d.), Untitled manuscript on Massim decorative art and technique, deposited with R. Firth in 1952.

Holm, B. (1965), *Northwest Coast Indian Art: An Analysis of Form*, Seattle: University of Washington Press.

Hutchins, E. L. (1980), *Culture and Inference: A Trobriand Case Study*, Cambridge, Mass.: Harvard University Press.

—— (n.d.), 'Technical Knowledge in the Trobriand Islands', Unpublished typescript.

Irwin, G. J. (1983), 'Chieftainship, Kula, and Trade in Massim Prehistory', in J. W. Leach and E. Leach (eds), *The Kula: New Perspectives on Massim Exchange*, Cambridge: Cambridge University Press.

Jones, R. and Meehan, B. (1978), 'Anbarra Concept of Colour', in L. R. Hiatt (ed.), *Australian Aboriginal Concepts*, Canberra: Institute of Aboriginal Studies.

Kasaipwalova, J. (1975a), 'Philosophy and Historical Reality of Kabisawali', *Gigibori: A Magazine of Papua New Guinea Cultures*, 2 (1): 16–17.

—— (1975b), 'Sopi: The Adaptation of a Traditional Aesthetic Concept for the Creation of a Modern Art School on Kiriwina', *Discussion Paper No. 5*, Port Moresby: Institute of Papua New Guinea Studies.

Lawton, R .S. (1978), 'Some Aspects of the Language of Kiriwina', Unsubmitted MA thesis, Australian National University.

—— (1980), 'The Kiriwinan Classifiers', Unpublished MA thesis, Australian National University.

Layton, R. (1991), *The Anthropology of Art*, Cambridge: Cambridge University Press.

—— (1992), 'Traditional and Contemporary Art of Aboriginal Australia: Two Case Studies', in J. Coote and A. Shelton (eds), *Anthropology, Art and Aesthetics*, Oxford: Clarendon Press.

Leach, E. R. (1950), 'Primitive Calendars', *Oceania*, 20: 245–262.

—— (1954), 'A Trobriand Medusa?', *Man*, 54: 103–105.

—— (1958), 'A Trobriand Medusa?: A Reply to Dr. Bernt', *Man*, 58: 79.

—— (1967a), 'Virgin Birth', *Proceedings of the Royal Anthropological Institute*: 39–50.

—— (1967b), 'Correspondence: Virgin Birth', *Man*, 3: 655–656.

—— (1973), 'Levels of Communication and Problems of Taboo in the Appreciation of Primitive Art', in A. Forge (ed.), *Primitive Art and Society*, London: Oxford University Press.

Leach, J. W. (1973), 'Making the Best of Tourism: The Trobriand Situation', in R. J. May (ed.), *Priorities in Melanesian Development*, Canberra: Australian National University.

—— (1978), 'The Kabisawali Movement in the Trobriand Islands', Unpublished Ph.D. thesis, Cambridge University.

—— (1981), 'Imdeduya: A Kula Folktale From Kiriwina', *Bikmaus: Journal of Papua New Guinea Affairs, Ideas, and the Arts,* II (1): 50–92.

—— (1982), 'The Conflict Underlying the Kabisawali Movement in the Trobriand Islands', in R. J. May (ed.), *Micronationalist Movements in Papua New Guinea*, Political and Social Change Monograph 1, Department of Political and Social Change, Research School of Pacific Studies, Canberra: Australian National University.

—— (1983), 'Trobriand Territorial Categories and the Problem of Who is Not in the Kula', in J. W. Leach and E. Leach (eds), *The Kula: New Perspectives on Massim Exchange*, Cambridge: Cambridge University Press.

—— and Leach, E (1983), *The Kula: New Perspectives on Massim Exchange*, Cambridge: Cambridge University Press.

Lepowsky, M. (1993), *Fruit of the Motherland: Gender in an Egalitarian Society*, New York: Columbia University Press.

Liep, J. (1983), 'A Note on Shells and Kula Valuables', in M. Macintyre, *The Kula: A Bibliography*, Cambridge: Cambridge University Press.

—— (1991), 'Great Man, Big Man, Chief: A Triangulation of the Massim', in M. Godelier and M. Strathern (eds), *Big Men and Great Men*, Cambridge: Cambridge University Press.

MacGregor, Sir W. (1890–91), *Annual Report on British New Guinea*, Brisbane: Government Printer.

—— (1891–92), *Annual Report on British New Guinea*, Brisbane: Government Printer.

—— (1892–93), *Annual Report on British New Guinea*, Brisbane: Government Printer.

—— (1893–94), *Annual Report on British New Guinea*, Brisbane: Government Printer.

—— (1897), *British New Guinea: Country and People*, London: John Murray.

Macintyre, M. (1983a), 'Kune on Tubetube and in the Bwanabwana Region of the Southern Massim', in J. W. Leach and E. Leach (eds), *The Kula: New Perspectives on Massim Exchange*, Cambridge: Cambridge University Press.

—— (1983b), 'Changing Paths: An Historical Ethnography of the Traders of Tubetube', Unpublished Ph.D. thesis, Australian National University.

—— (1983c), 'Warfare and the Changing Context of Kune on Tubetube', *The Journal of Pacific History*, 18 (1): 11–34

—— (1987), 'Flying Witches and Leaping Warriors: Supernatural Origins of Power and Matrilineal Authority in Tubetube Society', in M. Strathern (ed.), *In Dealing with Inequality: Analysing Gender Relations in Melanesia and Beyond*, Cambridge: Cambridge University Press.

—— (1994), 'Too Many Chiefs? Leadership in the Massim in the Colonial Era', in *History and Anthropology*, 7, (1–4): 241–262.

Malinowski, B. (1918), 'Fishing in the Trobriand Islands', *Man*, 17–18: 87–92.

—— (1920), 'Kula, the Circulatory Exchange of Valuables in the Archipelago of Eastern New Guinea', *Man*, 51: 97–105.

—— (1922), *Argonauts of the Western Pacific*, London: Routledge & Kegan Paul Ltd.

—— (1927a), *Sex and Repression in Savage Society*, London: Routledge & Kegan Paul Ltd.

—— (1927b), 'Lunar and Seasonal Calendar on the Trobriands', *Journal of the Royal Anthropological Institute*, 57: 203–215.

—— (1927c), *The Father in Primitive Psychology*, New York: W.W. Norton & Co. Inc.

—— (1932), *The Sexual Lives of the Savages*, London: Routledge & Kegan Paul Ltd.

—— (1935), *Coral Gardens and Their Magic*, Vols. I and II, London: George Allen & Unwin Ltd.

—— (1948a), 'Baloma, the Spirits of the Dead in the Trobriand Islands', in *Magic, Science, and Religion and Other Essays*, New York: Doubleday Anchor Books.

—— (1948b), 'Magic, Science, and Religion', in *Magic, Science, and Religion and Other Essays*, New York: Doubleday Anchor Books.

—— (1948c), 'Myth in Primitive Psychology', in *Magic, Science, and Religion and Other Essays*, New York: Doubleday Anchor Books.

—— (n.d.), Letter to A. C. Haddon, 25/6/1918, held in the Haddon Collection, University Library, Cambridge.

McCarthy, D. (1959), *South-West Pacific Area – First Year: Kokoda to Wau*, *Australia in the War of 1939–45*, Series one: Army, Vol. 5, Canberra: Canberra War Memorial.

Menzies, K. and Wilson, R. K. (1967), 'Production and Marketing of Artifacts in the Sepik District and the Trobriand Islands', *New Guinea Research Bulletin*, 20: 50–75.

Monckton, C. A. W. (1921), *Some Experiences of a New Guinea Resident Magistrate*, London: John Lane, The Bodley Head.

Montague, S. (1971), 'Trobriand Kinship and the Virgin Birth Controversy', *Man*, 6: 353–368.

—— (1989), 'To Eat for the Dead: Kaduwagan Mortuary Events', in F. H. Damon and R. Wagner (eds), *Death Ritual and Life in the Societies of the Kula Ring*, DeKalb: Northern Illinois University Press.

Moreton, M. H. (1894–95), 'Report of the Resident Magistrate for the Eastern Division', in *Annual Report for British New Guinea*, Brisbane: Government Printer.

—— (1896–97), 'Report of the Resident Magistrate for the Eastern Division', in *Annual Report for British New Guinea*, Brisbane: Government Printer.

Morphy, F. (1977), 'The Social Significance of Schematisation in Northwest Coast American Art', in P. J. Ucko (ed.), *Form in Indigenous Art: Schematisation in the Art of Aboriginal Australia and Prehistoric Europe*, Canberra: Australian Institute of Aboriginal Studies.

Morphy, H. (1977a), 'From Schematisation to Conventionalisation: A Possible Trend in Yirrkala Bark Paintings, in P. J. Ucko (ed.), *Form in Indigenous Art: Schematisation in the Art of Aboriginal Australia and Prehistoric Europe*, Canberra: Australian Institute of Aboriginal Studies.

—— (1977b), 'Schematisation, Meaning and Communication in Toas', in P. J. Ucko (ed.), *Form in Indigenous Art: Schematisation in the Art of Aboriginal Australia and Prehistoric Europe*, Canberra: Australian Institute of Aboriginal Studies.

—— (1983), 'Aboriginal Fine Art, the Creation of Audiences and the Marketing of Art', in P. Loveday and P. Cook (eds), *Aboriginal Arts and Crafts and the Market*, Darwin: North Australian Research Unit.

—— (1991), *Ancestral Connections: Art and an Aboriginal System of Knowledge*, Chicago: University of Chicago Press.

—— (1992), 'From Dull to Brilliant: The Aesthetics of Spiritual Power Among the Yolngu', in J. Coote and A. Shelton (eds), *Anthropology, Art and Aesthetics*, Oxford: Clarendon Press.

Mosko, M. S. (1995), 'Rethinking Trobriand Chieftainship', in *Journal of the Royal Anthropological Institute*, 1 (4): 763–785.

Mosuwadoga, G. (1978), 'The Making of an Artist', *Post-Courier*, Special Issue, Sept., Port Moresby: 30–32.

Munn, N. D. (1962), 'Walbiri Graphic Designs: An Analysis', *American Anthropologist*, 64 (5): 972–984.

—— (1973a), *Walbiri Iconography*, Ithaca, N.Y.: Cornell University Press.

—— (1973b), 'The Spatial Presentation of Cosmic Orders in Walbiri Icon-ography', in A. Forge (ed.), *Primitive Art and Society*, London: Oxford University Press.

—— (1977), 'The Spatiotemporal Transformations of Gawan Canoes', *Journal de la Société des Océanistes*, 33 (54–55): 39–52.

—— (1983), 'Gawan Kula: Spatiotemporal Control and the Symbolism of Influence', in J. W. Leach and E. Leach (eds), *The Kula: New Perspectives on Massim Exchange*, Cambridge: Cambridge University Press.

—— (1986), *The Fame of Gawa: A Symbolic Study of Value Transformation in a Massim (Papua New Guinea) Society*, Cambridge: Cambridge University Press.

Nalubutau (1975), 'Trobriand Canoe Prows: Fourteen Pieces from the National Collection in the Papua New Guinea Museum', *Gigibori: A Magazine of Papua New Guinea Cultures*, Institute of Papua New Guinea Studies in association with Niugini Press, 2 (1): 1–14.

—— (1979), 'Eleven Canoe Prows from the Trobriand Islands', *Gigibori: A Magazine of Papua New Guinea Cultures*, Institute of Papua New Guinea Studies in association with Niugini Press, 4: 40–46.

Nautical Magazine (1839), *The Nautical Magazine: A Journal of Papers on Subjects Connected with Maritime Affairs*, Glasgow: Brown, Son & Fergusson, 8: 37–39.

Niessen, S. (1999), 'Threads of Tradition, Threads of Invention: Unravelling Toba Batak Women's Expressions of Social Change', in R. B. Phillips and C. B. Steiner (eds), *Unpacking Culture: Art and Commodity in Colonial and Post-colonial Worlds*, Berkeley: University of California Press.

Newton, D. (1975), *Massim: Art of the Massim Area, New Guinea*, New York: The Museum of Primitive Art.

O'Hanlon, M. (1989), *Reading the Skin: Adornment, Display and Society Among the Wahgi*, London: British Museum Publications.

—— and Welsch, R. L. (2000), *Hunting the Gatherers: Ethnographic Collectors, Agents and Agency in Melanesia, 1870s–1930s*, New York: Berghahn Books.

Paijmans, K. (ed.) (1976), *New Guinea Vegetation*, Canberra: Commonwealth Scientific and Industrial Research Organisation in association with the Australian National University Press.

Phillips, R. B. and Steiner, C. B. (eds) (1999), *Unpacking Culture: Art and Commodity in Colonial and Postcolonial Worlds*, Berekely: University of California Press.

Pizzey, G. (1981) *A Field Guide to the Birds of Australia*, Sydney: Collins.

Powell, H. A. (1960), 'Competitive Leadership in Trobriand Political Organis-ation', *Journal of the Royal Anthropological Institute*, 90: 118–145.

—— (1968), 'Correspondence: Virgin Birth', *Man*, 3: 651–652.

—— (1969a), 'Genealogy, Residence and Kinship in Kiriwina', in *Man*, 4 (2): 177–202.

—— (1969b), 'Territory, Hierarchy and Kinship', *Man*, 4 (4): 580–604.

Price, S. (1989), *Primitive Art in Civilised Places*, Chicago: Chicago University Press.

Quinnell, M. (2000), "Before it has Become too Late': The Making and Repatriation of Sir William MacGregor's Official Collection from British New Guinea', in M. O'Hanlon and R. L. Welsch (eds), *Hunting the Gatherers: Ethnographic Collectors, Agents and Agency in Melanesia, 1870s–1930s*, New York: Berghahn Books.

Rand, A. L. and Gilliard, E. T. (1967), *Handbook of New Guinea Birds*, London: Weidenfeld & Nicolson.

Reichard, G. A. (1933), *Melanesian Design: A Study of Wood and Tortoiseshell Carving*, Vols. 1 and 2, New York: Columbia University Press.

—— (1939), *Navajo Medicine Men*, New York: J. J. Augustine.

Rentoul, C. A. (1931), 'Physiological Paternity and the Trobriands', *Man*, 31: 152–154.

—— (1932), 'Papuans, Professors, and Platitudes', *Man*, 32: 274–276.

Reynolds, V. (1958), 'Correspondence: "A Trobriand Medusa?"', *Man*, 58: 116.

Roheim, G. (1940), 'Professional Beauties of Normanby Island', *American Anthropologist*, 42 (4): 657–661.

—— (1945–46), 'Yaboaine, a War God of Normanby Island', *Oceania*, 16: 210–233, 311–334.

—— (1948), 'Witches of Normanby Island', *Oceania*, 28 (4): 279–308.

Salisbury, R. F. (1959), 'A Trobriand Medusa?', *Man*, 66–67: 50–51.

Saville, G. (1974), *King of Kiriwina: The Adventures of Sergeant Saville in the South Seas*, London: Leo Cooper.

Scheffler, H. W. (1973), 'Kinship, Descent, and Alliance', in J. J. Honigmann (ed.), *Handbook of Social and Cultural Anthropology*, Chicago: Rand-McNally.

Schindlbeck, M. (1980), *Sago bei den Sawos*, Basel: Ethnologisches Seminar der Universität und Museum für Volkerkunde.

Scoditti, G. G. (ed.) (1975), *Arte e Societ'a Primitive*, Rome: Giancarlo Serafini Editore.

—— (1977), 'A Kula Prowboard: An Iconological Interpretation', *L'Uomo*, 2: 199–232.

—— (1980), *Fragmenta Ethno-Graphica*, Rome: Giancarlo Serafini Editore.

—— (1990), *Kitawa: A Linguistic Aesthetic Analysis of Visual Art in Melanesia*, Berlin: Mouton de Gruyter.

—— and Leach, J. W. (1983), 'Kula on Kitava', in J. W. Leach and E. Leach (eds), *The Kula: New Perspectives on Massim Exchange*, Cambridge: Cambridge University Press.

Segall, M. H., Campbell, D. T. and Herskovits, M. J. (1966), *The Influence of Culture on Visual Perception*, New York: Bobbs-Merrill.

Seligman, C. C. (1909), 'A Type of Canoe Ornament with Magical Significance from South Eastern British New Guinea', *Man*, 16: 33–35.

—— (1910), *The Melanesians of British New Guinea*, Cambridge: Cambridge University Press.

—— and Dickson, T. E. (1946), ' "Rajim" and "Tabuya" of the D'Entrecasteaux Group', *Man*, 66: 112–122, and Nov.–Dec.: 129–134.

Silas, E. (1924), 'The Art of the Trobriand Islanders', *Studio*, 88: 132–135.

—— (1926), *A Primitive Arcadia: Being the Impressions of an Artist in Papua*, Boston, Mass.: Little, Brown & Co.

Silverman, E. K. (1999), 'Tourist Art as the Crafting of Identity in the Sepik River (Papua New Guinea)', in R. B. Phillips and C. B. Steiner (eds), *Unpacking Culture: Art and Commodity in Colonial and Postcolonial Worlds*, Berkeley: University of California Press.

Sperber, D. (1976), *Rethinking Symbolism*, Cambridge: Cambridge University Press.

Spiro, M. E. (1968), 'Virgin Birth, Parthenogenesis, and Physiological Paternity: An Essay in Cultural Interpretation', *Man*, 3: 242–261.

—— (1972), 'Correspondence: Reply to Montague', *Man*, 7: 315.

Strathern, A. and Strathern, M. (1971), *Self-Decoration in Mount Hagen*, London: Gerald Duckworth & Co. Ltd.

Tambiah, S. J. (1968), 'The Magical Power of Words', *Man*, 3: 175–206.

—— (1983), 'On Flying Witches and Flying Canoes: The Coding of Male and Female Values', in J. W. Leach and E. Leach (eds), *The Kula: New Perspectives on Massim Exchange*, Cambridge: Cambridge University Press.

Thomas, N. (1991), *Entangled Objects*, Cambridge, Mass.: Harvard University Press.

Thompson, R. F. (1973), 'Yoruba Artistic Criticism', in W. L. d'Azevedo (ed.), *Traditional Artist in African Societies*, Bloomington: Indiana University Press.

Tindale, N. (1959), 'A Trobriand Medusa?', *Man*, 66–67: 49–50.

Uberoi, J. P. Singh (1962), *Politics of the Kula Ring*, Manchester: Manchester University Press.

Ucko, P. J. (1977), *Form in Indigenous Art: Schematisation in the Art of Aboriginal Australia and Prehistoric Europe*, Canberra: Australian Institute of Aboriginal Studies.

Vargyas, G. (1980), 'Lime-Spatulae from the Massim Area of South-east New Guinea in the Ethnographical Museum, Budapest', *Acta Ethnographica Academiae Scientiarum Hungaricae*, 29 (3–4): 427–462.

Watt, W. (1966–67), *Morphology of the Nevada Cattle-brands and their Balsons*, Parts I and II: Part I, Washington, DC: US Dept of Commerce, National Bureau of Standards Report 9050; Part II, Pittsburgh,: Carnegie-Mellon University.

—— (1967), 'Structural Properties of the Nevada Cattle Brands', *Computer Science Research Review*, 2: 21–28.

Wayne, H. (ed.) (1995), *The Story of a Marriage: The Letters of Bronislaw Malinowski and Elsie Masson, Vol. 1, 1916–20*, London: Routledge.

Weiner, A. B. (1977), *Women of Value, Men of Renown: New Perspectives in Trobriand Exchange*, St Lucia: University of Queensland Press.

—— (1978), 'The Reproductive Model in Trobriand Society', *Mankind*, 11: 175–186.

—— (1980), 'Reproduction: A Replacement for Reciprocity', *American Ethnologist*, 7 (1): 71–85.

—— (1982), 'Ten Years in the Life of an Island', *Bikmaus: A Journal of Papua New Guinea Affairs, Ideas and the Arts*, 3 (4): 64–75.

—— (1983), ' "A World of Made is not a World of Born": Doing Kula on Kiriwina', in J. W. Leach and E. Leach (eds), *The Kula: New Perspectives on Massim Exchange*, Cambridge: Cambridge University Press.

—— (1988), *The Trobrianders of Papua New Guinea*, Fort Worth, Tex.: Harcourt Brace Jovanovich College Publishers.

Wilson, R. K. and Menzies, K. (1967), 'Production and Marketing of Artifacts in the Sepik Districts and the Trobriand Islands', *New Guinea Research Bulletin*, 20: 50–75.

Young, M. (1971), *Fighting with Food: Leadership, Values and Social Control in a Massim Society*, Cambridge: Cambridge University Press.

—— (1983a), 'The Theme of the Resentful Hero: Stasis and Mobility in Goodenough Mythology', in J. W. Leach and E. Leach (eds), *The Kula: New Perspectives on Massim Exchange*, Cambridge: Cambridge University Press.

—— (1983b), 'Ceremonial Visiting in Goodenough Island', in J. W. Leach and E. Leach (eds), *The Kula: New Perspectives on Massim Exchange*, Cambridge: Cambridge University Press.

—— (1983c), 'The Massim: An Introduction', The Journal of Pacific History, 18 (1): 4–10.

—— (1998) *Malinowski's Kiriwina: Fieldwork Photography 1915–1918*, Chicago: University of Chicago Press.

Index

above/below (*orakaiwa/otenauwa*), 180–3, 189
  of the village, 26
aesthetics, 57, 60, 62–4, 70, 91, 94, 98, 145,
  147–9
  of line, 76, 107
  terms, 77
age, 118–25, 134, 136, 144
  see also colour
Amphlett pots, 32
anchored, 155–6, 162–3, 173, 178–9, 182, 184,
  187–90, 192
Andrews, J., 22
animal associations, *see* representation
apprenticeship, 51, 54–7, 60, 65, 144
arm, *see* body–part terminology
armshell (*mwari*), 33–4, 119–21, 177
  see also shell valuables
astronomy, 53
Austen, L., 4, 19, 24, 46, 199n1
axe blades, 32, 36

baloma, 125, 141, 160, 178, 184, 186–7
banana, 26, 29, 51, 160
  leaf skirts, *see* skirts
Barthes, R., 8
Bartle Bay, 174
Barton, Captain F. R., 19
Basilisk, HMS, 3
bat (*kapaiyauwa*), 102–3, 131, 133–5, 138,
  146–7, 149
beach, 63, 130, 156–8, 163–4, 171–3, 183, 188
beak, *see* body–part terminology
beans, 29
beba, *see* butterfly
beche–de–mer, 2
Bellamy, Dr. R. L., 19–20
Beran, H., 5
betelnut, 26, 31, 37, 39, 57, 60, 112, 114,
  120–1, 159–60, 169
  in exchange, 36
  in magic, 61–2, 64, 66, 132, 164

bibisilasi, 164
binabina, *see* stones
black (bwabwau), *see* colour
birth, 35, 37, 118–20, 125, 177, 186, 189
  see also virgin birth
bisila, 164–5
Boas, F., 7
body decoration, 92–3
  face painting, 115
body-part terminology, 93, 113, 139, 192
  arm, 94, 139, 143
  beak, 70, 93, 97, 98, 128, 131–2, 139–40,
    142
  chest, 62, 93–4, 102–3, 108, 131–2, 135, 144
  elbow, 62
  eye, 49, 56, 93, 97, 103, 128–9, 131–2,
    135–6, 139–40, 142–4
  face, 94–5, 137, 142, 157, 168
  forehead, 62, 119
  head, 60, 63, 70, 93–4, 97, 103, 128, 131–3,
    135, 139–42
  intestine, 60
  mind, 49, 55–7, 60–4, 66, 93–4, 132, 135,
    141, 143, 146, 158, 164
  mouth, 62–3, 70, 93, 97, 114, 116, 120,
    139–40, 142, 144, 159
  neck, 70, 98, 129, 131–2, 139
  nose, 73, 99, 131, 136–7, 157–8, 164, 183–4
  penis, 131, 137, 160, 181
  shoulder, 62
  tail, 60, 63, 77, 82, 103, 131, 133, 183
  teeth, 93, 135, 159
  throat, 94
  vagina, 94, 141, 180, 203n4
  wing, 94–5, 103, 139, 141, 143, 153
  wrist, 62
boi, *see* egret
Bolutukwa myth, 179, 180–1
Boyowa, *see* Kiriwina Island
breadfruit, 29
Bromilow, Dr., 33

– 233 –

Index

Index

see also flying canoe myth, Imdeduya myth,
Kasibwaibwaireta myth, origin myths,
Tokosikuna myth, Tudava myth

name giving, 13, 17, 186
  achieving immortality, 6, 102, 129, 171,
    175–6, 179, 186, 189
  outrigger canoe, 156
  women, 175–6, 185–6
native almond (*seida*), 26
neck, *see* body-part terminology
necklace (*vaiguwa*), 33, 99, 121, 124, 177
  chama, 121
  spondylus, 121, 124
  see also shell valuables
Normanby Island, 161, 174
Northwest Coast Native Americans, 7, 70
nose, *see* body-part terminology

ocean, 38, 63–4, 66, 105, 115, 130, 157
ochre, 30, 32, 114–15
octopus (*kwita*), 115
oranges, 29
origabu, *see* yam garden
origin myths, 145
  Gawa, 196n5
  Kiriwina, 16
  love magic, 156, 183
  of *dala*, 26
  Vakuta, 16, 26, 180
osprey (*buribwari*), 98–100, 129–36, 138, 140,
  146, 149, 157–9, 163–4, 174, 177, 179, 180,
  182–3, 185–6, 192–3
outrigger canoe (*masawa*), 21, 38, 72–3, 102,
  115
  building of, 49, 54, 153, 155–7
  fishing, 38, 155
  hull, 6, 82, 155, 157, 159
  insertion of decorative boards, 99, 157, 159
  nagega, 72–3
  owner of (*toliwaga*), 92–3, 160
  painting of, 122, 159
  see also kewou, shipwreck, *tasasoria*
ovula ovum (*buna*), 140–1, 159

paint, 80, 88, 100, 111–12, 114–17, 159, 191
  European, 80, 111
  face paint, 115, 137, 157

painting of prow and splashboards, 82, 111,
  129, 136
  see also colour, pigment
pandanus streamer (*bisila*), 147, 164–5
papa, 105, 159
path (*keda*), 96, 177
  for colour, *see* colour
  in the village, 38–9
  kula, 33, 121, 169, 171
pearls, 20
  pearlers, 2
penis, *see* body-part terminology
pigment,
  applying, 117–18
  black, 114–16, 136–7, 140
  red, 114, 137, 140
  white, 114–17, 129
pigs, 42, 57
  as food, 29, 60
  in exchange, 31, 27
pineapple, 29
pokala, 27, 36, 53, 55, 57, 60, 66
Powell, H., 26, 29, 35
political alliances, 16, 23–4, 26, 37
pregnancy, 119, 157, 161, 181–2, 184
prowboards (*tabuya*), 6, 73, 93, 99–100, 114,
  127, 147, 149, 158, 162, 173, 192
  carving, 56–8, 65, 83, 132
  sections,
    section 1, 76–7, 86, 99, 129, 133–5
    section 2, 76, 86, 97–8, 132–3
    section 3, 76, 82, 86, 101, 103, 133–4
    section 4, 76, 80, 86, 135–6
    section 5, 76, 79, 82–3, 104, 108, 122,
      136–7
  see also dogina, uuna
pumpkin, 28–9, 60

rain, 39
  clouds, 112
  fertilising agent, 181
  see also magic
rank, 21, 29, 34–6, 121
  see also relationships
Rattlesnake, HMS, 3
red (*bweyani*), *see* colour
Reichard, G. A., 7
reincarnation, 118, 141, 145, 185–6, 188

Printed in the United States
100117LV00001B/128/A

9 781859 735183